T0235211

Quantitative Methods in the Humanities and Social Sciences

Quantitative Methods in the Humanities and Social Sciences is a book series designed to foster research-based conversation with all parts of the university campus – from buildings of ivy-covered stone to technologically savvy walls of glass. Scholarship from international researchers and the esteemed editorial board represents the far-reaching applications of computational analysis, statistical models, computer-based programs, and other quantitative methods. Methods are integrated in a dialogue that is sensitive to the broader context of humanistic study and social science research. Scholars, including among others historians, archaeologists, new media specialists, classicists and linguists, promote this interdisciplinary approach. These texts teach new methodological approaches for contemporary research. Each volume exposes readers to a particular research method. Researchers and students then benefit from exposure to subtleties of the larger project or corpus of work in which the quantitative methods come to fruition.

More information about this series at http://www.springer.com/series/11748

Matthew L. Jockers • Rosamond Thalken

Text Analysis with R

For Students of Literature

Second Edition

Matthew L. Jockers
College of Arts and Sciences
Washington State University
Pullman, WA, USA

Rosamond Thalken
Digital Technology and Culture Program
Washington State University
Pullman, WA, USA

ISSN 2199-0956   ISSN 2199-0964   (electronic)
Quantitative Methods in the Humanities and Social Sciences
ISBN 978-3-030-39645-9   ISBN 978-3-030-39643-5   (eBook)
https://doi.org/10.1007/978-3-030-39643-5

This Springer imprint is published by the registered company Springer Nature Switzerland AG.
The registered company address is: Gewerbestrasse 11, 6330 Cham, Switzerland

For our students,
past, present, and future

Preface to the Second Edition

A lot has changed in the R universe in the last 5 years. Almost as soon as I began teaching from this book, some of the content and approaches were already becoming old fashioned. Not obsolete, but old fashioned. The biggest change came with the rise of the "tidyverse." Tidyverse is a collection of R packages developed by Hadley Wickham and his team at RStudio. Before the advent of the tidyverse, there were ggplot and dplyr, two Wickham packages that I began using in 2013 and 2014 at precisely the moment that *Text Analysis with R* was going to the presses. I remember having had a brief "stop the presses" moment, but also realizing that I needed more time to adjust to the tidyverse before being able to teach it.

There is a pretty good chance that you have no idea what that last paragraph is about. The important thing to know here is that in around 2013 the way most people use R for data analytics began to change. The seeds of this change were sown as early as 2005, or maybe 2007 depending on what you want to count, when Hadley Wickham released an R package called ggplot2.[1] ggplot2, along with dplyr and later tidyr, readr, and stringr, radically changed the way that I write programs in R, and these packages simplified many of the most difficult programming challenges presented in the first edition of this book. So in many ways, these new packages are a driving force justifying the need for this second edition. But there were a few other reasons as well.

Most relevant, perhaps, is that I have learned a lot over the last 5 years. I have gotten feedback from students in my classes and from readers, and based on that learning and that feedback, I know there are ways to make the content in this book more relevant and easier to digest. And this time around, I have the benefit of a co-author. Rosamond Thalken, who joins me for this new edition, was a student in the first class I taught using this book.

---

[1]For a great (and pithy) history of the tidyverse revolution, see Roger Peng's article at simplystats.org.

She has lived through the transitions in R programming and joins me now in rethinking and rewriting this book for a new R universe.

But this isn't just the same book using `tidyverse` packages. We've changed a lot of other things as well: we've updated our programming conventions, completely overhauled several chapters, added a bunch of new material, including five new chapters, that deal with such things as parsing dramatic text, part of speech tagging, named entity recognition, and sentiment analysis.

Throughout all of this, however, we have stuck to the central principle of the first edition: You do not have to be a programmer or statistician to dive into this book. The subtitle, *For Students of Literature*, remains the guiding principle.

Pullman, WA, USA   Matthew L. Jockers
Kearney, NE, USA   Rosamond Thalken
March 2020

Preface from the First Edition
(Still Relevant)

This book provides an introduction to computational text analysis using the open source programming language R. Unlike other very good books on the use of R for the statistical analysis of linguistic data[2] or for conducting quantitative corpus linguistics,[3] this book is meant for students and scholars of literature and then, more generally, for humanists wishing to extend their methodological toolkit to include quantitative and computational approaches to the study of text. This book is also meant to be short and to the point. R is a complex program that no single textbook can demystify. The focus here is on making the technical palatable and more importantly making the technical useful and immediately rewarding! Here I mean rewarding not in the sense of satisfaction one gets from mastering a programming language, but rewarding specifically in the sense of quick return on your investment. You will begin analyzing and processing text right away and each chapter will walk you through a new technique or process.

Computation provides access to information in texts that we simply cannot gather using our traditionally qualitative methods of close reading and human synthesis. The reward comes in being able to access that information at both the micro and macro scale. If this book succeeds, you will finish it with a foundation, with a broad exposure to core techniques and a basic understanding of the possibilities. The real learning will begin when you put this book aside and build a project of your own. My aim is to give you enough background so that you can begin that project comfortably and so that you'll be able to continue to learn and educate yourself.

When discussing my work as a computing humanist, I am frequently asked whether the methods and approaches I advocate succeed in bringing new knowledge to our study of literature. My answer is a strong and resounding "yes." At the same time, that strong yes must be qualified a bit; not everything

---

[2]Baayen (2008).

[3]Gries (2009).

that text analysis reveals is a breakthrough discovery. A good deal of computational work is specifically aimed at testing, rejecting, or reconfirming the knowledge that we think we already possess. During a lecture about macro-patterns of literary style in the nineteenth century novel, I used an example from *Moby Dick*. I showed how *Moby Dick* is a statistical mutant among a corpus of 1000 other nineteenth century American novels. A colleague raised his hand and pointed out that literary scholars already know that *Moby Dick* is an aberration, so why, he asked, bother computing an answer to a question we already know?

My colleague's question was good; it was also revealing. The question said much about our scholarly traditions in the humanities. It is, at the same time, an ironic question. As a discipline, we have tended to favor a notion that literary arguments are never closed: but do we really know that *Moby Dick* is an aberration? Maybe *Moby Dick* is only an outlier in comparison to the other twenty or thirty American novels that we have traditionally studied alongside *Moby Dick*? My point in using *Moby Dick* was not to pretend that I had discovered something new about the position of the novel in the American literary tradition, but rather to bring a new type of evidence and a new perspective to the matter and in so doing fortify (in this case) the existing hypothesis.

If a new type of evidence happens to confirm what we have come to believe using far more speculative methods, shouldn't that new evidence be viewed as a good thing? If the latest Mars rover returns more evidence that the planet could have once supported life, that new evidence would be important. Albeit, it would not be as shocking or exciting as the first discovery of microbes on Mars, or the first discovery of ice on Mars, but it would be important evidence nevertheless, and it would add one more piece to a larger puzzle. So, computational approaches to literary study can provide complementary evidence, and I think that is a good thing.

The approaches outlined in this book also have the potential to present contradictory evidence, evidence that challenges our traditional, impressionistic, or anecdotal theories. In this sense, the methods provide us with some opportunity for the kind of falsification that Karl Popper and post-positivism in general offer as a compromise between strict positivism and strict relativism. But just because these methods *can* provide contradiction, we must not get caught up in a numbers game where we only value the testable ideas. Some interpretations lend themselves to computational or quantitative testing; others do not, and I think that is a good thing.

Finally, these methods can lead to genuinely new discoveries. Computational text analysis has a way of bringing into our field of view certain details and qualities of texts that we would miss with just the naked eye.[4] Using com-

---

[4]See, for example, Flanders (2005).

putational techniques, Patrick Juola recently discovered that J. K. Rowling was the real author of *The Cuckoo's Calling*, a book Rowling wrote under the pseudonym Robert Galbraith. Naturally, I think Juola's discovery is a good thing too.

This is all I have to say regarding a theory for or justification of text analysis. In my other book, I am a bit more polemical.[5] The mission here is not to defend the approaches but to share them.

Lincoln, NE, USA   Matthew L. Jockers
January 2014

References

Baayen RH (2008) Analyzing Linguistic Data: A Practical Introduction to Statistics using R, 1st edn. Cambridge University Press, Cambridge, UK; New York

Flanders J (2005) Detailism, digital texts, and the problem of pedantry. TEXT Technology (2):41–70

Gries ST (2009) Quantitative Corpus Linguistics with R: A Practical Introduction, 1st edn. Routledge, New York, NY

Jockers ML (2013) Macroanalysis: Digital Methods and Literary History, 1st edn. University of Illinois Press, Urbana

---

[5] Jockers (2013).

Contents

Part III Macroanalysis

About the Authors

Matthew L. Jockers is Professor of English and Data Analytics as well as Dean of the College of Arts and Sciences at Washington State University. Jockers leverages computers and statistical learning methods to extract information from large collections of books. Using tools and techniques from linguistics, natural language processing, and machine learning, Jockers crunches the numbers (and the words) looking for patterns and connections. This computational approach to the study of literature facilitates a type of literary "macroanalysis" or "distant reading" that goes beyond what a traditional literary scholar could hope to study. *The Bestseller Code*, his most recent book, with co-author Jodie Archer, has earned critical praise and the algorithms at the heart of the research won the University of Nebraska's Breakthrough Innovation of the year in 2018 (See: https://youtu.be/dWbVsWnQz1g). In addition to his academic research, Jockers has worked in industry, first as Director of Research at a data-driven book industry startup company and then as Principal Research Scientist and Software Development Engineer in iBooks at Apple Inc. In 2017, he and Jodie Archer founded "Archer Jockers, LLC," a text mining and consulting company that helps authors develop more successful novels through data analytics. In late 2019, Jockers and others founded a new text mining startup that focused on helping independent authors ("indies").

Rosamond Thalken is an Instructor of English and Digital Technology and Culture at Washington State University. Her research engages questions about the intersections and impacts between digital technology, language, and gender. She currently teaches College Composition and Digital Diversity, a course which analyzes the cultural contexts within digital spaces, including intersections of race, gender, class, and sexuality. In 2019, Thalken finished her Master's degree in English Literature at Washington State University. Her thesis combined text analysis and close reading to explore the female Supreme Court Justices' rhetorical strategies for reinforcing ethos in court opinions.

List of Figures

List of Tables

Part I
Microanalysis

Chapter 1
R Basics

Abstract This chapter explains how to download and install R and RStudio. Readers are introduced to the R console, to R Projects, and shown how to execute basic commands.

1.1 Introduction

There is a tradition in the teaching of programming languages in which students write a script to print out (to their screen) the words *hello world*. Though this book is about programming in R, this is not a programming book. Instead this text is designed to get you familiar with the R environment while engaging with, exploring, and even addressing some real text analysis questions. If you are like us, you probably launched R and started typing in commands a few hours ago. Maybe you got stuck, hit the wall, and are now turning to this book for a little shove in the right direction. If you are like us, you probably headed to the index first and tried to find some function name or keyword (such as *frequency list* or *count word occurrences*) to get you rolling. You are ready to jump in and start working, and if you've ever done any coding before, you may be wondering (maybe dreading) if this is going to be another one of those books that grinds its way through all sorts of data type definitions and then finally "teaches" you how to write an elegant little snippet of code with a tight descriptive comment.

This is not that type of book—not that there is anything wrong with books that are like that! This book is simply different; it is designed for the student and scholar of literature who doesn't already know a programming language,

© Springer Nature Switzerland AG 2020
M. L. Jockers, R. Thalken, *Text Analysis with R*, Quantitative Methods in the Humanities and Social Sciences,
https://doi.org/10.1007/978-3-030-39643-5_1

or at the very least does not know the R language, and, more importantly, is a person who has come to R because of some text-oriented question or due to some sense that computation might offer a new or particularly useful way to address, explore, probe, or answer some literary question. You are not coming to this book because you want to become a master programmer. You are a student or scholar (probably in the humanities or social sciences) seeking to learn just enough coding to probe some text-oriented research questions.

If you want to become a master R programmer, or someone who delivers shrink-wrapped programs, or R packages, then this is not the book for you; there are other books, and good ones, for that sort of thing.[1] Here, however, we'll take our cues from best practices in natural language instruction and begin with a healthy dose of full immersion in the R programming language. In the first section, *Microanalysis*, we will walk you through the steps necessary to complete some basic analysis of a single text. In the second part of the book, *Metadata*, we'll move from analysis of the words in a text to analysis that is based on metadata about those words. In the final section, *Macroanalysis*, we'll take on a larger corpus to engage in such crowd pleasers as clustering, classification, and even topic modeling. Along the way there will be some new vocabulary and even some new or unfamiliar characters for your alphabet. But all in good time. For now, let's get programming...

1.2 Download and Install R

Download the current version of R (at the time of this writing version 3.6.0) from the **c**omprehensive **R** **a**rchive **n**etwork (CRAN) website by clicking on the link that is appropriate to your operating system (see http://cran.at. r-project.org):

- If you use MS-Windows, click on "base" and then on the link to the executable (i.e. ".exe") setup file.
- If you are running Mac-OSX, choose the link to latest version that is compatible with your system.[2]
- If you use Linux, choose your distribution and then the installer file.

Follow the instructions for installing R on your system in the standard or "default" directory. You will now have the base installation of R on your system.

---

[1]See, for example, Wickham and Grolemund (2017); Venables and Smith (2009); Braun (2016); or any of the books in Springer's *Use R* Series: http://www.springer.com/series/6991?detailsPage=titles.

[2]To find what OS you are running, choose "About this Mac" from the Apple menu.

- If you are using a Windows or Macintosh computer, you will find the R application in the directory on your system where Programs (Windows) or Applications (Macintosh) are stored.

- If you are on a Linux/Unix system, simply type "R" at the command line to enter the R program environment.

New versions of R come out about once per year and there are any number of minor updates throughout the year. It's a good idea to keep your version of R up to date by checking the CRAN site every few months.

1.3 Download and Install RStudio

The R application you installed is fine for a lot of simple programming; you can launch the application and enter commands into the R console window, but RStudio is an application that offers an organized user environment for writing and running R programs. RStudio is an IDE, that's "Integrated Development Environment" for R. RStudio, like R, happily runs on Windows, Mac, and Linux. After you have downloaded R (by following the instructions above) you should download the "Desktop" version (i.e. not the Server version) of RStudio from http://www.rstudio.com. Follow the installation instructions and then launch RStudio like you would any other program/application. Just like R, new versions of RStudio come out several times a year. When an update is available, RStudio will notify you.

1.4 Download the Supporting Materials

Now that you have R and RStudio installed and running on your system, you will also need to download the directory of files used for the exercises and examples in this book. The materials consist of a directory titled "TAWR2" that includes an empty sub-directory titled "code" and another sub-directory titled "data" that contains two .csv files, a large .Rdata file that we use in Chap. 18, and five sub-directories containing the plain texts and XML files that you will work on throughout this book. You can download the supporting materials from: github.com/mjockers/TAWR2. Once on the github page, click on the button that says "Clone or Download" and then choose "Download Zip" to download a .zip archive titled "TAWR2-master.zip"

Unzip the file and save the resulting directory (aka "folder") as "TAWR2" (*not* "TAWR2-master") to a convenient location on your system. It's important that you rename the directory "TAWR2". If you are using a Mac, the file path to this new directory might look something similar to the following:

    "~/Documents/TAWR2"

It does not matter where you keep this new directory as long as you remember where you put it. In the R code that you write, you may need to include information that tells R where to find these materials.

1.5 RStudio

When you launch RStudio you will see the default layout which includes four *panes* (or *quadrants*) and within each of the panes you can have multiple *tabs*.[3] You can customize this pane/tab layout in RStudio's preferences area. We set up our layout a bit different from the default: we like to have the script editing pane in the upper right and the R console pane in the lower right. You will discover what is most comfortable for you as you begin to spend more time in the program.

The important point to make right now is that RStudio's four window panes each provide something useful, and you should familiarize yourself with at least two of these panes right away. These are the *script* editing pane and the *console* pane. The former provides an environment in which you can write R programs. This pane works just like a text editor but with the added benefit that it offers *syntax highlighting* and some other shortcuts for interacting with R. As you become a more experienced coder, you will learn to love the highlighting. RStudio's script editor understands the syntax of the R programming language and helps you read the code you write by highlighting variables in one color, literal characters, comments, and so on in other colors. If this does not make sense to you at this point, that is fine. The benefits of syntax highlighting will become clear to you as we progress, especially since the code samples shown throughout this book are highlighted to match what you will see in RStudio. A second point about the script editing pane is that anything you write in that pane can be saved to file. When you run commands in the R console, those commands do not get saved into a file that you can reuse.[4] When you write your code in the script editor, you intentionally save

---

[3]The first time you launch RStudio you will be able to see only three of the panes. The R scripting or *Source* pane will likely be *collapsed* so you will see only the word *Source* until you either create a new script (File > New > R Script) or un-collapse the *Source* window pane.

[4]This is not entirely true. RStudio does save your command history and, at least while your session is active, you can access that history and even save it to a file. Once you quit a session, however, that history may or may not be saved.

this code as a ".R" file. You can then close and reopen these files to run, revise, copy, etc.

Along with the scripting pane, RStudio provides a console pane. If you were simply running R by itself, then this is all you would get: a simple console.[5] In RStudio you can interact with the console just as you would if you had only launched R. You can enter commands at the R *prompt* (represented by a > symbol at the left edge of the console), hit return and see the results.

Because the scripting and console panes are integrated in RStudio, you can write scripts in the one pane and run them in the other without having to copy and paste code from the editor into the console. RStudio provides several shortcuts for running code directly from the script editing pane. We'll discuss these and other shortcuts later. For now just know that if you are working in the scripting pane, you can hit *command + return* to send the active line of code (i.e. where your cursor is currently located) directly to the console.

Throughout this book, we will assume that you are writing all of your code in the script editing pane and that you are saving your scripts to the "code" sub directory of the main "TAWR2" directory you downloaded from the book's github page. To help get you started, we'll provide specific instructions for writing and saving your files in this first chapter. After that, we'll assume you know what you are doing and that you are saving your files along the way.

1.6 Let's Get Started

If you have not already done so, launch RStudio.

The first thing to do is to set up an R project. Go to RStudio's "File" menu and select "New Project" from the drop-down menu. You will now have the option to create a "New Directory," choose an "Existing Directory" or check out a project from "Version Control" (see Fig. 1.1).

The first option, "New Directory," is useful if you are starting a new project from scratch. The last option is beyond the scope of this book, but is something to be mindful of once you have mastered the basics and want to use a version control repository, such as git. Here we are going to choose the second option and then navigate ("Browse") to the location of the "TAWR2" directory that you downloaded from the textbook's github page. Once you have navigated to the directory, click on the "Create Project" button. After you have created the new project, look for, and click on, the "Files" tab in

---

[5]The *Console* is a command line window where you enter commands. Sometimes this is called a *Terminal* or *Shell*.

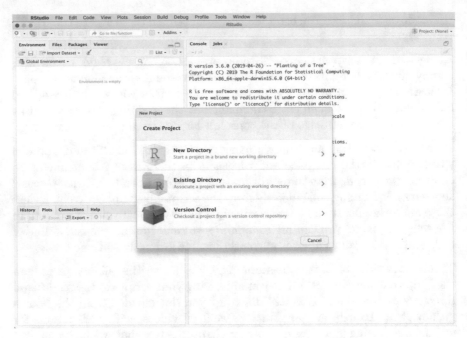

Fig. 1.1 Creating a new R project

RStudio to see the items that are currently in your project (see Fig. 1.2). Under the "Files" tab, you will see a directory labeled "data" and a new R project file titled "TAWR2.Rproj."

We'll come back to the advantages of having defined an R project as we progress through the next few chapters, but right now we want you to get your fingers dirty typing a few simple R commands in the console. By default, the RStudio console tab should be active, and you should see a bunch of information about the version of R that you have installed on your system and some boilerplate text about R being "free software and comes with ABSO-LUTELY NO WARRANTY." Underneath all that boilerplate, you will find a small blue greater than (>) symbol. That is the R "prompt". Next to the prompt, you will see a blinking cursor icon. If it's not blinking, just click on it to make that the active window pane in RStudio. You can now enter text on the command line of the console. At the prompt, type 1 + 10 and then hit return. You will then see a bracketed 1 ([1]) followed by a 11, like this: [1] 11. We'll discuss what that [1] tells us a bit later, for now just experiment with typing some other mathematical examples, such as 10 * 10 or 12 / 2.

The console is handy for entering quick, short commands that you you don't want to retain for later, but what you are really going to want to do is write and save longer scripts that can be rerun later. We'll cover that next.

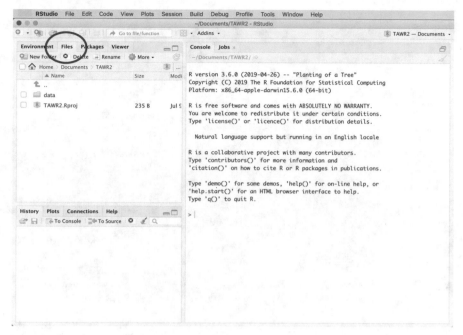

Fig. 1.2 Locating the Files Tab

1.7 Saving Commands and R Scripts

To create a new R script, go to the file menu and find "New File" in the drop-down. Now select "R Script" from the "New File" drop-down (i.e. File > New > R Script as in Fig. 1.3). Creating a new script file will add a fourth quadrant to the default RStudio layout; this is the script editor *pane*. The new script file will be given a temporary title of "Untitled1," which you should see represented as a tab at the top of the pane. Save this new file to your "code" directory as "chapter1.R" by either clicking on the blue disk icon just below the "Untitled1" tab or by choosing "save" from the File menu. Notice when you do this, that RStudio already understands that your project is located inside the "TAWR2" directory where there is already a "code" (and "data") sub-directory. If you have any experience with programming or even with building web sites with html, you may already understand the advantages of relative versus absolute paths. When you define an R project, as we have done here, you don't have to worry about setting a working directory or using absolute paths; RStudio handles all that for you!

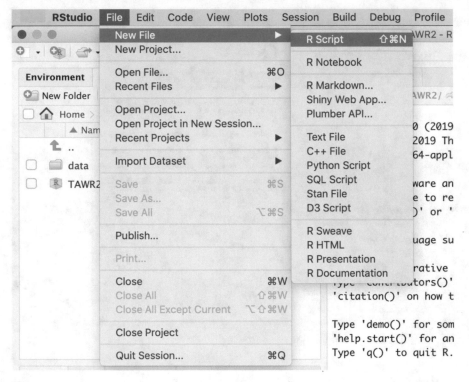

Fig. 1.3 Saving an R script

At the top of your freshly saved script file, type in the mathematics expression 1 + 10. Unlike the example above where we typed commands into the console, now we are typing commands into a script, which is essentially just a plain text file. If we hit return, all that will happen is that the cursor will move to the next line. If you want to see the output from the commands in your script, you have to execute them in the console. You could copy and paste the command into the console, but RStudio gives us a couple of quick shortcuts for running scripts. You can execute any line of code in your script by hitting *command + return* when your cursor is on that line. You can execute multiple lines of code from your script by selecting them and hitting *command + return*. If you want to run your entire script, you can click on the "Run" icon in the tool bar at the top of the script editing pane. Try this with a few more examples:

```
10 + 5
```

If all proceeded correctly, then R should perform the simple addition, and you'll see the following appear in your console[6]:

---

[6]Throughout this book, we will show output from the console proceeded by two hash marks (##). These hash marks will not appear in your console output.

```
## [1] 15
```

Like this example, to execute basic mathematical calculations in R, you use a plus sign (+) for addition, a minus sign or hyphen (-) for subtraction, an asterisk (*) for multiplication, a forward slash (/) for division, and a caret sign (^) for exponents. Other examples of useful built-in mathematical functions in R include square root (sqrt), absolute value (abs), and (round) for rounding. R also has some preset values, such as pi:

```
10 * pi
## [1] 31.41593
```

If you want to create a sequence of numbers, called a *vector*, you can use a colon:

```
1:10
##  [1]  1  2  3  4  5  6  7  8  9 10
```

1.8 Assignment Operators

Assignment operators are used to assign a value to a variable. You will find assignment operators to be increasingly important as you begin building more complicated projects. R's assignment operator is the *less than* symbol followed by the *hyphen*: <- (The two symbols form an icon that looks like a left facing arrow.) R also allows the "#" symbol for adding comments into your scripts; anything you write after a "#" will be ignored by the R processor.

```
x <- 10  # Assign 10 to the variable "x"
x - 3 # subtract 3 from x
```

1.9 Practice

Go to the "Files" tab in RStudio and click on the "New Folder" icon to create a new directory in your R project. Name the new directory "Practice." Now create a new R script and title it "practice1.R"). Save this file to the newly created Practice directory in your "TAWR2" R project. Write the following practice exercises into your new practice1.R script and then run them either using the *control + return* shortcut or the *run* icon in the script editing pane of RStudio.

1. As in mathematics, in programming there are conventions around the order
   in which mathematical expressions are evaluated. The expression 2 + 3
   * 4 is interpreted to be 2 + (3 * 4) = 14 not (2 + 3) * 4 = 20. Run
   the following two expressions and explain how the answers were derived.

```
10 * 2 / 5  - 1
10 * 2 / (5  - 1)
```

2. Variables can be set to contain specific values (x in the example below), or
   they can be the result of a calculation (y in the example). Variables can
   also be combined using the c function. The sum function will calculate the
   sum of the items in a numerical vector. Explain the difference between the
   output of sum(xy) and sum(xyz) in the example below.

```
x <- 5
y <- 24/4
xy <- c(x, y)
xy
z <- "whale"
xyz <- c(x, y, z)
xyz
sum(xy)
sum(xyz)
```

3. The == operator is used to test for equivalence, meaning "exactly equal to."
   Why is the result of the first expression "TRUE" and the second expression
   "FALSE"?

```
x <- 5
y <- 10/2
x == y
"x" == "y"
```

4. In the following example, x is a vector containing 3 values. Explain how
   the values of y are derived.

```
x <- (1:3)
y <- 2 * x
y
```

5. Vectors can be combined to create data frames, which are like tables (or
   spreadsheets) with rows and columns. In the following example, we create
   a data frame from two vectors and then call the dim function to access the
   data frame's dimensions. This tells us that there are 3 rows and 2 columns.
   Using brackets ([]) we can access specific cells (or a range of cells) in the
   data frame. The fifth line of code below shows how to access the first row
   of the data frame. The sixth line shows how to access the second column.
   How would you access the value in the third row, second column?

```
x <- (1:3)
y <- 2 * x
df <- data.frame(x,y)
dim(df)
df[1, ]
df[, 2]
```

Answers to all practice questions can be found at the back of the book.

References

Braun W (2016) A First Course in Statistical Programming with R, 2nd edn. Cambridge University Press, New York, NY, USA

Venables WN, Smith DM (2009) An Introduction to R, 2nd edn. Network Theory Ltd.

Wickham H, Grolemund G (2017) R for Data Science: Import, Tidy, Transform, Visualize, and Model Data, 1st edn. O'Reilly Media, Sebastopol, CA

Chapter 2
First Foray into Text Analysis with R

Abstract In this chapter readers learn how to load, tokenize, and search a text. Several methods for exploring word frequencies and lexical makeup are introduced. The practice exercise at the end of the chapter introduces the `plot` function.

2.1 Loading the First Text File

If you have not already done so, open your R project in RStudio. Now create a new R script and title it "chapter2.R." We will now write the R code needed to read and analyze Herman Melville's novel *Moby Dick*. We will do this using the `scan` function.[1]

```
text_v <- scan("data/text/melville.txt", what = "character", sep = "\n")
```

Type this command into your new R script, and then run it by either copying and pasting into the console or using RStudio's *command + return* shortcut when your cursor is positioned on the line of code you have just written.

This is as good a place as any to mention that the `scan` function can also be used to grab text (or html) files from the Internet. If you have an Internet

---

[1]Throughout this book we will use a naming convention when instantiating new R objects. In the example seen here, we have named the object `text_v`. The `_v` extension is a convention we have adopted to indicate the R data type of the object, in this case a *vector* object, hence the v. This will make more sense as you learn about R's different data types. For now, just understand that you can name R objects in ways that will make sense to you as a human reader of the code.

© Springer Nature Switzerland AG 2020

M. L. Jockers, R. Thalken, *Text Analysis with R*, Quantitative Methods in the Humanities and Social Sciences,
https://doi.org/10.1007/978-3-030-39643-5_2

connection, you can enter a URL in place of the file path and load a file directly from the web. In the example below, we show how you can download the novel directly from Project Gutenberg.[2]

```
# Not run
gutentext_v <- scan(
  "http://www.gutenberg.org/cache/epub/2701/pg2701.txt",
  what = "character",
  sep = "\n"
  )
```

Whether you load the file from your own system—as you will do for the exercises in this book—or from the Internet, if the code has executed correctly, you should see something like the following result:

```
Read 18172 items
```

We will explain what this "Read 18172 items" means in just a moment. In case you do not see this result, or you get an error, check your code carefully for typos. Programming code is extremely finicky. If you do not type the commands exactly as they appear here, you will likely get an error. In our experience about 95% of the errors and bugs one sees when coding are the result of careless typing. If the program is not responding the way you expect or if you are getting errors, check your typing. Everything counts: capital letters must be consistently capitalized, commas between arguments must be outside of the quotes and so on.

Remember that the > symbol seen here is simply a new R prompt indicating that R has completed its operation and is ready for the next command. At the new prompt, enter:

```
> text_v
```

You will see the entire text of *Moby Dick* flash before your eyes.[3] Now try examining just the first item using bracketed sub-setting. You will see the contents of the first *item* in the text_v variable.[4]

```
> text_v[1]
## [1] "MOBY DICK; OR THE WHALE"
```

---

[2]Bear in mind, however, that the copy of *Moby Dick* on the Project Gutenberg website contains all of the Project Gutenberg boilerplate metadata at the top and bottom. The plain text files used in this book were acquired from Project Gutenberg but we have removed the metadata.

[3]Actually, you may only see the first 1000 or 10,000 lines. That is, because R has set the max.print option to 1000 by default. If you wish to increase the default for a given work session, just begin by entering options(max.print = 1000000).

[4]From this point forward, we will not show the R prompt in the code examples.

When you used the **scan** function, you included an *argument* (**sep**) that told the **scan** function to separate the file using **\n**. **\n** is a *regular expression* or *meta-character* (that is, a kind of computer shorthand) representing (or standing in for) the newline (carriage return) characters in a text file.[5] What this means is that when the **scan** function loaded the text, it broke the text up into chunks according to where it found newlines in the text.[6] These chunks were then stored in what is called a *vector*, or more specifically a *character vector*.[7] In this single R expression, you invoked the **scan** function and put the results of that invocation into a new object named **text_v**, and the **text_v** object is an object of the type known as a character vector.[8] Deep breath.

It is important to understand that the data inside this new **text_v** object is *indexed*. Each line from the original text file has its own special container inside the **text_v** object, and each container is numbered. You can access lines from the original file by referencing their *container* or *index* number within a set of square brackets.

Entering **text_v[1]** returns the contents of the first indexed container, in this case, the first line of the text file, that is, the first part of the text file you loaded up to the first newline character. If you enter **text_v[2]**, you will retrieve the second item, that is, the line between the first and second newline characters.[9]

2.2 A Word About Warnings, Errors, Typos, and Crashes

We did not want to scare you off in the first chapter, but when running R scripts and installing and using R packages, you are bound to encounter an error or warning message at some point.

---

[5] *Wikipedia* provides a fairly good overview of regular expressions and a web search for "regular expressions" will turn up all manner of useful information.

[6] Be careful not to confuse newline with "sentence" break or even with "paragraph" break. Also note that depending on your computing environment, there may be differences between how your machine interprets \n, \r and \n\r.

[7] If you have programmed in another language, you may be familiar with this kind of data structure as an *array*.

[8] As noted above, we have found it convenient to append suffixes to the variable names to indicate the type of data being stored in the variable. So, for example, *text_v* has a _v suffix to indicate that the variable is a vector: *v = vector*. Later you will see *data frame* variables with _df extensions and lists with a _l, and so on.

[9] Those who have programming experience with another language may find it disorienting that R (like FORTRAN) begins indexing at 1 and not 0 like C, JAVA, and many other languages.

Warnings Warning messages in R caution you about something that is going on, but warnings do not halt your script from running. Sometimes warnings can be ignored; other times they provide valuable information about something that might be a real problem. You should always investigate any code that throws a warning to be sure you understand whether or not it can be ignored.

Errors Errors are fatal (for your R code). They stop your code from executing. If you encounter an error, you will need to troubleshoot the problem. Most errors that you encounter will be errors that other people have had before. Luckily, many of the folks who got these errors for the first time posted them online and then other folks helped with the troubleshooting. We rarely encounter errors today that have not been talked about somewhere online. *Googling* the error will usually turn up a solution.

Typos The most common mistakes you will make (that we make) are typographical. A slip on the keyboard can ruin your day. A lowercase l where you really needed a number 1 can cause all kinds of hair pulling. If your code is not working, the first step is to read through it very carefully. Another common mistake is to forget to close a parenthetical expression. In the code at the beginning of this chapter, we loaded a text file using the `scan` function. But if for some reason we forgot to add the closing parentheses, then we might have seen a strange plus (+) sign show up in the console, like this:

```
> text_v <- scan("data/text/melville.txt",
                  what = "character",
                  sep = "\n"
+
```

If you hit the return key again, you will see another + sign and so on. That + is there to tell you that you forgot something. It is a signal to you that R is expecting something more before it can close out and execute the command. If you see that you forgot a) (as in this example), just click into the console window and hit the `escape` key to cancel the command. You can then edit your code to include the) and rerun.

Crashes Sometimes you do something in R that causes RStudio to freeze up or show an "R Session Aborted" message (Fig. 2.1). The only thing to do is to take a deep breath and restart the RStudio program and then try to figure out what happened. Generally RStudio does a good job of reopening the script you were working on, but you might need to reopen your R Project by going to the *File* menu and selecting *Open Project*.

2.3 Separate Content from Metadata

The electronic text that you loaded into `text_v` is the plain text version of *Moby Dick* that is available from *Project Gutenberg*. Along with the text of the novel, however, you also get a wee bit of metadata: specifically the title of the book and the fact that it is "By Herman Melville." Since you do not want to analyze the metadata, you need to determine where the text of the novel begins and, in some cases, ends.[10] As it happens, the main text of the novel, or more specifically, the first chapter heading, is found at index 3 (`text_v[3]`). One way to figure this out is to visually inspect the output you saw (above) when you typed the object name `text_v` at the R prompt

Fig. 2.1 R crashed

and hit return. If you had lightning fast eyes, you might have noticed that item `text_v[3]` contained the text string: "CHAPTER 1. Loomings." Instead of removing the book title and byline in advance, we opted to leave it in so that we might explore ways of accessing the indices of a character vector.

Let us assume that you did not already know about index 3, but that you did know that the first line of the book contained the character string "CHAPTER 1. Loomings." You could use this information, along with R's `which` function to isolate the main text of the novel. To do this on your own, enter the code below, but be advised that in R, and any other programming language

---

[10]As our friend Ryan Cordell likes to point out, this is not always a simple thing to determine. In this book, we have removed of lot of front matter material from the beginning of the novel so that our text here begins with the first chapter. Some people might want to retain that preliminary material depending on their research goals.

for that matter, accuracy counts. The great majority of the errors you will encounter as you write and test your first programs will be the results of careless typing.[11]

```
start_v <- which(text_v == "CHAPTER 1. Loomings.")
```

In reality, of course, you are not likely to know in advance the exact contents of the text items that scan created by locating the *newline* characters in the file, and the which function requires that you identify an exact match. Later on we will show a better way of handling this situation using the grep function. For now just pretend that you know where all the chunks begin and end.

You can now check to see if which correctly found the third index by entering the new variable name at the prompt:

```
start_v
```

You should now see the following returned from R:

```
start_v
## [1] 3
```

In a moment we will use this information to separate the main text of the novel from the metadata, but first a bit more about character vectors...

When you loaded *Moby Dick* into the text_v object, you asked R to divide the text (or delimit it) using the carriage return or *newline* character, which was represented using \n. To see how many newlines there are in the text_v variable, and, thus, how many lines of text, use the length function:

```
length(text_v)
## [1] 18172
```

You will see that there are 18,172 lines of text in the file. But not all of these lines, or *character strings*, of text are part of the actual novel that you wish to analyze.[12] Text files, especially novels, often come with some baggage such as title pages, prefaces, introductions, afterwords, author's notes, etc., and so you will probably want to remove the non-narrative material and just keep the story: everything from "CHAPTER 1. Loomings..." to "...orphan," which is the last word of the book. To get the meat of the novel, you need to reduce the contents of the text_v variable to just the lines of the narrative proper. Rather than throwing out the metadata, you can opt to save it to a

---

[11]In this expression, the two equal signs serve as a comparison operator that translates to "exactly equal to" or "equivalent." You got a bit of experience with this operator in the Chap. 1 practice exercises. You cannot use a single equals sign because the equals sign can also be used in R as an *assignment* operator, similar to <-. This is an idiosyncrasy of R. For now just know that you need to use two equals signs to compare values.

[12]Sentences, lines of text, etc. are formally referred to as *strings* of text.

new variable called `metadata_v`, and then keep the text of the novel itself in a new variable called `novel_lines_v`. Enter the following two lines of code:

```
metadata_v <- text_v[1:start_v -1]
novel_lines_v <- text_v[start_v:length(text_v)]
```

The first line copies the text from the first and second indexed positions in the `text_v` vector and puts them into a new vector called `metadata_v`. If you are wondering about that `start_v -1`, remember that the `start_v` variable you created earlier contains the value 3 and refers to a place in the text vector that contains the words "CHAPTER 1. Loomings." Since you want to keep that line of the text (that is, it is not metadata but part of the novel) you must subtract 1 from the value inside the `start_v` variable to get the 2.

The second line does something similar; it grabs all of the lines of text beginning at the third index position (currently stored inside the `start_v` variable) and then continues all the way to the end of the vector, which we reference by calling the `length` function.

You can now compare the size of the original file to the size of the new `novel_lines_v` variable that excludes the metadata:

```
length(text_v)
## [1] 18172
length(novel_lines_v)
## [1] 18170
```

If you want, you can even use a little subtraction to calculate how much smaller the new object is: `length(text_v) - length(novel_lines_v)`. The answer should be 2.

The main text of *Moby Dick* is now in an object titled `novel_lines_v`, but the text is still not quite in the format we need for further processing. Right now the contents of the novel are spread over 18,170 line items derived from the original decision to delimit the file using the newline character. Sometimes, it is important to maintain line breaks: for example, some literary texts are encoded with purposeful line breaks representing the lines in the original print publication of the book or sometimes the breaks are for lines of poetry. For our purposes here, maintaining the line breaks is not important, so we will get rid of them using the `paste` function to *join* and *collapse* all the lines into one long string:

```
novel_v <- paste(novel_lines_v, collapse = " ")
```

The `paste` function with the `collapse` argument provides a way of *gluing* together a bunch of separate *pieces* using a *glue character* that you define as the value for the `collapse` argument. In this case, we are gluing together the lines (the *pieces*) using a blank space character (the *glue*). After entering this expression, you will have the entire contents of the novel stored as a single string of words, or more precisely, a string of characters. You can check the size of the novel object by typing:

```
length(novel_v)
## [1] 1
```

At first you might be surprised to see that the length is now 1. The variable called `novel_v` is a vector just like `novel_lines_v`, but instead of having an indexed slot for each line, it has just one slot in which the entire text is held. If you are not clear about this, try entering:

```
novel_v[1]
```

A lot of text is going to flash before your eyes, but if you were able to scroll up in your console window to where you entered the command, you would see something like this:

```
novel_v[1]
## [1] "CHAPTER 1. Loomings. Call me Ishmael. Some years ago..."
```

R has dumped the entire contents of the novel into the console. Go ahead, read the book!

2.4 Reprocessing the Content

Now that you have the novel loaded as a single string of characters, you are ready to have some fun. First use the `tolower` function to convert the entire text to lowercase characters.

```
novel_lower_v <- tolower(novel_v)
```

You now have a big blob of *Moby Dick* in a single, lowercase string, and this string includes all the letters, numbers, and marks of punctuation in the novel. For the time being, we will focus on the words, so we need to extract them out of the full text string and put them into a nice organized list. R provides an aptly named function for splitting text strings: `strsplit`.

```
moby_word_l <- strsplit(novel_lower_v, "\\W")
```

The `strsplit` function, as used here, takes two arguments and returns what R calls a *list*.[13] The first argument is the object (`novel_lower_v`) that you want to split, and the second argument, \\W, is another example of a *regular expression*. Remember, a *regular expression* is a special type of character string that is used to represent a pattern. In this case, the regular expression

---

[13]Because this new object is a *list*, we have appended "underscore l" (_l) to the variable name.

will match any non-word character. Using this simple *regex*, `strsplit` can detect *word boundaries*.

So far we have been working with vectors. Now you have a list. Both vectors and lists are data types, and R, like other programming languages, has other data types as well. At times you may forget what kind of data type one of your variables is, and since the operations you can perform on different R objects depends on what kind of data they contain, you may find yourself needing the `class` function.

R's `class` function returns information about the data type of an object you provide as an argument to the function. Here is an example that you can try:

```
class(novel_lower_v)
## [1] "character"
class(moby_word_l)
## [1] "list"
```

To get even more detail about a given object, you can use R's `str` or *structure* function.

This function provides a compact display of the internal structure of an R object. If you ask R to give you the structure of the `moby_word_l` list, you will see the following:

```
str(moby_word_l)
## List of 1
##  $ : chr [1:253992] "chapter" "1" "" "loomings" ...
```

The output tells you that this object (`moby_word_l`) is a list with one item and that the one item is a character (`chr`) vector with 253,992 items. R then shows you the first few items, which happen to be the first few words of the novel. If you look closely, you will see that the third item in the `chr` vector is an empty string represented by two quotation marks: `""`. We will deal with that in a moment...

Right now, though, you may be asking, why a list? The short answer is that the `strsplit` function that you used to split the novel into words returns its results as a list object. The long answer is that sometimes the object being given to the `strsplit` function is more complicated than a simple character string, so `strsplit` is designed to deal with more complicated situations. A list is a special type of object in R. You can think of a list as being like a file cabinet. Each drawer is an item in the list and each drawer can contain different kinds of objects. In our file cabinet, for example, we have three drawers full of file folders and one full of old diskettes, CDs, and miscellaneous hard drives. You will learn more about lists as we go on.

It is worth mentioning here that anytime you want some good technical reading about the nature of R's functions, just enter the function name proceeded by a question mark, e.g., `?strsplit`. Try this now, and you will activate the help tab in RStudio and an explanation for how `strsplit` works to "Split the Elements of a Character Vector."

This "question mark function name" sequence is how you access R's built in "help" files.[14] Be forewarned that your mileage with R-help may vary. Some functions are very well documented and others are like reading tea leaves.[15] One might be tempted to blame poor documentation on the fact that R is open source, but it is more accurate to say that the documentation often assumes a degree of familiarity with programming and with statistics. R-help is not geared toward the novice, but, fortunately, R has now become a popular language, and if the built-in help is not always kind to newbies, the resources that are available online have become increasingly easy to use and newbie friendly.[16] For the novice, the most useful part of the built-in documentation is often found in the code examples that almost always follow the more technical definitions and explanations at the bottom of the help record. Be sure to read all the way down in the help files, especially if you are confused. When all else fails, or even as a first step, consider searching for answers and examples on sites such as http://www.stackexchange.com.

Because you used `strsplit`, you have a list, and since you do not need a list for this particular problem, you can simplify it to a vector using the `unlist` function:

```
moby_word_v <- unlist(moby_word_l)
```

When discussing the `str` function above, we mentioned that the third item in the vector was an empty character string. Calling `str(moby_word_l)` revealed the following:

```
str(moby_word_l)
## List of 1
##  $ : chr [1:253992] "chapter" "1" "" "loomings" ...
```

---

[14]Note that in RStudio the help window pane also has a search box where you can enter search terms instead of entering them in the console.

[15]`?functionName` is a shortcut for R's more verbose *help(functionName)*. If you want to see an example of how a function is used, you can try *example(functionName)*. *args(functionName)* will display a list of arguments that a given function takes. Finally, if you want to search R's documentation for a single keyword or phrase, try using *"??your keyword"* which is a shorthand version of *help.search("your keyword")*. We wish we could say that the documentation in R is always brilliant; we cannot. It is inevitable that as you learn more about R you will find places where the documentation is frustratingly incomplete. In these cases, the Internet is your friend, and there is a very lively community of R users who post questions and answers on a regular basis. As with any web searching, the construction of your query is something of an art form, perhaps a bit more so when it comes to R since using the letter *r* as a keyword can be frustrating.

[16]This was not always the case, but a recent study of the R-help user base shows that things have improved considerably. Trey Causey's analysis "Has *R*-help gotten meaner over time? And what does Mancur Olson have to say about it?" is available online at http://badhessian.org/2013/04/has-r-help-gotten-meaner-over-time-and-what-does-mancur-olson-have-to-say-about-it.

As it happens, that empty string between *1* and *loomings* is where a period character used to be. The \\W regular expression that you used to split the string ignored all the punctuation in the file, but then left these little blanks, as if to say, "if I'd kept the punctuation, it'd be right here."[17] Since you are ignoring punctuation, at least for the time being, these blanks are a nuisance. You will want to identify where they are in the vector and then remove them. Or more precisely, you will identify where they are not!

First you must figure out which items in the vector are not blanks, and for that you can use the which function in combination with the "not equal" operator.

```
not_blanks_v  <-  which(moby_word_v != "")
```

Notice how the which function has been used in this example. which performs a logical test to identify those items in the moby_word_v that are not equal (represented by the "!=" operator in the expression) to blank (represented by the empty quote marks "" in the expression). If you now enter "not_blanks_v" into R, you will get a list of all of the index *positions* in moby_word_v where there is not a blank. Try it:

```
not_blanks_v
```

If you tried this, you just got a screen full of numbers. Each of these numbers corresponds to an indexed *position* in the moby_word_v vector where there is *not* a blank. If you scroll up to the top of this mess of numbers, you will find that the series begins like this: [1] 1 2 4. . .

Notice specifically that position 3 is missing. That is because the item in the third position was an empty string! If you want to see just the first few items in the not_blanks_v vector, try showing just the first ten items, like this:

```
not_blanks_v[1:10]
## [1]  1  2  4  6  7  8 10 11 12 14
```

With the non-blanks identified, you can overwrite moby_word_v like this[18]:

```
moby_word_v <-  moby_word_v[not_blanks_v]
```

---

[17]There are much better, but more complicated, regular expressions that can be created for doing word tokenization. One downside to \\W is that it treats apostrophes as word boundaries. So the word *can't* becomes the words *can* and *t* and *John's* becomes *John* and *s*. These can be especially problematic if, for example, the eventual analysis is interested in negation or possession. You will learn to write more sophisticated *regular expressions* in later chapters.

[18]Overwriting an object is generally not a good idea, especially when you are writing code that you are unsure about, which is to say code that will inevitably need debugging. If you overwrite your variables, it makes it harder to debug later. Here we are making an exception because we are quite certain we are not going to need the vector with the blanks in it.

Only those items in the original `moby_word_v` that are not blanks are retained.[19] Just for fun, now enter:

```
moby_word_v
```

After showing you the first 1000 words of the novel, R will give up and return
a message saying something like `[[ reached getOption("max.print") --`
`omitted 213891 entries ]]`. Even though R will not show you the entire
vector, it is still worth seeing how the word data has been stored in this vector
object, so you may want to try the following:

```
moby_word_v[1:10]
##  [1] "chapter"   "1"         "loomings" "call"      "me"
##  [6] "ishmael"   "some"      "years"    "ago"       "never"
```

The numbers in the square brackets are the *index* numbers showing you the
position in the vector where each of the words is found.

R put a bracketed number at the beginning of each row. For instance, the
word "chapter" is stored in the first (`[1]`) position in the vector and the word
some is in the 7th (`[7]`) position. An instance of the word *ago* is found in
the 9th position and so on. If, for some reason, you wanted to know what the
99986th word in *Moby Dick* is you could simply enter

```
moby_word_v[99986]
## [1] "by"
```

This is an important point (not that the 99986th word is *by*). You can access
any item in a vector by referencing its index. And, if you want to see more
than one item, you can enter a range of index values using a *colon* such as
this:

```
moby_word_v[4:6]
## [1] "call"     "me"        "ishmael"
```

Alternatively, if you know the exact positions, you can enter them directly
using the `c` combination function to create a vector of positions or index
values. First enter this to see how the `c` function works:

```
mypositions_v <- c(4,5,6)
```

Now simply combine this with the vector:

```
moby_word_v[mypositions_v]
## [1] "call"     "me"        "ishmael"
```

You can do the same thing without putting the vector of values into a new
variable. Simply use the `c` function right inside the square brackets:

---

[19]A shorthand version of this whole business could be written as `moby_word_v <-`
`moby_word_v[which(moby_word_v != "")]`.

```
moby_word_v[c(4,5,6)]
## [1] "call"      "me"        "ishmael"
```

Admittedly, this is only useful if you already know the index positions you are interested in. But, of course, R provides a way to find the indexes by also giving us access to the contents of the vector. Say, for example, we want to find all the occurrences of *whale*. For this we can use the `which` function and ask R to find *which* items in the vector satisfy the condition of being the word *whale*.

```
which(moby_word_v == "whale")
```

Go ahead and enter the line of code above. R will return the index positions in the vector where the word *whale* was found. Now remember from above that if you know the index numbers, you can find the items stored in those index positions. Before entering the next line of code, see if you can predict what will happen.

```
moby_word_v[which(moby_word_v == "whale")]
```

2.5 Beginning Some Analysis

Putting all of the words from *Moby Dick* into a vector of words (or, more precisely, a *character* vector) provides a handy way of organizing all the words in the novel in chronological order; it also provides a foundation for some deeper quantitative analysis. You already saw how to find a word based on its position in the overall vector (the word *by* was the 99986th word). You then saw how you could use `which` to figure out which positions in the vector contain a specific word (the word *whale*). You might also wish to know how many occurrences of the word *whale* appear in the novel. Using what you just learned, you can easily calculate the number of *whale* tokens using `length` and `which` together[20]:

```
length(moby_word_v[which(moby_word_v == "whale")])
## [1] 1150
```

Perhaps you would now also like to know the total number of tokens (words) in *Moby Dick*? Simple enough, just ask R for the `length` of the entire vector:

---

[20]In R, as in many languages, there are often alternative ways of achieving the same goal. A more *elegant* method for calculating the number of *whale* hits might look like this: `length(moby_word_v[moby_word_v == "whale"])`. For beginners, the explicit use of `which` can be easier to understand.

```
length(moby_word_v)
## [1] 214891
```

With this information, you can easily calculate the percentage of *whale* occurrences in the novel by dividing the number of whale *hits* by the total number of word tokens in the book. To divide, simply use the forward slash character.[21]

```
# Put a count of the occurrences of whale into whale_hits_v
whale_hits_v <-length(moby_word_v[which(moby_word_v == "whale")])

# Put a count of total words into total_words_v
total_words_v <- length(moby_word_v)

# Now divide
whale_hits_v / total_words_v
## [1] 0.00535155
```

More interesting, perhaps, is to have R calculate the number of unique word types in the novel. R's **unique** function will examine all the values in the character vector and identify those that are the same and those that are different. By combining the **unique** and **length** functions, you can easily calculate the number of unique words in Melville's *Moby Dick* vocabulary.

```
length(unique(moby_word_v))
## [1] 16872
```

It turns out that Melville has a fairly big vocabulary: In *Moby Dick* Melville uses 16,872 unique words. That is interesting, but let us kick it up another notch. What we really want to know is how often he uses each of his words and which words are his favorites. We may even want to see if *Moby Dick* abides by Zipf's law regarding the general frequency of words in English.[22] No problem. R's **table** function can be used to build a "contingency" table of word types and their corresponding frequencies.

```
moby_freqs_t <- table(moby_word_v)
```

You can view the first few items in the table using `moby_freqs_t[1:10]`, and the entire frequency table can be sorted from most frequent to least frequent words using the **sort** function like this:

---

[21] In these next few lines of code, we have added some comments to explain what the code is doing. This is a good habit for you to adopt; explaining or *commenting* your code so that you and others will be able to understand it later on. In R you insert comments into code by using a # symbol before the comment. When processing your code, R ignores everything between that # and the next full line return.

[22] According to Zipf's law, the frequency of any word in a corpus is inversely proportional to its "rank" or position in the overall frequency distribution. In other words, the second most frequent word will occur about half as often as the most frequent word.

```
sorted_moby_freqs_t <- sort(moby_freqs_t, decreasing = TRUE)
```

If you then want to see the first six items in the sorted table, you can use the
head function as a shortcut instead of bracketed sub-setting.

```
head(sorted_moby_freqs_t)
## moby_word_v
##    the     of    and      a     to     in
## 14176   6469   6325   4636   4539   4077
```

2.6 Practice

1. Having sorted the frequency table as described above, how do you find the
   top ten most frequent words in the novel? Save the top ten words into a
   new object called top_ten_t.

2. Once you have the top ten most frequent words stored in a vector, use R's
   built in plot (Fig. 2.2) function to visualize whether the frequencies of the
   words correspond to Zipf's law. The plot function is fairly straightforward.
   To learn more about the plot's complex arguments, just enter: ?plot. To
   complete this exercise, consider this example:

```
mynums_v <- c(1:10)
plot(mynums_v)
```

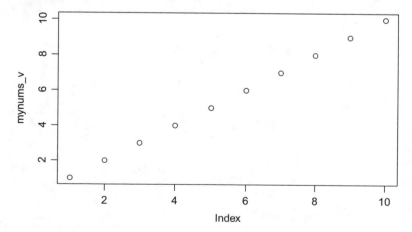

Fig. 2.2 Example plot

You only need to substitute the `mynums_v` variable with the top ten values from `sorted_moby_freqs_t`. You do not need to enter them manually![23]

---

[23]When generating plots in RStudio, you may get an error saying: "Error in plot.new() : figure margins too large." This is because you have not given enough *screen real estate* to the *plots* pane of RStudio. You can click and drag the frames of the plotting pane to resolve this issue.

Chapter 3
Accessing and Comparing Word Frequency Data

Abstract In this chapter, we derive and compare word frequency data. We learn about vector recycling, and the exercises invite you to compare the frequencies of several words in Melville's *Moby Dick* to the same words in Jane Austen's *Sense and Sensibility*.

3.1 Introduction

This chapter expands upon the code that we developed in the last chapter to access word frequencies. Before beginning to work through this chapter, create a new R script file, title it "chapter3.R" and save it in your code directory. Now you can copy the necessary code from your chapter2.R script, or use the chapter start up code provided here:

3.2 Start Up Code

```
text_v <- scan("data/text/melville.txt", what = "character", sep = "\n")
start_v <- which(text_v == "CHAPTER 1. Loomings.")
novel_lines_v <-  text_v[start_v:length(text_v)]
novel_v <- paste(novel_lines_v, collapse = " ")
novel_lower_v <- tolower(novel_v)
moby_words_l <- strsplit(novel_lower_v,"\\W")
moby_word_v <- unlist(moby_words_l)
not_blanks_v  <-  which(moby_word_v != "")
moby_word_v <-  moby_word_v[not_blanks_v]
```

© Springer Nature Switzerland AG 2020
M. L. Jockers, R. Thalken, *Text Analysis with R*, Quantitative Methods in the Humanities and Social Sciences,
https://doi.org/10.1007/978-3-030-39643-5_3

```
moby_freqs_t <- table(moby_word_v)
sorted_moby_freqs_t <- sort(moby_freqs_t, decreasing = TRUE)
```

3.3 Accessing Word Data

While it is no surprise to find that the word *the* is the most frequently occurring word in *Moby Dick*, it is a bit more interesting to see that the ninth
most frequently occurring word is *his*. Put simply, there are a lot of men and
not a lot of women in *Moby Dick*. In fact, you can easily compare the usage
of *he* vs. *she* and *him* vs. *her* as follows:

```
sorted_moby_freqs_t["he"]
##   he
## 1876
sorted_moby_freqs_t["she"]
## she
## 114
sorted_moby_freqs_t["him"]
##  him
## 1058
sorted_moby_freqs_t["her"]
## her
## 330
```

Notice how unlike the original `moby_word_v` in which each word was indexed
at a *position* in the vector, here the word types *are* the indexes, and the
values are the frequencies, or counts, of those word tokens. When accessing
values in `moby_word_v`, you had to first figure out where in the vector those
word tokens resided. Recall that you can do this with vector indexing, as in

```
moby_word_v[4:6]
## [1] "call"     "me"       "ishmael"
```

and that you can find specific matches using the `which` function to test for
the presence of a word, such as *whale*, in the vector.

With the data in a *table* object (`sorted_moby_freqs_t`), however, you get
both numerical indexing and *named* indexing. In this way, you can access a
value in the table either by its numerical position in the table or by its *name*.
Thus, the expression

```
sorted_moby_freqs_t[1]
```

returns the same value as this one:

```
sorted_moby_freqs_t["the"]
```

These each return the same result because the word type *the* happens to be the first (`[1]`) item in the vector. If you want to know just how much more frequent *him* is than *her*, you can use the / operator to perform division.

```
sorted_moby_freqs_t["him"]/sorted_moby_freqs_t["her"]
##      him
## 3.206061
```

him is 3.206061 times more frequent than *her*, but, as you will see in the next code snippet, *he* is 16.45614 times more frequent than *she*.

```
sorted_moby_freqs_t["he"]/sorted_moby_freqs_t["she"]
##       he
## 16.45614
```

Often when analyzing text, what you really need are not the raw number of occurrences of the word types but the *relative* frequencies of word types expressed as a percentage of the total words in the file. Converting raw counts to relative frequencies allows you to more easily compare the patterns of usage from one text to another. For example, you might want to compare Jane Austen's use of male and female pronouns to Melville's. Doing so requires compensating for the different lengths of the novels, so you convert the raw counts to percentages by dividing each individual word count by a count of all of the words in the whole text. These are called *relative* frequencies because the frequencies are relative to the length of the text.

As it stands we have a sorted table of raw word counts. We want to convert those raw counts to percentages, which requires dividing each count by the total number of word tokens in the entire text. We can access the total number of words using the **length** function on the original word vector.

```
length(moby_word_v)
## [1] 214891
```

It is worth mentioning, however, that we could also find the total by calculating the sum of all the raw counts in the tabled and sorted vector of frequencies.

```
sum(sorted_moby_freqs_t)
## [1] 214891
```

3.4 Recycling

To convert the raw counts into relative frequencies, we will use division and then a little multiplication by 100 (multiplication in R is done using an asterisk) to express the results as percentages:

```
moby_length_v <- sum(sorted_moby_freqs_t)
sorted_moby_rel_freqs_t <- 100*(sorted_moby_freqs_t/moby_length_v)
```

The key thing to note about this expression is that R understands that it needs to *recycle* the result of `sum(sorted_moby_freqs_t)` and apply that result to each and every value in the `sorted_moby_freqs_t` variable. This recycling also works with definite values. In other words, if you wanted to multiply every value in a vector by ten, you could do so quite easily. Here is a simple example for you to try.

```
num_vector_v  <-  c(1, 2, 3, 4, 5)
num_vector_v * 10
## [1] 10 20 30 40 50
```

Having applied the above calculation to the `sorted_moby_freqs_t` object, you can now access any word type and return its relative frequency as a percentage. Because you have multiplied by 100, this percentage shows the number of occurrences per every 100 words.

```
sorted_moby_rel_freqs_t["the"]
##       the
## 6.596833
```

The word token *the* occurs 6.5968328 times for every 100 words in *Moby Dick*.

If you want to plot the top ten words by their percentage frequency, you can use the `plot` function as you learned in the practice exercise in Chap. 2. Here we will add a few more arguments to `plot` in order to convey more information about the resulting image, and then we will call the `axis` function to reset the values on the x-axis with the names of the top ten words (Fig. 3.1).

Notice that the `names` function can be used to *set*, or in this case, *get* the names of an object. The shape of the line in this plot is the same as in the exercise for Chap. 2, but now the values on the y-axis have been converted from raw counts to counts per hundred.

```
plot(
  sorted_moby_rel_freqs_t[1:10], type = "b",
  xlab = "Top Ten Words in Moby Dick",
  ylab = "Percentage of Full Text",
  xaxt = "n"
```

```
  )
axis(
  1, 1:10,
  labels = names(sorted_moby_rel_freqs_t [1:10])
  )
```

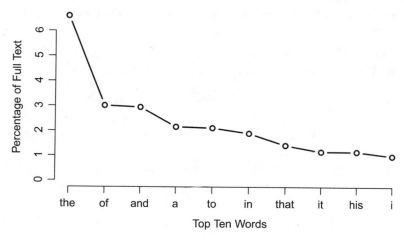

Fig. 3.1 Top ten words in *Moby Dick*

3.5 Practice

1. In the same directory in which you found *melville.txt*, locate *austen.txt* and produce a relative word frequency table for Austen's *Sense and Sensibility* that is similar to the one created in the Chap. 2 exercise using *Moby Dick*.[1] Keep in mind that you will need to separate out the metadata from the actual text of the novel just as you did with Melville's text. Once you have the relative frequency table (i.e., `sorted_sense_rel_freqs_t`), plot it as above for *Moby Dick* and visually compare the two plots.

2. In the previous exercise, you should have noticed right away that the top ten most frequent words in *Sense and Sensibility* are not identical to those found in *Moby Dick*. You will also have seen that the order of words, from most to least frequent, is different and that the two novels share eight of the same words in the top ten. Using the `c` combination function join the names of the top ten values in each of the two tables and then use the `unique` function to show the twelve word types that occur in the combined

[1] The text of Austen's *Sense and Sensibility* was acquired from Project Gutenberg. We have stripped out the Project Gutenberg metadata.

name list. Hint: look up how to use the functions by entering a question mark followed by function name (i.e., ?unique).

3. The %in% operator is a special *matching* operator that returns a logical (as in TRUE or FALSE) vector indicating if a match is found for its left operand in its right operand. It answers the question "is x found in y?" Using the which function in combination with the %in% operator, write a line of code that will compute which words from the two top ten lists are shared.

4. Write a similar line of code to show the words in the top ten of *Sense and Sensibility* that are *not* in the top ten from *Moby Dick*.

Chapter 4
Token Distribution and Regular Expressions

Abstract This chapter explains how to use the positions of words in a vector to create distribution plots showing where words occur across a narrative. We introduce the `grep` function and show how to use regular expressions for more nuanced pattern matching.

4.1 Introduction

By now you should be familiar with the process of creating a new R script file. From here on out, we will assume that for each chapter you begin by creating a new "chapter#.R" script in order to work through the code presented in the chapters and in the practice exercises at the end. Remember that many of the chapters in this book build on each other and that you will often be able to recycle code from previous chapters to use in subsequent ones. In cases where a new chapter depends upon code written in a previous chapter, we will always provide the necessary code at the beginning of the chapter.

4.2 Start Up Code

```
text_v <- scan("data/text/melville.txt", what = "character", sep = "\n")
start_v <- which(text_v == "CHAPTER 1. Loomings.")
novel_lines_v <- text_v[start_v:length(text_v)]
novel_v <- paste(novel_lines_v, collapse = " ")
novel_lower_v <- tolower(novel_v)
moby_words_l <- strsplit(novel_lower_v, "\\W")
```

© Springer Nature Switzerland AG 2020

M. L. Jockers, R. Thalken, *Text Analysis with R*, Quantitative Methods in the Humanities and Social Sciences,
https://doi.org/10.1007/978-3-030-39643-5_4

```
moby_word_v <- unlist(moby_words_l)
not_blanks_v  <-  which(moby_word_v != "")
moby_word_v <-  moby_word_v[not_blanks_v]
```

4.3 A Word About Coding Style

If you previously read the first edition of this book you might notice a few
changes to the way we are coding things in this new edition. For one thing, we
are now using the underscore (_) character in variable and function names. In
the first edition, there were periods (.) instead. We prefer the underscore because other programming languages use the period character in special ways,
and we do not want to confuse those who may have experience working in
one of these other languages. Another thing you might notice is the way that
we use spacing (white space). For example, before and after every assignment
operator (<-) we have a blank space. This is not required by R, but it makes
reading our code a lot easier. We also try to put spaces after commas between
arguments in a function, and on either side of an equals (=) sign. The truth
is that the spacing does not matter as far as whether the code will execute
or not. The spacing is just a "coding convention" that we have adopted to
make our code look better and be easier to read. You will also see that we
will sometimes break up a very long line of code onto multiple lines. Again,
this is not necessary, but it makes reading and troubleshooting our code a lot
easier.

4.4 Dispersion Plots

You have seen how easy it is to calculate the raw and relative frequencies
of words. These are *global* statistics that show something about the central
tendencies of words across a book as a whole. But what if you want to see
exactly where in the text different words tend to occur; that is, where the
words appear and how they behave over the course of a novel instead? At
what points, for example, does Melville really *get into* writing about *whales*?

For this analysis you will need to treat the order in which the words appear
in the text as a measure of time, *novelistic* time in this case.[1] You now need
to create a sequence of numbers from 1 to n, where n is the position, or index
number, of the last word in *Moby Dick*. You can create such a sequence using

---

[1] For some very interesting work on modeling narrative time, see Mani (2010).

the `seq` (*sequence*) function. For a simple sequence of the numbers, one to ten, you could enter:

```
seq(from = 1, to = 10)
## [1]  1  2  3  4  5  6  7  8  9 10
```

Instead of one through ten, however, you will need a sequence *from* one *to* the last word in *Moby Dick*. You already know how to get this number n using the `length` function. Putting the two functions together allows for an expression like this:

```
n_time_v <- seq(from = 1, to = length(moby_word_v))
```

This expression returns an integer vector (`n_time_v`) containing the positions of every word in the book.[2] We have titled this object `n_time_v` because it is a vector (`_v`) that will serve to represent narrative time (`n_time`) in the novel.

Now you need to locate the position of every occurrence of *whale* in the novel, or, more precisely, in the `moby_word_v` object. You have already learned how the `which` function can be used to locate items meeting certain conditions, so you can use `which` to identify the positions in the vector that are an occurrence of *whale* and store them in a new integer vector called `whales_v`, like this:

```
whales_v <- which(moby_word_v == "whale")
```

If you now enter the object name (`whales_v`) into the console and hit enter, R will return a vector of the numerical index positions in the `moby_word_v` object where it found an exact match for the character string *whale*.

Our goal here is to create a dispersion plot where the *x*-axis is novelistic time. You have those *x*-axis values in the `n_time_v` object. Another vector containing the values for plotting on the *y*-axis is now needed, and in this case, the values need only be some reflection of the logical condition of TRUE where a *whale* is found and FALSE or *none found* when an instance of *whale* is not found. In R you can represent the logical value TRUE with a number 1 and FALSE with a 0. Here, however, since we are not really counting items but, instead, noting their presence or absence, we will introduce a special character sequence NA—as in "not available"—for places where there is no found match. Begin, therefore, by initializing a new vector object called "`w_count_v`" that will be full of NA values. It needs to be the same length as the `n_time_v` object, so you can use the `rep` or *repeat* function to repeat NA as many times as there are items in the `w_count_v` variable.

---

[2]Remember that you can find out the data type of any R object using the `class` function. For example, `class(n_time_v)`.

```
w_count_v <- rep(NA, times = length(n_time_v))
```

Now you simply need to reset the NA values to 1 in those places in the
moby_word_v where a match for *whale* is found. You already have those
numerical positions stored in the whales_v object, so the resetting is simple
with this expression:

```
w_count_v[whales_v] <- 1
```

With the places where each *whale* was found now set to a value of 1 and
everything else set to a value of NA, you can produce a very simple plot
showing the distribution of the word *whale* across the novel (Fig. 4.1)[3]:

```
plot(
  w_count_v,
  main = "Dispersion Plot of 'whale' in Moby Dick",
  xlab = "Novel Time",
  ylab = "whale",
  type = "h",
  ylim = c(0, 1), yaxt = 'n'
  )
```

Dispersion Plot of 'whale' in Moby Dick

Fig. 4.1 Dispersion plot of "whale" in Moby Dick

This simple dispersion plot shows that the greatest concentration of the word
whale occurs in what is, roughly, the third quarter of the novel. The first
significant concentration of *whale* begins just before 50,000 words, and then
there is a fairly sustained *pod* of *whale* occurrences from 100,000 to about
155,000, and then there is a final patch at the end of the novel, just after
200,000.

By changing just a few lines of code, you can generate a similar plot (Fig. 4.2)
showing the occurrences of *ahab*.

---

[3]Remember, if you get an error saying: "Error in plot.new() : figure margins too
large" you may not have enough screen real estate devoted to the plot pane of RStudio. You can solve this problem by increasing the size of the plots pane (just click and drag
the frame). Your plot may also appear a lot taller (or thicker) than the one seen here. We
have shrunk the plotting pane height in RStudio to make the image fit this page better.

```
ahabs_v <- which(moby_word_v == "ahab") # find 'ahab'
a_count_v <- rep(NA, length(n_time_v))
# change 'w' to 'a' to keep whales and ahabs in separate variables
a_count_v[ahabs_v] <- 1 # mark the occurrences with a 1
plot(
  a_count_v,
  main = "Dispersion Plot of 'ahab' in Moby Dick",
  xlab = "Novel Time",
  ylab = "ahab",
  type = "h",
  ylim = c(0, 1),
  yaxt = 'n'
  )
```

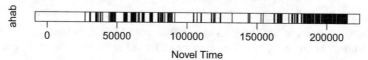

Fig. 4.2 Dispersion plot of 'ahab' in Moby Dick

4.5 Searching with grep

Comparing the two plots seems to indicate that when the word *ahab* appears, there are less appearances of *whale*. Given that the novel is about Ahab's long search for a whale, this might be an interesting result. In terms of sheer occurrences, *whale* dominates throughout the novel and appears especially prominent in the third quarter of *Moby Dick*. Overall, there are twice as many occurrences of the string *whale* than the string *ahab*. (There are 1150 occurrences of *whale* and 511 of *ahab*). But Melville does not always refer to Ahab as *ahab* or to the whale as *whale*. As you can imagine, Ahab might be referred to as *captain* or, more often, with the simple pronoun *he*. The whale, on the other hand, might be referred to as *it*, as *the monster, the leviathan*, and so on. In addition to synonyms and pronouns, our current accounting has not considered possessives or plurals such as *Ahab's* and *whales*. For finding these variants, the which function is quite impoverished—it only allows for exact matching.

Fortunately, we have an alternative to which in grep, which is a function for searching a text for *patterns* that match a regular expression. You have already seen two examples of regular expressions in action. We used \n as an argument in the scan function to find the line breaks when reading the novel into the text_v object. And we used \\W as an argument in the strsplit function to find word boundaries.[4] In this next code example, we create two *very simple* regular expressions that allow us to find some of these more subtle variants of *whale* and *ahab*.[5] Both of these expressions introduce the | (or) operator allowing us to search for multiple variants.

```
whale_hits <- grep(
  "whale|whales|whale's|monster|leviathan",
  moby_word_v
  )
ahab_hits <- grep(
  "ahab|ahabs|ahab's|captain",
  moby_word_v
  )
```

You can read the first line as "search for occurrences of 'whale' or 'whales' or 'whale's' or 'monster' or 'leviathan' in the moby_word_v vector." Run these two lines and then compare the number of found matches, to what you found previously using which.

```
length(whales_v); length(whale_hits)
## [1] 1150
## [1] 1746
length(ahabs_v); length(ahab_hits)
## [1] 511
## [1] 863
```

Instead of 1150 occurrences of *whale*, we now have 1746 occurrences of *whale* and the variants. And instead of 511 instances of *ahab*, we have 863 of *ahab* and the variants.[6]

You can now use the index positions held in these two new objects to create new dispersion plots. But before doing that, there is a problem that needs to be resolved. As you may recall, the regular expression, \\W, that we used as an argument of strsplit tokenized the text by treating all marks of punctuation as non-word characters. What this means is that occurrences of the possessives, *ahab's* and *whale's* do not actually exist in the moby_word_v object. Before our new grep-based approach can be fully useful, we need to rethink the way that we tokenized the text so that we keep the apostro-

---

[4]grep, by the way, is an acronym for Globally search a Regular Expression and Print.

[5]A full introduction to regular expressions is beyond the scope of this book, but you can learn a lot more over at https://www.regular-expressions.info.

[6]Note in the code example we have introduced the use of a semi-colon between two expressions. In R you can separate expressions on the same line using the semi-colon. It is just a short cut.

phes as word characters. For this, we need an alternative to the \\W regular expression.

It is often useful in programming to create "dummy" examples upon which to test and iterate your code. Here we will create a very simple string of text and place it into a variable called eg_v. The dummy text includes a couple of words using an apostrophe. We can then try different regular expressions as arguments to strsplit until we get one that achieves the desired outcome. First let us examine how our current expression works.

```
eg_v <- "this is a _test_ to see if we can keep ahab's and
other words such as contractions like can't and ain't. it
will also allow us to see some other oddities."
strsplit(eg_v, "\\W")
## [[1]]
##  [1] "this"       "is"         "a"            "_test_"
##  [5] "to"         "see"        "if"           "we"
##  [9] "can"        "keep"       "ahab"         "s"
## [13] "and"        ""           "other"        "words"
## [17] "such"       "as"         "contractions" "like"
## [21] "can"        "t"          "and"          "ain"
## [25] "t"          ""           "it"           ""
## [29] "will"       "also"       "allow"        "us"
## [33] "to"         "see"        "some"         "other"
## [37] "oddities"
```

When you run this code, you will see that the "s" from *ahab's* and the two "t" characters in *can't* and *ain't* are all being treated as individual word tokens because \\W treats them as marks of punctuation and breaks the strings in those places. It is worth mentioning here that \\W does treat one non-alphanumeric mark of punctuation as a word character. The underscore (_) is passed through as a word character. You might have noticed this when you were looking at the frequency table we created in the last chapter. If you enter the expression head(sort(table(moby_word_v))) you will find the tokens _ile_ and _you_. This is because both of these strings were present in the text file of *Moby Dick* that we got from *Project Gutenberg*. You will see in the example text here that we have included underscores around the word *test* so that you can see how things change with the new regular expression we are developing in this chapter; it will treat the underscore character just like other non-word characters.

The \\W regular expression that we used initially is a shortcut for a more complex regular expression that behind the scenes might look something like this: [^A-Za-z0-9_]. When placed inside square brackets, the caret (^) character at the beginning of this pattern is interpreted as a negation operator that you can read to mean "not." What follows after the *not* are three types of character classes: the capital letters A through Z, the lowercase letters a through z, and then all the numbers 0 through 9. After the numbers, you will also see the underscore character. When this expression is provided to strsplit, the function "splits" the text on any characters that are *not* (^) in the set of characters represented by A-Za-z0-9_. In other words, the text gets split on all the remaining characters, which include other marks of punctuation and, of course, the space character. With this knowledge, it is not too difficult to create a similar expression that substitutes the apostrophe for the underscore, like this:

```
strsplit(eg_v, "[^A-Za-z0-9']")
## [[1]]
##  [1] "this"      "is"        "a"         ""
##  [5] "test"      ""          "to"        "see"
##  [9] "if"        "we"        "can"       "keep"
## [13] "ahab's"    "and"       ""          "other"
## [17] "words"     "such"      "as"        "contractions"
## [21] "like"      "can't"     "and"       "ain't"
## [25] ""          "it"        ""          "will"
## [29] "also"      "allow"     "us"        "to"
## [33] "see"       "some"      "other"     "oddities"
```

With this new expression, we retain the words that use apostrophes, and we do not retain the underscores. We still have to deal with the empty "blanks" as we did with the \\W, but now we have got a slightly more nuanced expression for tokenizing the text.[7] After testing on this dummy example, we can now load and tokenize the text using the new expression:

```
text_v <- scan("data/text/melville.txt", what = "character", sep = "\n")
start_v <- which(text_v == "CHAPTER 1. Loomings.")
novel_lines_v <-  text_v[start_v:length(text_v)]
novel_v <- paste(novel_lines_v, collapse=" ")
novel_lower_v <- tolower(novel_v)
moby_words_l <- strsplit(novel_lower_v, "[^A-Za-z0-9']")
moby_word_v <- unlist(moby_words_l)
not_blanks_v  <-  which(moby_word_v != "")
moby_word_v <-  moby_word_v[not_blanks_v]
```

When we search for *whale* and *ahab* along with the variants using this new expression, we will actually get the same number of hits. Recall that the original expression that excluded apostrophes resulted in 1746 hits for variants of *whale* and 863 for variants of *ahab*.

---

[7] As you may have gathered from this example, tokenization is not a simple matter, and this is in no way meant to be an exhaustive discussion. One takeaway here, however, is that you need to be very conscious of your decisions. In the new expression that we have created, any single quotation mark will now be retained, and it is possible that some of these might not be being used for contractions or possessives. Consider, for example, the way that single quotes get used in a quotation of a quotation: e.g., Bob asked, "Did you really hear Mary say 'Holy Cow!' when she saw the sacred bovine?" Tokenizing this text with the regular expression [^A-Za-z0-9'] will result in tokens for both "'Holy" and "'".

```
whale_hits_new <- grep(
  "whale|whales|whale's|monster|leviathan",
  moby_word_v
  )
ahab_hits_new <- grep(
  "ahab|ahabs|ahab's|captain",
  moby_word_v
  )
```

With the new expression we still get 1746 total hits for variants of *whale* and 863 for variants of *ahab*. That is because the first method was breaking *ahab's* into *ahab* and *s* and *whale's* into *whale* and *s*; all the *ahab* and *whale* instances still got counted, they just were not being counted in their possessive form. Depending on what we are interested in, this may or may not be important. To see why it might matter, let us use these hits to create some new frequency tables that let us see how the variants are being used. Given that the values contained inside the `whale_hits_new` and `ahab_hits_new` are index positions within the larger `moby_word_v` object, we can use sub-setting to pull them out:

```
whale_varients_v <- moby_word_v[whale_hits_new]
ahab_varients_v <- moby_word_v[ahab_hits_new]
```

We can now build two new frequency tables to see the relative use of the variants and to reveal something else that we might not have even considered:

```
sort(table(whale_varients_v), decreasing = TRUE)
## whale_varients_v
```

##	whale	whales	whale's	leviathan	whalemen
##	1030	246	120	79	68
##	monster	whaleman	whaler	whalers	leviathans
##	42	36	19	19	17
##	narwhale	whalebone	whaleman's	leviathanic	monsters
##	11	11	9	8	6
##	leviathan's	monster's	whaleboats	whalemen's	narwhales
##	4	4	4	3	2
##	whaleships	leviathanism	whaleboat's	whaleboning	whaled
##	2	1	1	1	1
##	whaleship	whalesmen			
##	1	1			

```
sort(table(ahab_varients_v), decreasing = TRUE)
## ahab_varients_v
```

##	ahab	captain	ahab's	captains	captain's	ahabs
##	436	306	75	24	21	1

The first thing these new tables reveal, seen especially in the data about whales, is that there are a variety of other token variants in the text that

did not come immediately to mind. *Whaleship* and *whalebone* were probably
not what we were thinking about when considering occurrences of *whale*.
The second thing revealed here is a key difference between using the `which`
function and a regular expression. Where `which` finds exact matches, regular
expressions find patterns. Consider this example:

```
length(which(whale_varients_v == "whale"))
## [1] 1030
length(grep("whale", whale_varients_v))
## [1] 1585
```

The first line, using `which`, only finds exact matches, whereas the second
line, using `grep`, finds all the strings that *include* the sub-string *whale*. Naturally, there are ways we could tweak the regular expression so that it also
finds the exact match. For this we might use the special regular expression
metacharacters `^` and `$`. Instead of having the meaning of *not* that we described previously when placed inside square brackets, the `^` when placed at
the beginning of a search string has the meaning of *start* and it acts as an anchor. Anchor metacharacters do not match a specific character; instead, they
match a position (anchor) before, after, or between characters. The caret `^`
matches the position before the first character in the string. The `$` sign, is
similar, but it matches the position right after a character. These special
characters can, therefore, be used as start of string and end of string anchors.
To recreate the behavior of `which`, we could use the following:

```
length(grep("^whale$", whale_varients_v))
## [1] 1030
```

Again, this section on regular expressions is meant to be a very general introduction. There is a lot more to learn, and how you write your expressions
can radically change the way your text is tokenized. The other thing to keep
in mind, especially if you have used regular expressions elsewhere, is that we
have been searching for matches in a vector of tokens, and not in the entire
text file. Because we have already tokenized the novel into a vector of words,
`grep` is being recycled over all the values in the vector. But you can use
`grep` to search for patterns in a larger text. The exercises below will help you
explore a few more features and idiosyncrasies of using `grep`.

4.6 Practice

1. Now that you have a vector of all variations of the word *whale* (stored in
   `whale_variants_v`), create a dispersion plot of the *whale* variants grouped
   together. Compare this to your previous dispersion plot of the word *whale*
   alone. What do you notice?

2. In addition to ^ and $, the "dot" (.), or period is another special metachar-
acter within regular expressions. The . serves as a wildcard that can be
used to match any character. If you wanted to find and tally up all the
five character strings in *Moby Dick* that begin with w and ending with e,
you might write the following expression using three . wildcards:

```
table(moby_word_v[grep("^w...e$", moby_word_v)])
##
## waive waste we're we've weave wedge whale where while white
##     1     2     2     2     2     2  1030   205   242   280
## whole whose worse write wrote
##   137    85    21     4     3
```

Rewrite this expression to find five letter words that begin with wh and end
with e.

3. Adverbs often end with "ly." Write an R script that finds all the words
ending in "ly" and then use table and sort(with the decreasing = TRUE
argument) to identify the three most frequently occurring adverbs in *Moby
Dick*. (You can do this as several lines of code or in one line by function
embedding. The solution at the back of the book shows both methods.)

Reference

Mani I (2010) The Imagined Moment: Time, Narrative, and Computation.
University of Nebraska Press, Lincoln

Chapter 5
Token Distribution Analysis

Abstract This chapter expands upon the introduction to regular expressions and introduces several new functions including `seq_along`, `rbind`, `apply`, and `do.call`. `if` conditionals and `for loops` are also presented as we explore how to identify chapter breaks and build a distribution plot based on chapters.

5.1 Cleaning the Workspace

If you have been working through the chapters in the book without quitting RStudio, then it is very likely that you have a bunch of variables instantiated in memory. If you click on the "Environment" tab, you will be able to see what is currently in memory. Recall, for example, that you have a variable (`novel_lines_v`) containing the entire text from the original *Project Gutenberg* file as a list of lines. If you have had the same R session opened for a while, and especially if you have been experimenting with your own code as you work your way through the examples and exercises in this book, it might be a good idea to clear your *workspace* before moving on. As you work in a given R session, R is keeping track of all of your variables in memory. When you switch between different tasks during the same session, you can avoid a lot of potential variable conflict (and headache) if you refresh, or clear, your workspace. Since you are about to do something new with chapter breaks instead of looking at the novel as a single string, now is a good time to get a fresh start. In RStudio you can clean the slate by selecting *Clear Workspace* from the *Session* menu. Alternatively, you can just enter `rm(list = ls())` into the R console. Be aware that both of these commands will delete all of your currently instantiated objects.

© Springer Nature Switzerland AG 2020

M. L. Jockers, R. Thalken, *Text Analysis with R*, Quantitative Methods in the Humanities and Social Sciences,
https://doi.org/10.1007/978-3-030-39643-5_5

Enter the following expression to create a fresh session.

```
rm(list = ls())
```

If you now enter ls (short for "list objects") you will simply see character(0).

```
ls()
## character(0)
```

ls is a *listing* function that returns a list of all of your currently instantiated objects. This character(0) lets you know that there are no variables instantiated in the session. Now that you have cleared everything, you will need to reload *Moby Dick* using the same code you learned earlier.

5.2 Start Up Code

```
text_v <- scan("data/text/melville.txt", what = "character", sep = "\n")
start_v <- which(text_v == "CHAPTER 1. Loomings.")
novel_lines_v <-  text_v[start_v:length(text_v)]
```

You may recall from earlier that you can view the whole text of *Moby Dick* in your R console, newline by newline, by entering the name of the variable:

```
novel_lines_v
```

If you try this now, it might take a few seconds to load, and the results you will see are not going to be very pretty.[1] One thing you might notice in this long list is that the beginning of each new chapter follows a specific *pattern*. Each new chapter starts with a new line followed by the capitalized word *CHAPTER* and then a space character and then one or more digits. For example, [1] "CHAPTER 1. Loomings." and [185] "CHAPTER 2. The Carpet-Bag."

Because the *Project Gutenberg* text uses this *CHAPTER* convention to mark the chapters, you can *split* the text into chapters by using this character sequence (CHAPTER) as delimiter in a manner similar to the way that you split the text into words using \\W.

---

[1]Do not be alarmed if you see a series of backslash characters in the text. These are escape characters that R adds before quotation marks and apostrophes so that they will not be treated as special characters and parsed by R.

5.3 Identifying Chapter Breaks with grep

In text analysis grep and its related functions are your ever-loyal friends. If you have not already done so, be sure to access the grep help file by typing ?grep at the R prompt.

As we learned in the last chapter, grep is an R function for performing regular expression pattern matching. Using the regular expression ^CHAPTER \\d will allow grep to identify lines in the novel_lines_v vector that begin[2] with the capitalized letters CHAPTER followed by a space and then, using the shorthand \\d, any digit. Here is the full expression.

```
chap_positions_v <- grep("^CHAPTER \\d", novel_lines_v)
```

To check your work, enter the next R expression:

```
novel_lines_v[chap_positions_v]
```

If grep and the *regex* did their job, you will now see a character vector containing all 135 of the chapter headings. Here is a truncated version showing only the first six items:

```
head(novel_lines_v[chap_positions_v])
## [1] "CHAPTER 1. Loomings."            "CHAPTER 2. The Carpet-Bag."
## [3] "CHAPTER 3. The Spouter-Inn." "CHAPTER 4. The Counterpane."
## [5] "CHAPTER 5. Breakfast."            "CHAPTER 6. The Street."
```

The object chap_positions_v holds the positions from the novel_lines_v where the search string ^CHAPTER\\d was found. The goal now will be to find a way to collect all of the lines of text that occur *between* these positions: the chunks of text that make up each chapter.

That sounds simple, but we do not yet have a marker for the *ends* of the chapters; we only know where they *begin*. To get the ends, we can subtract 1 from the known position of the following chapter. In other words, if *CHAPTER 10* begins at position 1524, then you know that *CHAPTER 9* ends at 1524 - 1 or 1523.

This technique works perfectly except for the last chapter where there is no following chapter! There are several ways we might address this situation, but since the last item in the novel_lines_v contains the phrase *THE END*, we can just add this final index number to the chap_positions_v object. If we did not already know that *THE END* was the last item in the novel_lines_v there are a couple of ways that we could have found it. One option would be to use an expression such as this: novel_lines_v[length(novel_lines_v)]. But R provides two very handy functions for showing us either the first or

---

[2]Recall that the start of a line is marked by use of the caret symbol: ^.

last six items in any vector. These functions are **head** and **tail**. To view the
last few items in the **novel_lines_v** vector, use **tail**:

```
tail(novel_lines_v)
## [1] "they glided by as if with padlocks on their mouths; the s..."
## [2] "sailed with sheathed beaks. On the second day, a sail dre..."
## [3] "and picked me up at last. It was the devious-cruising Rac..."
## [4] "her retracing search after her missing children, only fou..."
## [5] "orphan."
## [6] "THE END"
```

Now that you know that the last item in the **novel_lines_v** is *THE END*
and not part of the text of the chapter, which ends with the word *orphan*, you
can simply add the index number of *THE END* (**length(novel_lines_v)**)
to your **chap_positions_v** object.

But let us slow down so that you can see exactly what is happening:

1. Enter **chap_positions_v** at the prompt to see the contents of the current
   vector:

```
chap_positions_v
##   [1]     1   185   301   790   925   989  1062  1141  1222  1524
##  [11]  1654  1712  1785  1931  1996  2099  2572  2766  2887  2997
##  [21]  3075  3181  3323  3357  3506  3532  3635  3775  3893  3993
##  [31]  4018  4084  4532  4619  4805  5023  5273  5315  5347  5371
##  [41]  5527  5851  6170  6202  6381  6681  6771  6856  7201  7274
##  [51]  7360  7490  7550  7689  8379  8543  8656  8742  8828  8911
##  [61]  9032  9201  9249  9293  9555  9638  9692  9754  9854  9894
##  [71]  9971 10175 10316 10502 10639 10742 10816 10876 11016 11097
##  [81] 11174 11541 11638 11706 11778 11947 12103 12514 12620 12745
##  [91] 12843 13066 13148 13287 13398 13440 13592 13614 13701 13900
## [101] 14131 14279 14416 14495 14620 14755 14835 14928 15066 15148
## [111] 15339 15377 15462 15571 15631 15710 15756 15798 15873 16095
## [121] 16113 16164 16169 16274 16382 16484 16601 16671 16790 16839
## [131] 16984 17024 17160 17473 17761
```

2. Add a new item referencing the last position in the **novel_lines_v** object
   to the end of the **chap_positions_v** object using the **c** function. In the
   code below we have made this very explicit and then provided a commented
   line of code that simplifies the command into one line.

```
last_position_v <- length(novel_lines_v)
chap_positions_v <- c(chap_positions_v , last_position_v)
# alternatively,
# chap_positions_v <- c(chap_positions_v , length(novel_lines_v))
```

3. Enter `chap_positions_v` at the prompt again, this time to see the entire
   vector but now with a new value (18170) appended to the end[3]:

```
chap_positions_v
##   [1]      1    185    301    790    925    989   1062   1141   1222   1524
##  [11]   1654   1712   1785   1931   1996   2099   2572   2766   2887   2997
##  [21]   3075   3181   3323   3357   3506   3532   3635   3775   3893   3993
##  [31]   4018   4084   4532   4619   4805   5023   5273   5315   5347   5371
##  [41]   5527   5851   6170   6202   6381   6681   6771   6856   7201   7274
##  [51]   7360   7490   7550   7689   8379   8543   8656   8742   8828   8911
##  [61]   9032   9201   9249   9293   9555   9638   9692   9754   9854   9894
##  [71]   9971  10175  10316  10502  10639  10742  10816  10876  11016  11097
##  [81]  11174  11541  11638  11706  11778  11947  12103  12514  12620  12745
##  [91]  12843  13066  13148  13287  13398  13440  13592  13614  13701  13900
## [101]  14131  14279  14416  14495  14620  14755  14835  14928  15066  15148
## [111]  15339  15377  15462  15571  15631  15710  15756  15798  15873  16095
## [121]  16113  16164  16169  16274  16382  16484  16601  16671  16790  16839
## [131]  16984  17024  17160  17473  17761  18170
```

The trick now is to figure out how to process the text, that is, the actual
content of each chapter that appears between each of these chapter markers.
For this we introduce the `for` loop.

5.4 The `for` Loop and `if` Conditional

Most of what follows from here will be familiar to you from what we have
already learned about tokenization and word frequency processing. The main
difference is that now all of that code will be wrapped inside of a looping
function. A `for` loop allows us to do a task over and over again for a set
number of iterations. In this case, the number of iterations will be equal to
the number of chapters found in the text.

As a simple example, let us say you just want to print (to the screen) the
various chapter positions you found using `grep`. Instead of printing them all at
once, like you did above by dumping the contents of the `chap_positions_v`
variable, you want to show them one at a time. You already know how to
return specific items in a vector by putting an index number inside brackets,
like this

---

[3]You might be wondering what to do if the text you are analyzing does not happen to
include the final line *THE END*. A simple solution would be to add a new line to the end
of the `novel_lines_v` vector. You could add the words *THE END* as a final line, or it
could simply be blank. And, naturally, there are other more sophisticated ways of writing
your code so that you do not have to do any of this, but that is more than we want to get
into in this introductory text.

```
chap_positions_v[1]
chap_positions_v[2]
```

Instead of entering the vector indexes (1 and 2 in the example above), you can use a `for` loop to go through the entire vector and *automate* the bracketing of the index numbers in the vector. Here is a simple way to do it using a `for` loop:

```
for(i in 1:length(chap_positions_v)){
  print(chap_positions_v[i])
}
```

Notice the `for` loop syntax; it includes two arguments inside the parentheses: a variable (`i`) and a sequence (`1:length(chap_positions_v)`). These are followed by a set of opening and closing *braces*. These braces contain (or encapsulate) the instructions to perform within each iteration of the loop.[4] Upon the first iteration, `i` gets set to 1. With `i == 1` the program prints the contents of whatever value is held in the 1st position of `chap_positions_v`. In this case, the value is 1, which can be a bit confusing. When the program gets to the second iteration, the value printed is 185, which is less confusing. After each iteration of the loop, `i` is advanced by 1, and this looping continues until `i` is equal to the length of `chap_positions_v`.

To make this even more explicit, we will add a `paste` function that will print the value of `i` along with the value of the chapter position, making it all easy to read and understand. Try this now.

```
for(i in 1:length(chap_positions_v)){
  print(paste("Chapter ", i, " begins at position ",
    chap_positions_v[i]), sep="")
}
```

When you run this loop, you will get a clear sense of how the parts are working together. With this example under your belt, you can now return to the chapter-text problem. As you iterate over the `chap_positions_v` vector, you are going to be grabbing the text of each chapter and performing some analysis. Along the way, you do not want to print the results to the R console (as in our example above), so you will need a place to store the results of the analysis during the `for` loop. For this you will create two empty *list* objects. These will serve as containers in which to store the calculated result of each iteration:

```
chapter_raws_l <- list()
chapter_freqs_l <- list()
```

---

[4]Using `i` is a matter of convention. You could name this variable anything that you wish: e.g., `my.int`, `x`, etc.

Remember from Chap. 2 that a *list* is a special type of object in R. You can think of a list as being like a file cabinet. Each drawer is an item in the list and each drawer can contain different kinds of objects.

To summarize, the for loop will iterate over each item in the chap_positions_v vector. When it gets to each item, it will use the chapter position information stored in the vector to figure out the *beginning* and the *end* of each chapter. With the chapter boundaries determined, the script will then collect the lines and word tokens found within those boundaries and calculate both the *raw* and *relative* frequencies of those word types using the table function that you learned about earlier. The frequencies (both the raw counts and the relative frequencies) will then be stored in the two list variables that are instantiated prior to the loop.

Though the processing inside the loop is similar to what was done in the previous chapters, there are one or two complicating factors that must be addressed. The most problematic of these involves what to do when i is equal to the length of chap_positions_v. Since there is no text following the last position, you need a way to break out of the loop. For this an if conditional is perfect. Below we have written out the entire loop. Before moving on to the line-by-line explication that follows, take a moment to study this code and see if you can explain each step.

```
for(i in 1:length(chap_positions_v)){
  if(i != length(chap_positions_v)){
    chapter_title <- novel_lines_v[chap_positions_v[i]]
    start <- chap_positions_v[i] + 1
    end <- chap_positions_v[i + 1] - 1
    chapter_lines_v <- novel_lines_v[start:end]
    chapter_words_v <- tolower(paste(chapter_lines_v, collapse = " "))
    chapter_words_l <- strsplit(chapter_words_v, "\\W")
    chapter_word_v <- unlist(chapter_words_l)
    chapter_word_v <- chapter_word_v[which(chapter_word_v != "")]
    chapter_freqs_t <- table(chapter_word_v)
    chapter_raws_l[[chapter_title]] <-  chapter_freqs_t
    chapter_freqs_t_rel <- 100*(chapter_freqs_t/sum(chapter_freqs_t))
    chapter_freqs_l[[chapter_title]] <- chapter_freqs_t_rel
  }
}
```

Now that you have had a chance to think through the logic of this loop for yourself, here is a line-by-line explication:

5.5 The for Loop in Eight Parts

5.5.1

Initiate a for loop that iterates over each item in chap_positions_v.

```
for(i in 1:length(chap_positions_v)){
```

5.5.2

As long as the value of i is not equal to the length of the vector, keep iterating over the vector.

```
 if(i != length(chap_positions_v)){
```

Here we introduce the conditional if. if allows us to set a condition that will evaluate to either TRUE or FALSE. If the condition is found to be TRUE, then the code inside the curly braces of the if statement will be executed. This has the effect of saying "so long as this condition is met, continue iterating." The condition here is that i not be equal (!=) to the length of the vector. The reason we must set this condition is because there is no chapter text after the last item in chap_positions_v. We do not want to keep the loop going once it gets to the end!

Assuming that the condition stated in the if statement is met, we proceed to the next line.

5.5.3

At this stage the program captures the chapter title which is found at the place in the novel_lines_v indicated by the value held in the chap_positions_v.

```
chapter_title <- novel_lines_v[chap_positions_v[i]]
```

If this is confusing, try this: In your console, set i to 1.

```
i <- 1
```

Now enter:

```
novel_lines_v[chap_positions_v[i]]
```

When you hit return, you will see [1] "CHAPTER 1. Loomings.

If that is still not clear, you can break it down even further, like this:

```
i <- 1
chap_positions_v[i]
## [1] 1
novel_lines_v[chap_positions_v[i]]
## [1] "CHAPTER 1. Loomings."
i <- 2
chap_positions_v[i]
## [1] 185
novel_lines_v[chap_positions_v[i]]
## [1] "CHAPTER 2. The Carpet-Bag."
```

5.5.4

We know that the title of the chapter is at the *ith* line in novel_lines_v, so we can add 1 to i and get the values of the next line in the vector. i + 1 will give us the position of the first line of the chapter text (i.e., excluding the chapter title).

```
start <- chap_positions_v[i] + 1
```

5.5.5

What is done next is a bit more subtle. Instead of adding 1 to the value held in the *ith* position of chap_positions_v, we must add 1 to i in its capacity as an *index*. Instead of grabbing the value of the *ith* item in the vector, the program is going to grab the value of the *item* in the *next* position beyond i in the vector.

```
end <- chap_positions_v[i + 1] - 1
```

If this is not clear, you can break it down like this:

```
i <- 1
chap_positions_v[i]
```

```
## [1] 1
chap_positions_v[i + 1]
## [1] 185
```

When i == 1, the value held in `chap_positions_v[i]` will be 1 because 1 happens to be the first value stored in the vector. When i == i + 1, in this case 2, R will return the value held in the 2nd position in `chap_positions_v`, or 185. In the next iteration, i will be 2 and so [i + 1] will be 3 and the result will be 301, which is the third value stored in the vector.

`chap_positions_v[i + 1]` will return the next item in the vector, and the value held in that spot is the position for the start of a new chapter. Since we do not want to count the words in the chapter heading, we must subtract 1 from that value in order to get the line number in `novel_lines_v` that comes just before the start of a new chapter. Thus we subtract 1 from the value found in the [i + 1] position.

5.5.6

The code that follows should be familiar to you from previous sections. With the `start` and `end` points defined, we grab the lines, paste them into a single block of text, lowercase everything, and then split it all into a vector of words that is tabulated into a frequency count of each word type.

```
chapter_lines_v <- novel_lines_v[start:end]
chapter_words_v <- tolower(paste(chapter_lines_v, collapse = " "))
chapter_words_l <- strsplit(chapter_words_v, "\\W")
chapter_word_v <- unlist(chapter_words_l)
chapter_word_v <- chapter_word_v[which(chapter_word_v != "")]
chapter_freqs_t <- table(chapter_word_v)
```

5.5.7

This next line of code is where the resulting table of raw frequency counts is stuffed into the list object that was created before entering the loop. The double bracketing here is used to assign a *name* or *label* to the list item, and here each item in the list is named with the chapter heading extracted a few lines above. It is not *necessary* to assign labels to list items in this way. If you leave out the label, the list will just be created with numerical indexes. The utility of this labeling will become clear later on.

```
chapter_raws_l[[chapter_title]] <-  chapter_freqs_t
```

5.5.8

The last two lines in the loop simply convert the raw counts to relative frequencies based on the number of words in the chapter. This relative frequency table is then stuffed into the other list object that was created before entering the `for` loop.

```
chapter_freqs_t_rel <- 100*(chapter_freqs_t/sum(chapter_freqs_t))
chapter_freqs_l[[chapter_title]] <- chapter_freqs_t_rel
```

5.6 Accessing and Processing List Items

With the two lists now populated with data, we need a way of accessing the data and putting it into a usable structure that allows for easy comparisons of word frequencies across chapters. For this we will utilize three functions: `rbind`, `lapply`, and `do.call` and along the way you will learn something more about *vector recycling*.

5.6.1 rbind

`rbind` is the simplest of the three functions introduced in this section. As the name suggests, `rbind` is a function for *binding* rows of data together. For `rbind` to work, the rows being bound must have the same number of columns. Enter the following R code into your console window:

```
x <- c(1, 2, 3, 4, 5)
y <- c(6, 7, 8, 9, 10)
```

These expressions create two vectors of five numerical values each. If you now use `rbind` to combine them, you get a matrix object with two rows and five columns.

```
rbind(x, y)
##    [,1] [,2] [,3] [,4] [,5]
```

```
## x      1     2     3     4     5
## y      6     7     8     9    10
```

Notice, however, what happens when we recreate the y vector so that x and y are not of the same length:

```
y <- c(6, 7, 8, 9, 10, 11)
rbind(x, y)
## Warning in rbind(x, y): number of columns of result is not a
## multiple of vector length (arg 1)
##    [,1] [,2] [,3] [,4] [,5] [,6]
## x     1    2    3    4    5    1
## y     6    7    8    9   10   11
```

First, R reports a warning message that the vectors were not of the same length. In R, a warning is just a warning; your script did not fail to execute. In fact, you now have a sixth column. Take a moment to experiment with this example and see if you can figure out what R is doing when it has two vectors of different lengths.

5.6.2 More Recycling

What you should have discovered is something called *recycling*. The recycling occurs because you are binding vectors of differing lengths. At some point R discovers that the shorter vector is at its end and that the longer vector still has uncombined elements. So R simply returns to the beginning of the shorter vector and begins *recycling* its elements. R will keep recycling from the shorter vector until it reaches the end of the process. The elements of the shorter vector will be reused over and over again until the process is complete. Sometimes this recycling is particularly useful. Say you want to multiply every item in one vector by a value held in some other vector. Here, for example, we multiply each number in the x vector by the number held in the y vector.[5]

```
x <- c(1, 2, 3, 4, 5, 6)
y <- 2
x * y
## [1]  2  4  6  8 10 12
```

---

[5]It might seem a bit odd, but in R even objects containing only one item are vectors. So in this example the y object is a vector of one item. If you simply enter y into the console, you will get a bracketed number 1 [1] followed by the value 2, which is the value held in the first (and only) position of the y vector.

This recycling can get a bit confusing when you have more complicated vectors. In the example above, each value in the x vector is multiplied by the value in the y vector. When the y vector contains more than one item then the recycling gets a bit more complicated. Consider this example:

```
x <- c(1, 2, 3, 4, 5, 6)
y <- c(2, 3)
x * y
## [1]  2  6  6 12 10 18
```

Here, the 2 and 3 get recycled over and over again, in order, such that the first item in the x vector is multiplied by the first item in the y vector (the number 2), the second item in the x vector is multiplied by the second item in the y vector (the number 3). But then when R gets to the third item in the x vector it recycles the y vector by going back to the first item in the y vector (the number 2) again. Deep breath.

5.6.3 apply

lapply is one of several functions in the apply family. lapply (with an "l" in front of "apply") is specifically designed for working with lists. Remember that you have two lists that were filled with data using a for loop. These are:

```
chapter_freqs_l
chapter_raws_l
```

lapply is similar to a for loop. Like for, lapply is a function for iterating over the elements in a data structure. The key difference is that lapply requires a list as one of its arguments, and it requires the name of some other function as one of its arguments. When run, lapply returns a new list object of the same length as the original one, but it does so after having applied the function it was given in its arguments to *each* item of the original list. Say, for example, that you have the following list called x:

```
x  <-  list(a = 1:10, b = 2:25, b=100:1090)
```

This is a list of three integer objects (vectors), each containing a series of numbers. Enter x at the R prompt to look at the contents of the x list. Basically, x is like a file cabinet with three drawers, and each one of the drawers contains an integer vector. If you now enter: lapply(x, mean), R will return a new list in which the function (mean) is applied to each object in the list called x.

```
lapply(x, mean)
## $a
```

```
## [1] 5.5
##
## $b
## [1] 13.5
##
## $b
## [1] 595
```

R has calculated the mean for each of the integer vectors in the x list.

Now consider the construction of the lists you filled up using the for loop. Each list contains a series of frequency tables. Each item in chapter_raws_l contains a table of raw counts of each word type in each chapter, and each list item in chapter_freqs_l contains a table of the relative frequencies of each word type in a chapter.

If you want to know the relative frequency of the word type whale in the first chapter of *Moby Dick*, you could get the value using bracketed sub-setting, like this:

```
chapter_freqs_l[[1]]["whale"]
```

This expression tells R that you want to go to the first item in the chapter_freqs_l list (list items are accessed using the special double bracket [[]] notation), which is a frequency table of all the words from chapter one, i.e.,

```
chapter_freqs_l[[1]]
```

But you also instruct R to return only those values for the word type *whale*. Try it for yourself:

```
chapter_freqs_l[[1]]["whale"]
##     whale
## 0.1336898
```

The result indicates that the word *whale* occurs 0.1336898 times for every one hundred words in the first chapter. Since you know how to get this data for a single list item, it should not be too hard then to now use lapply to grab the *whale* values from the entire list. In fact, you can get that data by simply entering this:

```
lapply(chapter_freqs_l, '[', 'whale')
```

Well, OK, we will admit that using "[" as the function argument here is not the most intuitive thing to do, and we will admit further that knowing you can send another argument to the main function is even more confusing. So let us break this down a bit. The lapply function is going to handle the iteration over the list by itself. So basically, lapply handles calling each chapter from

the list of chapters. If you wanted to do it by hand, you would have to do
something like this:

```
chapter_freqs_l[[1]]
chapter_freqs_l[[2]]
# . . .
chapter_freqs_l[[135]]
```

By adding "[" as the *function* argument to `lapply`, you tell `lapply` to "apply
bracketed sub-setting" to each item in the list. Recall again that each item
in the list is a table of word counts or frequencies. `lapply` allows us to add
another *optional* argument to the function that is being called; in this case
the function is "bracketed sub-setting." When you send the keyword *whale* in
this manner, then behind the scenes R executes code for each item that looks
like this:

```
chapter_freqs_l[[1]] ["whale"]
chapter_freqs_l[[2]] ["whale"]
# . . .
chapter_freqs_l[[135]] ["whale"]
```

If you enter a few of these by hand, you will begin to get a sense of where
things are going with `lapply`.

Here is how to put all of this together in order to generate a new list of the
whale values for each chapter.

```
whale_l <- lapply(chapter_freqs_l, '[', 'whale')
```

Instead of just printing out the values held in this new list, you can then
capture the results into a single matrix using `rbind`.

One option would be to `rbind` each item in the `whale_l` list object by hand:
something like what follows here (but including more than just the first three
list items):

```
# Not run
rbind(whale_l[[1]], whale_l[[2]], whale_l[[3]], . . . whale_l[[133]])
```

While this method works, it is not very scalable or elegant. Fortunately R
has another function for just this kind of problem: the function is `do.call`
and is pronounced *do dot call*.

5.6.4 do.call (do dot call)

Like lapply, do.call is a function that takes another function as an argument. In this case the other function will be rbind. The do.call function will take rbind as an input argument and call it over the different elements of the list object. Consider this very simple application of the do.call function: First create a list called x that contains 3 integer vectors.

```
x  <-  list(1:3, 4:6, 7:9)
x
## [[1]]
## [1] 1 2 3
##
## [[2]]
## [1] 4 5 6
##
## [[3]]
## [1] 7 8 9
```

To convert this list into a matrix where each row is one of the vectors and each column is one of the three integers from each of the list items, use do.call.

```
do.call(rbind, x)
##      [,1] [,2] [,3]
## [1,]   1    2    3
## [2,]   4    5    6
## [3,]   7    8    9
```

Using do.call in this way binds the contents of each list item *row-wise*.

The list of *whale* occurrences in *Moby Dick* is fairly similar to the list (x) that was used in this example. In some ways whale_l is even simpler than x because each integer vector only contains one item. You can use do.call, therefore, to activate the rbind function across the list of *whale* results. Doing this will generate a matrix object of 135 chapter *rows* by 1 *column* of relative frequency values. A *matrix* object is like a very simple spreadsheet; a matrix has rows and columns. One special (or limiting) thing about matrix objects in R, however, is that they can only contain one type of data. That is, they cannot contain text values in one column and numerical values in another. R has another object for handling mixed data, and we will cover that later on. For now, just think about a matrix as a simple spreadsheet. We will call this new matrix whales_m:

```
whales_m <- do.call(rbind, whale_l)
```

After you have entered this expression, look at the results by entering `whales_m` at the R prompt. Here is a truncated version showing just the first six items:

```
head(whales_m)
##                              whale
## CHAPTER 1. Loomings.         0.13368984
## CHAPTER 2. The Carpet-Bag.   0.06882312
## CHAPTER 3. The Spouter-Inn.  0.10000000
## CHAPTER 4. The Counterpane.          NA
## CHAPTER 5. Breakfast.                NA
## CHAPTER 6. The Street.       0.24067389
```

Using what you have learned thus far, you can create another matrix of chapter-by-chapter values for occurrences of *ahab*. The only thing you need to change in the code described already is the keyword: you will use *ahab* in place of *whale*:

```
ahab_l <- lapply(chapter_freqs_l, '[', 'ahab')
ahabs_m <- do.call(rbind, ahab_l)
```

5.6.5 cbind

With both `whales_m` and `ahabs_m` instantiated in memory, you can easily bind them together *column-wise* using `cbind`. As it happens, the individual columns in a matrix object are individual vectors. In this example, the data in the first column of the `whales_m` matrix is a numeric vector.

```
class(whales_m[,1])
```

Remember that a matrix is like a spreadsheet with rows and columns. You can access any *cell* in the matrix by identifying its row and column number. Here is a simple matrix created by `cbind`-ing several vectors together:

```
x <- c(1, 2, 3, 4, 5, 6)
y <- c(2, 4, 5, 6, 7, 8)
z <- c(24, 23, 34, 32, 12, 10)
test_m <- cbind(x, y, z)
test_m
##      x y  z
## [1,] 1 2 24
## [2,] 2 4 23
```

```
## [3,] 3 5 34
## [4,] 4 6 32
## [5,] 5 7 12
## [6,] 6 8 10
```

To access the value held in the second row and third column in this matrix, you use bracketed sub-setting similar to what you have been using when accessing values in a vector. Here, you will need to put both row and column information into the brackets.

```
test_m[2, 3] # show the value in the second row third column
##  z
## 23
```

Inside the brackets 2 was entered to indicate the row number. This was followed by a comma and then a 3 to indicate the third column. If you wanted to see an entire row or an entire column, you would just leave the field before or after the comma empty:

```
test_m[2,] # show all values in the second row
##  x  y  z
##  2  4 23
test_m[,1] # show all values in the first column
## [1] 1 2 3 4 5 6
```

It is also worth knowing that if the columns have names, you can access them by name. By default cbind names columns based on their original variable name:

```
test_m[,"y"]
## [1] 2 4 5 6 7 8
```

Now that you know how to access specific values in a matrix, you can easily pull them out and assign them to new objects. You can pull out the *whale* and *ahab* values into two new vectors like this:

```
whales_v <- whales_m[,1]
ahabs_v <- ahabs_m[,1]
```

You can now use cbind to bind these vectors into a new, two-column matrix. The resulting matrix will have 135 rows and 2 columns, a fact you can check using the dim function.

```
whales_ahabs_m <- cbind(whales_v, ahabs_v)
dim(whales_ahabs_m)
## [1] 135   2
```

Previously we mentioned that by default cbind titles columns based on the input variable names. You can reset the column names manually using the `colnames` function in conjunction with the c function. To rename the two columns in this example, use this expression:

```
colnames(whales_ahabs_m) <- c("whale", "ahab")
```

Once you have reset the column names, you can plot the results side by side using the `barplot` function with the `beside` argument set to `TRUE` (Fig. 5.1).

```
barplot(whales_ahabs_m, beside = TRUE)
```

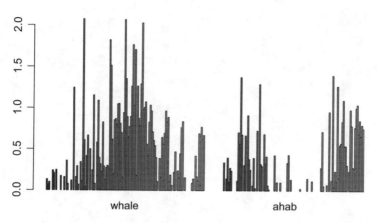

Fig. 5.1 Bar plot of "whale" and "ahab" side by side

5.7 Practice

1. In section 5.6.3 we saw how we could use `lapply` with the `mean` function to calculate the mean of numerical vectors that were stored in a list, x. Instead of using `lapply`, write a `for` loop that achieves the same end. Then, instead of saving the output to a new object, just print the results of each iteration to the console.

2. Write code that will find the relative frequencies, per chapter, for another word (e.g., *queequeg*) from the same `chap_freqs_l` object. Once you have isolated all relative frequencies for that word in a list, convert the list to a matrix by using `rbind`. Next, like you created `whales_v` from `whales_m`, develop a single vector holding the chapter relative frequencies for *queequeg*. After you have done this, bind `whales_v`, `ahabs_v`, and the new vector into a single matrix with three columns.

3. These bar plots were derived from the list of *relative* frequency data. Write a script to plot the *raw* occurrences of *whale* and *ahab* per chapter using the `chapter_raws_l` you created.

Chapter 6
Correlation

Abstract This chapter introduces data frames, random sampling, and correlation. Readers learn how to perform permutation tests to assess the significance of derived correlations.

6.1 Introduction

It might be tempting to look at the graphs you have produced thus far and begin forming an argument about the relative importance of Ahab versus the whale in Melville's novel. Occurrences of *whale* certainly appear to occupy the central portion of the book, whereas *Ahab* is present at the beginning and at the end. It might also be tempting to begin thinking about the structure of the novel, and this data does provide some evidence for an argument about how the human dimensions of the narrative frame the more naturalistic. But is there, in fact, an inverse relationship?

6.2 Start Up Code

```
rm(list = ls()) # Clear Workspace
text_v <- scan("data/text/melville.txt", what = "character", sep = "\n")
start_v <- which(text_v == "CHAPTER 1. Loomings.")
novel_lines_v <-  text_v[start_v:length(text_v)]
chap_positions_v <- grep("^CHAPTER \\d", novel_lines_v)
last_position_v <-  length(novel_lines_v)
chap_positions_v  <-  c(chap_positions_v , last_position_v)
```

© Springer Nature Switzerland AG 2020
M. L. Jockers, R. Thalken, *Text Analysis with R*, Quantitative Methods in
the Humanities and Social Sciences,
https://doi.org/10.1007/978-3-030-39643-5_6

```
chapter_raws_l <- list()
chapter_freqs_l <- list()
for(i in 1:length(chap_positions_v)){
  if(i != length(chap_positions_v)){
    chapter_title <- novel_lines_v[chap_positions_v[i]]
    start <- chap_positions_v[i] + 1
    end <- chap_positions_v[i + 1] - 1
    chapter_lines_v <- novel_lines_v[start:end]
    chapter_words_v <- tolower(paste(chapter_lines_v, collapse = " "))
    chapter_words_l <- strsplit(chapter_words_v, "\\W")
    chapter_word_v <- unlist(chapter_words_l)
    chapter_word_v <- chapter_word_v[which(chapter_word_v != "")]
    chapter_freqs_t <- table(chapter_word_v)
    chapter_raws_l[[chapter_title]] <-  chapter_freqs_t
    chapter_freqs_t_rel <- 100*(chapter_freqs_t/sum(chapter_freqs_t))
    chapter_freqs_l[[chapter_title]] <- chapter_freqs_t_rel
  }
}
whale_l <- lapply(chapter_freqs_l, '[', 'whale')
whales_m <- do.call(rbind, whale_l)
ahab_l <- lapply(chapter_freqs_l, '[', 'ahab')
ahabs_m <- do.call(rbind, ahab_l)
whales_v <- as.vector(whales_m[,1])
ahabs_v <- as.vector(ahabs_m[,1])
whales_ahabs_m <- cbind(whales_v, ahabs_v)
colnames(whales_ahabs_m) <- c("whale", "ahab")
```

6.3 Correlation Analysis

Using the frequency data you compiled for *ahab* and *whale*, you can run a correlation analysis to see if there is a statistically significant relationship between the two variables. A correlation analysis attempts to determine the extent to which there is a relationship, or linear dependence, between two sets of points. Thought of another way, correlation analysis attempts to assess the way that the occurrences of *whale* and *ahab* behave in unison or in opposition to each other over the course of the novel. You can use a correlation analysis to answer a question such as: to what extent does the usage of *whale* change (increase or decrease) in relation to the usage of *ahab*? R offers a simple function, `cor`, for calculating the strength of a possible correlation. But before you can employ the `cor` function on the `whales_ahabs_m` object, you need to deal with the fact that there are some cells in the matrix that contain the value NA. Not every chapter in *Moby Dick* had an occurrence of *whale* (or *ahab*), so in the previous practice exercise when you ran

```
whale_l  <-  lapply(chapter_freqs_l, "[", "whale")
```

R found no *hits* for *whale* in some chapters of the novel and recorded an NA, as in *not available* or *missing*. You may recall seeing this NA output when you viewed the contents of whales_ahabs_m matrix:

```
whales_ahabs_m[1:16, ]
##              whale      ahab
##  [1,] 0.13368984        NA
##  [2,] 0.06882312        NA
##  [3,] 0.10000000        NA
##  [4,]        NA        NA
##  [5,]        NA        NA
##  [6,] 0.24067389        NA
##  [7,] 0.21097046        NA
##  [8,]        NA        NA
##  [9,] 0.24711697        NA
## [10,]        NA        NA
## [11,]        NA        NA
## [12,]        NA        NA
## [13,] 0.17341040        NA
## [14,]        NA        NA
## [15,]        NA        NA
## [16,] 0.16037063 0.3385602
```

As you see here, there are no occurrences of *whale* in chapters 4 or 5 and no occurrences of *ahab* until chapter 16. Because cor is a mathematical function that requires numerical data, you need to replace the NA values before running the correlation analysis. Since the appearance of an NA in these cases is equivalent to *zero* (there are exactly *zero* occurrences of the keyword in the given chapter), you can safely replace all the occurrences of NA in the whales_ahabs_m matrix with zero. One way to do this is by embedding the conditional is.na function inside a call to the which function as in: which(is.na(whales_ahabs_m)). To set the values to 0, place the entire expression inside the brackets of whales_ahabs_m and assign a 0 to those items that meet the condition:

```
whales_ahabs_m[which(is.na(whales_ahabs_m))] <- 0
```

This is the short and easy way to achieve our objective, but for the sake of illustration we will break it down with comments added to explain what is going on:

```
# identify the position of NA values in the matrix
the_na_positions <- which(is.na(whales_ahabs_m))
# set the values held in the found positions to zero
whales_ahabs_m[the_na_positions] <- 0
```

With the NAs set to zero, the correlation can be run.

```
cor(whales_ahabs_m)
##               whale        ahab
## whale  1.0000000 -0.2411126
## ahab  -0.2411126  1.0000000
```

Because whales_ahabs_m is a matrix of two columns, the result of calling cor
is a new matrix containing two rows and two columns. The row and column
names are the same, and the values held in the cells are the correlation values.
It is no surprise to see that *whale* is perfectly correlated with *whale* and *ahab*
with *ahab*. The positive 1.0000000 in these cells is not very informative,
which is to say that running cor over the entire matrix as we have done
here results in a lot of extraneous information. That is because cor runs the
correlation analysis for every possible combination of columns in the matrix.
With a two column matrix such as this, it is really overkill. The results could
be made a lot simpler by just giving cor the two vectors that you really want
to correlate:

```
mycor <- cor(whales_ahabs_m[,"whale"], whales_ahabs_m[,"ahab"])
mycor
## [1] -0.2411126
```

The resulting number (−0.2411126) is a measure of the strength of linear
dependence between the values in the *whale* column and the values in the
ahab column. This result, called the *Pearson Product-moment correlation
coefficient*, is expressed as a number between -1 and +1. A negative one
(-1) coefficient represents perfectly negative correlation; if the correlation
between *ahab* and *whale* were -1, then we would know that as the usage of
whale increases, the usage of *ahab* decreases proportionally. Positive one (+1)
represents perfect positive correlation (as one variable goes up and down the
other variable does so in an identical way). Zero (0) represents no correlation
at all.

The further the coefficient is from zero, in either a positive or negative direction, the stronger the correlation; conversely the closer the result is to
0, the less dependence there is between the two variables. Here, with *whale*
and *ahab* a correlation coefficient of −0.2411126 is observed. This suggests
that while there is a slight inverse relationship (i.e., negative correlation), it
is not strongly correlated since the result is closer to 0 than to -1. Having
said that, how one interprets the meaning, or significance, of the correlation
indicated by this coefficient is largely dependent upon the context of the analysis and upon the number of observations or data points under consideration.
Generally speaking a coefficient between -0.3 and -0.1 on the negative side
of 0 and between 0.1 and 0.3 on the positive side of 0 is considered quite
small. Strong correlation is usually seen as existing at levels less than -0.5
or greater than 0.5.

This correlation test does not lead us to any easy conclusions about the relationship between occurrences of *whale* and occurrences of *ahab*. These two data points, for *ahab* and *whale*, appear to show only a weak inverse relationship. Nevertheless, there is much more to be considered.

Consider, for example, what we explored in Chap. 4, and how the use of synonyms and pronouns complicates these results. When *Ahab* is not being referred to by name, he is undoubtedly appearing as either *he* or *him*. The same may be said for the *whale* and the various appellations of *whale* that Melville evokes: *monster, leviathan, etc.* Using the techniques described in Chap. 4, you could investigate all of these and more. But before leaving this seemingly weak correlation, it might be useful to run a few more experiments to see just how significant or insignificant the result really is.

As noted above, the number of samples can be a factor in how the importance of the correlation coefficient is judged, and in this case there are 135 observations for each variable: one observation for each chapter in the novel.

One way of contextualizing this coefficient is to calculate how likely it is that we would observe this coefficient by mere chance alone. In other words, assuming there is no relationship between the occurrences of *whale* and *ahab* in the novel, what are the chances of observing a correlation coefficient of -0.2411126? A fairly simple test can be constructed by randomizing the order of the values in either the *ahabs* or the *whales* column and then retesting the correlation of the data.

6.4 A Word About Data Frames

Before explaining the randomization test in detail, we want to return to something mentioned earlier about the R matrix object and its limitations and then introduce you to another important data object in R: the *data frame*.

Thus far we have barely used data frames, but as it happens, data frames are R's bread and butter data type, and they offer us some flexibility that we do not get with matrix objects. Like a matrix, a data frame can be thought of as similar to a table in a database or a sheet in an Excel file: a data frame has some number of rows and some number of columns, and each column contains a specific type of data. A major difference between a matrix and a data frame, however, is that in a data frame, one column may contain character values and another numerical values. To see how this works, enter the following code to create a simple matrix of three rows by three columns:

```
x <- matrix(1, 3, 3)
x
##        [,1] [,2] [,3]
## [1,]    1    1    1
## [2,]    1    1    1
## [3,]    1    1    1
```

If you ask R to return the data type (class) of any one of the values in this matrix, it will return the class *numeric*.

```
class(x[1,2]) # get class of cell in first row second column
## [1] "numeric"
```

Now change the value of one cell in this matrix so that it contains *character* data instead of a number.

```
x[1,2] <- "Sam I am"
x
##        [,1]  [,2]        [,3]
## [1,] "1"   "Sam I am" "1"
## [2,] "1"   "1"         "1"
## [3,] "1"   "1"         "1"
```

You will notice right away that all of the values in the matrix are now shown inside quotation marks. This is because the entire matrix has been converted to character data. Those 1's are no longer numbers, they are the 1 *character*. Among other things, this means that you cannot perform mathematical operations on them anymore! If you check the class, R will report the change:

```
class(x[1,2]) # get class of cell in first row second column
## [1] "character"
class(x[1,3]) # get class of cell in first row third column
## [1] "character"
```

To see the difference between a matrix and a data frame, recreate the first matrix example and then convert it to a data frame, like this:

```
x <- matrix(1, 3, 3)
x_df <- as.data.frame(x)
x_df
##    V1 V2 V3
## 1   1  1  1
## 2   1  1  1
## 3   1  1  1
```

You can see immediately that a data frame displays differently. Instead of bracketed row and column numbers, you now see column headers (V1, V2, V3) and simple row numbers without the brackets. You can now repeat the experiment from above and assign some character data into one of the cells in this data frame.

```
x_df[1,2] <- "Sam I am"
class(x_df[1,2]) # get class of cell in first row second column
## [1] "character"
class(x_df[1,3]) # get class of cell in first row third column
## [1] "numeric"
x_df
##    V1        V2 V3
## 1  1 Sam I am  1
## 2  1         1  1
## 3  1         1  1
```

When using a matrix, the assignment of character data to any one cell resulted in all the cells in the matrix being converted into character data. Here, with a data frame, only the data in the column containing the target cell are converted to character data, not the entire table of data. The takeaway is that a data frame can have columns containing different types of data. This will be especially useful as your data get more complicated. You may, for example, want a way of storing character based metadata (such as *author gender*, or *chapter title*) alongside the numerical data associated with these metadata facets.

Another handy thing about data frames is that you can access columns of data using a bit of R shorthand. If you want to see all the values in the second column of the x_df variable, you can do so using bracketed index references, just as you have done previously with matrix objects. To see the entire second column, for example, you might do this:

```
x_df[,2]
## [1] "Sam I am" "1"         "1"
```

Alternatively, you can use the fact that the data frame has a header to get column information by referencing the column name, like this:

```
x_df[,"V2"]
## [1] "Sam I am" "1"         "1"
```

And, most alternatively, you can use the shorthand ($) to get column data like this:

```
x_df$V2
## [1] "Sam I am" "1"         "1"
```

That is a basic overview of data frames. Now we will return to correlating values in *Moby Dick*.

6.5 Testing Correlation with Randomization

In this section you will use your new knowledge of data frames. First convert the matrix object `whales_ahabs_m` into a data frame called `cor_data_df`:

```
cor_data_df <- as.data.frame(whales_ahabs_m)
```

As a gut check, you can use the `cor` function on the entire data frame, just as you did with the matrix object. The output should be the same.

```
cor(cor_data_df)
##            whale       ahab
## whale  1.0000000 -0.2411126
## ahab  -0.2411126  1.0000000
```

The goal now is to determine if that observed correlation coefficient of -0.2411126 could have been likely to occur by mere chance. To assess this you are going to take the values for one of the two columns in the data frame and *shuffle* them into a random order. You will then run a new correlation test with the randomized column. In this way, a chance distribution of the values that is independent of the actual structure of the chapters in the book can be simulated. If the correlation of the shuffled data is similar to the actual (as in *unshuffled*) data, then you will have to concede that the relationship between *whale* and *ahab* observed in the actual data is really no different from what might be observed if you threw all the occurrences of *whale* and *ahab* up in the air and then created 135 arbitrary piles.

The first step is to randomize the order of the values (the word frequency measurements) in one of the two columns of data in. `cor_data_df`. Since the columns contain chapter-by-chapter measurements, this randomizing will have the effect of shuffling the chapter order for one set of measurements and leaving the other set in chronological order. R provides a function called `sample` for generating a random shuffling of data. At its most simple, the `sample` function requires a vector of values to shuffle. So, to get a random ordering of the values in the *whale* column of `cor_data_df` you can simply enter:

```
sample(cor_data_df$whale)
```

Go ahead and try entering this a few times and you will see that each time `sample` randomly shuffles the order of the values from the *whale* column.

With the ability to randomize the values, you now need to correlate these randomized values against the ordered values in the unshuffled *ahab* column. Using the dollar sign to reference the columns in the data frame, the expression can be written as simply as this:

```
cor(sample(cor_data_df$whale), cor_data_df$ahab)
```

In our first test of this code, R returned a correlation coefficient of -0.0094803.
Your results will be different given the random sampling. We then copied
and pasted this code ten more times and observed the following correlation
coefficients for the various shuffles of the data.

```
## [1] 0.122331
## [1] 0.00818978
## [1] -0.01610114
## [1] -0.1289073
## [1] 0.05115036
## [1] 0.0443622
## [1] 0.08513762
## [1] -0.1019796
## [1] 0.07842781
## [1] 0.04410211
```

As you see, in this small sample of ten randomizations, the highest positive
correlation coefficient was `0.122331` and the lowest negative correlation coefficient was `-0.1289073`. Remember that the actual correlation coefficient
before we began shuffling anything was `-0.2411126`. In other words, the actual data seems to be quite a bit below (i.e., further from 0) what is observed
when shuffling the data and simulating a chance distribution of values. Still,
10 randomizations are not very many. Instead of copying and pasting the code
over and over again, you can develop a more programmatic way of testing
the correlation using a `for` loop and `10,000` iterations!

With a `for` loop you can repeat the randomization and correlation test process multiple times and at each iteration capture the result into a new vector.
With this new vector of `10,000` correlation values, it will be easy to generate
some statistics that describe the distribution of the random data and offer
a better way of assessing the significance of the actual observed correlation
coefficient in the unshuffled data.

The code required for this is simple. Begin by creating an empty container
variable called `mycors_v`, and then create a `for` loop that iterates a set number of times (`10,000` in our example). Within the curly braces of that loop,
you will add code for shuffling and then correlating the vectors. At each step
in the loop, you will capture the correlation coefficient by adding it to the
`mycors_v` vector using the `c` function. Here is how we wrote it:

```
mycors_v <- NULL
for(i in 1:10000){
  mycors_v <- c(
    mycors_v,
```

```
    cor(sample(cor_data_df$whale),
        cor_data_df$ahab)
    )
}
```

With this step completed, you can now use some basic R functions such as
min, max, range, mean, and sd to get a general sense of the results.

Here is what our randomization tests returned; your results will be similar
but not identical:

```
min(mycors_v)
## [1] -0.2992775
max(mycors_v)
## [1] 0.3484449
range(mycors_v)
## [1] -0.2992775  0.3484449
mean(mycors_v)
## [1] -0.0003656731
sd(mycors_v)
## [1] 0.08633026
```

What these descriptive statistics reveal is that our actual observed value is
more typical of the extremes than the norm. A low **standard deviation**
suggests that most of the values recorded are close to the **mean**, and here the
mean is very close to zero ($-3.6567306 \times 10^{-4}$), which you will recall from
above can be interpreted as meaning very little correlation. A high **standard
deviation** would indicate that the values are spread out over a wide range
of values. So even though the min value of -0.2992775 is slightly less than
our actual observed value of -0.2411126, that -0.2992775 is very *atypical*
of the randomized data. In fact, using a bit of additional code that we will
not explain here, we can generate a plot showing the distribution of all the
values in mycors_v (Fig. 6.1).

```
h <- hist(mycors_v, breaks = 100, col="grey",
          xlab = "Correlation Coefficient",
          main = "Histogram of Random Correlation Coefficients\n
          with Normal Curve",
          plot = T)
xfit <- seq(min(mycors_v), max(mycors_v), length = 1000)
yfit <- dnorm(xfit, mean = mean(mycors_v), sd = sd(mycors_v))
yfit <- yfit * diff(h$mids[1:2]) * length(mycors_v)
lines(xfit, yfit, col = "black", lwd = 2)
```

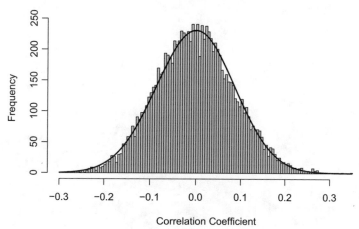

Fig. 6.1 Histogram plot of random correlation coefficients

The plot reveals, in dramatic fashion, just how much the data clusters around the **mean**, which as you recall from above is nearly 0. It also dramatizes the outlier status of the actual value (−0.2411126) that was observed. In 10,000 random iterations, only 19 correlation coefficients were calculated to be less than the actual observed value and the actual observed value was nearly 3 (2.79) **standard deviations** away from the **mean**. In short, the probability of observing a random value as extreme as the actual value observed (−0.2411126) is just 0.48%.[1]

6.6 Practice

1. Add two more columns to the matrix with data for the words *i* and *my* and then rerun the **cor** function. Though we have only used **cor** for two columns so far, we can use it just as easily on a matrix with two or more columns. Do not forget to set the frequencies for any chapters where the word *does not* occur to zero. What does the result tell you about the usage of the words *i* and *my*?

2. Calculate the correlation coefficient for *i* and *my* and run a randomization test to evaluate whether the results are significant.

---

[1]Another way to test the significance of a correlation coefficient is to use the **cor.test** function. Use ?**cor.test** to learn about this function and then run it using the **method = "pearson"** argument. To make more sense out of the results, consider consulting http://en.wikipedia.org/wiki/P-value on t-tests.

Chapter 7
Measures of Lexical Variety

Abstract In this chapter we will begin to transition from microanalysis to macroanalysis. We will leave behind the study of single terms and begin to explore two global measures of lexical variety: mean word frequency and type-token ratios.

7.1 Lexical Variety and the Type-Token Ratio

Moby Dick is a complicated book with a complex vocabulary. Readers of the book inevitably remember chapter 32. This is the cetology chapter in which Melville offers a zoological and pseudo-scholarly, pseudo-comical account of whale history and physiology. Students frequently complain that this section of the novel is more complex or *difficult*. One way to measure the complexity of the language is to calculate a measure of vocabulary richness. Such a measure can be represented as a mean word frequency or as a relationship between the number of unique words used (i.e., the working lexicon) and a count of the number of word tokens in the document. Using either measure as a proxy for lexical complexity or variety, you can compare the lexical variety in the cetology chapter to the other chapters of the novel.

Vocabulary richness is more commonly expressed as a percentage or ratio of unique word types to the total number of word tokens. A *type-token* ratio, or *TTR* as it is generally called, is calculated by dividing the total number of unique word types by the total number of word tokens. The result is then typically multiplied by 100 so as to end with a percentage. As you can surmise, a lower type-token ratio (TTR) is suggestive of less lexical variety.

© Springer Nature Switzerland AG 2020
M. L. Jockers, R. Thalken, *Text Analysis with R*, Quantitative Methods in the Humanities and Social Sciences,
https://doi.org/10.1007/978-3-030-39643-5_7

In the previous chapters, you learned how to use a `for` loop to generate two list objects containing tables of words and their frequencies for each chapter of *Moby Dick*. The list titled `chapter_raws_l` contains the raw counts of each word type and `chapter_freqs_l` contains the relative frequencies of each word type in the given chapter. To calculate the mean word frequency and TTR values for each chapter of *Moby Dick*, you will need `chapter_raws_l`.

7.2 Start Up Code

```
rm(list=ls())
text_v <- scan("data/text/melville.txt", what = "character", sep = "\n")
start_v <- which(text_v == "CHAPTER 1. Loomings.")
novel_lines_v <-  text_v[start_v:length(text_v)]
chap_positions_v <- grep("^CHAPTER \\d", novel_lines_v)
last_position_v <-  length(novel_lines_v)
chap_positions_v  <-  c(chap_positions_v , last_position_v)
chapter_raws_l <- list()
chapter_freqs_l <- list()
for(i in 1:length(chap_positions_v)){
  if(i != length(chap_positions_v)){
    chapter_title <- novel_lines_v[chap_positions_v[i]]
    start <- chap_positions_v[i] + 1
    end <- chap_positions_v[i + 1] - 1
    chapter_lines_v <- novel_lines_v[start:end]
    chapter_words_v <- tolower(paste(chapter_lines_v, collapse = " "))
    chapter_words_l <- strsplit(chapter_words_v, "\\W")
    chapter_word_v <- unlist(chapter_words_l)
    chapter_word_v <- chapter_word_v[which(chapter_word_v != "")]
    chapter_freqs_t <- table(chapter_word_v)
    chapter_raws_l[[chapter_title]] <-  chapter_freqs_t
    chapter_freqs_t_rel <- 100*(chapter_freqs_t/sum(chapter_freqs_t))
    chapter_freqs_l[[chapter_title]] <- chapter_freqs_t_rel
  }
}
```

7.3 Mean Word Frequency

To calculate mean word frequency on a chapter by chapter basis, you will first get the total number of word tokens in each chapter by summing the raw frequency counts in each, and then you will calculate the number of unique word types in each chapter. These are two very simple calculations that you can derive from the `chapter_raws_l` list object. It is worth taking

a moment to recall just exactly what this list contains. The first thing you
will want to know is the *size* or *length* of the list.

```
length(chapter_raws_l)
## [1] 135
```

The `length` function reveals that there are 135 items in the list. As you will
recall, each list item corresponds to a chapter in the novel. If you want to see
the chapter titles, you can find them in another part of the list object that is
accessed via the `names` function. Here we will just look at the first six using
`head`.

```
head(names(chapter_raws_l))
## [1] "CHAPTER 1. Loomings."      "CHAPTER 2. The Carpet-Bag."
## [3] "CHAPTER 3. The Spouter-Inn." "CHAPTER 4. The Counterpane."
## [5] "CHAPTER 5. Breakfast."      "CHAPTER 6. The Street."
```

Any item in a list may also be accessed and examined individually. Like so
much in R, such access is facilitated through bracketed sub-setting. In this
case, since you have also stored the chapter titles as *names* for each list item,
you can also use the `$` shortcut character in the way that you did with data
frames in the previous chapter. The `chapter_raws_l` object contains a series
of *table* objects, which you can check by calling the `class` function on one
item of the list:

```
class(chapter_raws_l$"CHAPTER 1. Loomings.")
## [1] "table"
```

Or, if you do not know the exact name, you can achieve the same result using
the numerical index:

```
class(chapter_raws_l[[1]])
## [1] "table"
```

As you can see, the first item in the list is a table object. To access the
word frequency table for this first chapter, just remove the call to the `class`
function:

```
chapter_raws_l$"CHAPTER 1. Loomings."
```

Or you can use this expression:

```
chapter_raws_l[[1]]
```

You have already learned how to find useful information about R objects
using the `class` function. For even more detailed information, you saw how
to use `str`, the *structure* function. The `class` function tells us something
general about the kind of data an R object contains. For example, entering
`class(chapter_raws_l)` shows us that the object is a list. Alternatively,
`str(chapter_raws_l)` returns additional information about the size (135

items) and construction of the list, including a long string of output containing information about each of the 135 items in the list.

Enter str(chapter_raws_1) in the console and examine the output. Calling str reveals that the first item of the main list is a table object with 854 items. The line of output that begins with the word *table* shows the counts for the first 10 items in the table. The *int* that you see tells you that the items are stored in an *integer* vector. Two lines below that is another line showing a series of words: "a" "abandon," etc. These are prefaced with the *chr* marker. *chr* indicates that these values are stored as a *character* vector. These, of course, are the actual word types from the chapter, and the integers above them are the raw counts of the occurrences of these word types in the chapter. The word *a*, for example, occurs 69 times in the first chapter. The fourth word in the vector, *about*, occurs 7 times in the chapter and so on.

With an understanding of how and where the data are stored, it is a fairly routine matter to calculate the mean word frequency for each chapter. Summing the integer values held in each chapter *table* will give you a count of all word tokens in the chapter, and you can use the length function to return the total number of word types.

```
sum(chapter_raws_1[[1]])
## [1] 2244
length(chapter_raws_1[[1]])
## [1] 854
```

Using these two results, the mean word frequency can be calculated by dividing the total number of tokens by the total number of unique word types.

```
sum(chapter_raws_1[[1]])/length(chapter_raws_1[[1]])
## [1] 2.627635
```

The result shows that each word type in the first chapter is used an average of 2.6276347 times. A much simpler way of doing this is to just use R's built in mean function.

```
mean(chapter_raws_1[[1]])
## [1] 2.627635
```

7.4 Extracting Word Usage Means

Since the chapters are already in a list object, all that you need now is a method for extracting the frequency data from all of the chapters at once. For this you can employ the lapply function that we have learned a bit about in previous chapters. lapply is an alternative to for that in some sense simply hides the operations of a `for` loop. In another sense, `lapply` simplifies the code needed by automatically generating a new `list` object for a result. That is, we do not need to create an empty list outside of a loop and then fill it with each iteration of the loop. `lapply` takes two arguments: a list object and a function to apply to the items in the list. To get the `mean` word usage for each chapter in *Moby Dick*, for example, you could use the following command:

```
lapply(chapter_raws_l, mean)
```

Calling `lapply` in this way generates a new `list` object. In the example here, we have just printed the results to the screen instead of saving the output into a new object.

Since a list is not very handy for further manipulation, you can wrap this `lapply` expression inside a `do.call` function, which will take the list output from `lapply` and apply another function (`rbind`) to the results. This has the effect of putting all of the results into neat rows in a matrix object. Since you want to be able to plot this data, you can direct the results of all of this into a new object called `mean_word_use_m`.

```
mean_word_use_m <- do.call(rbind,
  lapply(chapter_raws_l, mean)
  )
```

The dimensions of the resulting matrix can be obtained using the `dim` function (for *dimensions*):

```
dim(mean_word_use_m)
## [1] 135    1
```

`dim` reports that the matrix has 135 rows and 1 column. But there is a bit more information stored in this matrix object, and you can get a hint of that content by using the `str` function discussed above. During the creation of this matrix, the individual chapter names were retained and assigned as *rownames*. Entering `rownames(mean_word_use_m)` returns the names.

At this point, you can plot the values and visualize the mean word usage pattern across the novel (Fig. 7.1). Calling `plot` with the type argument as "h" returns a simple bar plot in which chapters with higher bars are, in one manner of speaking, *less rich*.

```
plot(mean_word_use_m,
     type = "h",
     xlab = "Chapter",
     ylab = "Mean Word Use"
     )
```

In the chapters with high values, individual word types are used more often; there is more repetition of the same word types. Alternatively, in chapters

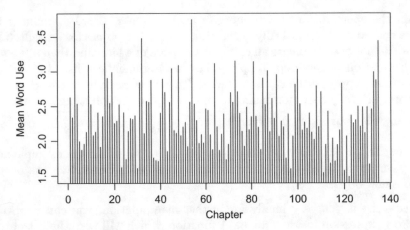

Fig. 7.1 Bar plot of mean word use

where the bar is low, each word type has a lower overall usage frequency. In the chapters with high bars, the reader can expect to see the same words repeated rather frequently, in the lower bar chapters the reader is treated to a collection of words that might give the impression of greater variety for being repeated less often.

By this measure of mean word use, the cetology chapter (chapter 32), which readers so often remember as being one of denser, richer vocabulary is not exceptional at all. Words in the cetology chapter are repeated fairly often. In fact, each unique word type is used an average of 3.48 times.

To be more interpretable, you may want to consider normalizing these values across the entire text. R provides a `scale` function for normalizing or *scaling* data. In such scaling, the overall mean for all of the chapters is first calculated and then subtracted from each of the individual chapter means. This method has the effect of subtracting away the expected value (expected as calculated by the overall mean) and then showing only the deviations from the mean. The result is a vector of values that includes both positive and negative numbers. You can look at the scaled values by entering:

```
scale(mean_word_use_m)
```

Instead of just studying the numbers, however, it might be better to visualize the results as a bar plot similar to the one above. In the resulting plot, 0 on the y-axis will correspond to the mean across the entire novel. You will only see the deviations from the mean (Fig. 7.2).

```
plot(scale(mean_word_use_m),
    type = "h",
    xlab = "Chapter",
    ylab = "Mean Word Use (scaled)"
    )
```

7.5 Ranking the Values

To see where the cetology chapter ranks in terms of average word use, you can employ the **order** function to arrange the data in decreasing rank order. Beware, however, that the **order** function can be confusing. If you enter:

```
order(mean_word_use_m)
```

R will return a vector of numbers corresponding to the ranked *positions* of each item in the **mean_word_use_m** vector. What this vector reveals is that the first item in the **mean_word_use_m** object, the *mean* of the word usage in chapter one of the novel, is the 122nd in rank when the means are sorted in increasing order, from smallest to largest.

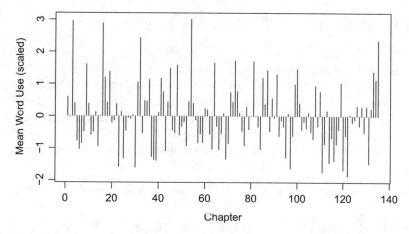

Fig. 7.2 Mean word usage plot with scaling

If you want to order them according to decreasing rank, you need to set the *decreasing* argument of **order** to *TRUE*.

```
order(mean_word_use_m, decreasing = TRUE)
```

Again, just to emphasize this point, `order` does not sort the means; it returns
a vector of ranks in which the vector positions correspond to the positions in
the vector being ranked. The vector of means can then be reordered, *sorted*,
using this new vector of *rank positions* inside the brackets:

```
mean_word_use_m[order(mean_word_use_m, decreasing = TRUE),]
```

Here is a truncated look at the results:

```
## CHAPTER 54. The Town-Hos Story.
## 3.748727
## CHAPTER 3. The Spouter-Inn.
## 3.719777
## CHAPTER 16. The Ship.
## 3.692105
## CHAPTER 32. Cetology.
## 3.477622
```

After sorting you will see that the cetology chapter has the *fourth* largest
mean of the 135 chapters. Only three other chapters recycle words at the rate
of the cetology chapter! By this measure, it is not an especially interesting
chapter at all.

7.6 Calculating the TTR Inside `lapply`

The last few sections demonstrated how to use R's built in `mean` function
with `lapply` to calculate the mean word frequency of each chapter. Mean
word usage is one way of thinking about lexical variety. A Type-Token Ratio
(TTR) provides a similar value for assessing lexical richness, but since R does
not already have a function for calculating TTR, you will need to modify the
arguments given to `lapply`. Instead of using `mean`, you will create your own
function.

Above, you saw that you could calculate the mean for one chapter using this
expression:

```
sum(chapter_raws_l[[1]])/length(chapter_raws_l[[1]])
```

You can calculate the TTR using a similar expression in which the numerator
and denominator are reversed, and here we will also multiply the result by
100.

```
length(chapter_raws_l[[1]])/sum(chapter_raws_l[[1]]) * 100
## [1] 38.05704
```

To run a similar calculation for all of the chapters as part of a call to `lapply`, a generalized version of this calculation needs to be provided to `lapply` as the *function* argument. As you have seen, `lapply` takes a function argument such as `mean` or `sum`, etc. Since there is no function for TTR, you can provide `lapply` with your own custom function. In place of an existing function such as `mean` you can insert an *inline* function definition using a variable `x` to stand in for each item in the main list.

```
ttr_l <- lapply(
  chapter_raws_l,
  function(x) {length(x) / sum(x) * 100}
  )
```

Within the parentheses of `lapply` the TTR function is defined as follows: `function(x) {length(x) / sum(x) * 100`. When executed, `lapply` will treat each item in the `chapter_raws_l` list as the value for `x` (much in the same way that we have been using `i` inside of a `for` loop). The calculations will be performed on each item and the results returned in a new list object. You can then run `do.call` with `rbind` just as you did when calculating the means.

```
ttr_m <- do.call(rbind, ttr_l)
```

Now you can order and inspect the results:

```
ttr_m[order(ttr_m, decreasing = TRUE),]
```

Or you can visualize the results using a plot (Fig. 7.3):

```
plot(ttr_m, type = "h", xlab = "Chapter", ylab = "TTR")
```

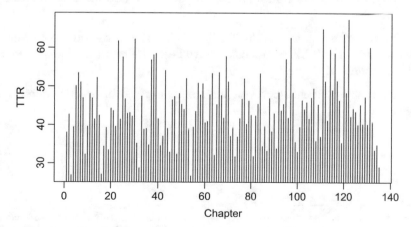

Fig. 7.3 Plot of type-token ratios

7.7 A Further Use of Correlation

Unfortunately, measures such as mean word frequency and TTR are not terribly useful because text length, or chapter length in this case, can be a strong determiner in the rate at which words get recycled. As chapter length increases you can generally expect more new words to be introduced. At the same time, many of the existing words will see repeated use because they provide the necessary structure or scaffolding for the introduction of new words. The practice exercises that follow provide you an opportunity to test these assertions.[1]

7.8 Practice

1. To test the assertion that document length is a strong determiner in the rate at which words get recycled, measure the strength of correlation between chapter length and TTR. For this you need two vectors of data. You already have the TTR values in the `ttr_m` matrix. Convert that data to a vector using `as.vector`. You now need another vector of chapter lengths. For this you can use `lapply` with the sum function instead of using *mean*. Once you have the two vectors, run a correlation analysis similar to the correlation you did previously with occurrences of *whale* and *ahab*. Write up your code and an analysis of the result.

2. Run a similar correlation test using the values in the `mean_word_use_m` instead of the TTR values. Write up your code and an interpretation of the result.

3. Use randomization to test the likelihood that the correlation coefficient observed with the TTR values could have been the result of chance. Explain the outcome of the test.

4. Explain the difference between the results derived in practice questions 1 and 2.

---

[1] In addition to the two measures of lexical variety offered in this chapter, and another approach offered in the next, readers may wish to consider *Yule's K* (see Yule (2014)). Yule attempts to compensate for text length and provide a stable measure of lexical variety in what he called the *K characteristic*. A function for computing Yule's characteristic constant K can be found in the `languageR` R package.

Reference

Yule CU (2014) The Statistical Study of Literary Vocabulary, 1st edn. Cambridge University Press

Chapter 8
Hapax Richness

Abstract This chapter expands the analysis of vocabulary by focusing on words that occur very infrequently. Readers learn how to use `sapply` and create another simple inline function.

8.1 Introduction

Another way of thinking about vocabulary richness and the *experience* of reading a particular text is to consider how many words appear quite infrequently or even just once. These words that occur just once are sometimes referred to as *singletons* or even *one-zies*, but they are more formally called *hapax legomena*. *Hapax* (for short) may provide a different way of assessing the lexical richness of a given segment of prose. In this chapter you will learn how to calculate the total number of *hapax* and test if there is a correlation between the number of *hapax* and the length of a chapter. The working hypothesis will be that as chapter length increases, you would expect to see an increase in the number of *hapax legomena*.

8.2 Start Up Code

```
rm(list = ls())
text_v <- scan("data/text/melville.txt", what = "character", sep = "\n")
start_v <- which(text_v == "CHAPTER 1. Loomings.")
novel_lines_v <-  text_v[start_v:length(text_v)]
chap_positions_v <- grep("^CHAPTER \\d", novel_lines_v)
```

© Springer Nature Switzerland AG 2020

M. L. Jockers, R. Thalken, *Text Analysis with R*, Quantitative Methods in the Humanities and Social Sciences,
https://doi.org/10.1007/978-3-030-39643-5_8

```
last_position_v <-  length(novel_lines_v)
chap_positions_v  <-  c(chap_positions_v, last_position_v)
chapter_raws_l <- list()
chapter_freqs_l <- list()
for(i in 1:length(chap_positions_v)){
  if(i != length(chap_positions_v)){
    chapter_title <- novel_lines_v[chap_positions_v[i]]
    start <- chap_positions_v[i] + 1
    end <- chap_positions_v[i + 1] - 1
    chapter_lines_v <- novel_lines_v[start:end]
    chapter_words_v <- tolower(paste(chapter_lines_v, collapse = " "))
    chapter_words_l <- strsplit(chapter_words_v, "\\W")
    chapter_word_v <- unlist(chapter_words_l)
    chapter_word_v <- chapter_word_v[which(chapter_word_v != "")]
    chapter_freqs_t <- table(chapter_word_v)
    chapter_raws_l[[chapter_title]] <-  chapter_freqs_t
    chapter_freqs_t_rel <- 100*(chapter_freqs_t/sum(chapter_freqs_t))
    chapter_freqs_l[[chapter_title]] <- chapter_freqs_t_rel
  }
}
chapter_lengths_m <- do.call(rbind, lapply(chapter_raws_l, sum))
```

8.3 sapply

For this analysis, you must return to the `chapter_raws_l` list. Instead of extracting a count of all word tokens, you will compute a `sum` of all of the word types *that appear only once* in each chapter. To extract a count of the *hapax*, you can use the `sapply` function in combination with an argument that identifies the values that are equal to `1`. `sapply` is a simplified, or, as the R documentation calls it, a *user-friendly* version of `lapply`. The main difference between `lapply` and `sapply` is that `sapply` returns a *vector* instead of a *list*. The arguments that you provide to `sapply` are going to be very similar to those given to `lapply`, but here we are going to add some additional conditions in the form of a *custom function* that calculates a `sum` of only those values that meet the condition of being equal to `1`. The function is going to count how many words in the vector are used only once.

8.4 An Inline Conditional Function

Instead of using built in functions such as `mean` or `sum`, for this task we need to construct our own function using the inline `function(x)` argument of `sapply` followed by a definition, or declaration, of that function. This is similar to what we did in Chap. 7 when we computed the *Type-Token Ratio* (TTR) of each chapter. In this case the custom function will enclose a conditional expression that sums all the values in the raw counts table that are equal to one. It is important to emphasize here that to express equivalence, R expects us to use two *equal signs* (==). As you recall, this is done to avoid confusing the use of a single equals sign, which can be used in R as an assignment operator.[1] The code required for counting the number of *hapax* in each chapter, therefore, looks like this:

```
chapter_hapax_v  <-  sapply(chapter_raws_l, function(x) sum(x == 1))
```

Translating this code block into plain English, we might say something like this: "For each item in `chapter_raws_l`, return the `sum` of the values that are equal to one." Since the *values* in this case are all `one`, `sum` will return a *count* of the words that occur just once in each chapter. If you print the contents of `chapter_hapax_v` to the console, you will see the *hapax* counts for each chapter. Here we just show the first five values:

```
chapter_hapax_v[1:5]
##        CHAPTER 1. Loomings.   CHAPTER 2. The Carpet-Bag.
##                        605                          433
## CHAPTER 3. The Spouter-Inn.  CHAPTER 4. The Counterpane.
##                       1054                          465
##        CHAPTER 5. Breakfast.
##                        266
```

This is a start, but now we need to divide the number of *hapax* in each chapter by the total number of words in each chapter. As it happens, we already have these values in the `chapter_lengths_m` variable from the practice exercise in the last chapter. Here it is again:

```
chapter_lengths_m <- do.call(rbind, lapply(chapter_raws_l, sum))
```

Since R easily facilitates matrix division (that is, R allows you to divide one matrix of values by the corresponding values in another matrix) the code is simple. Instead of having to perform the division on one value at a time, like this:

```
chapter_hapax_v[1] / chapter_lengths_m[1]
## CHAPTER 1. Loomings.
##            0.2696078
chapter_hapax_v[2] / chapter_lengths_m[2]
## CHAPTER 2. The Carpet-Bag.
##                  0.2980041
```

---

[1] In R values can be assigned to an object using either <- or =. Throughout this book we use <- because it is the most common convention among users of R, and it avoids the whole = vs. == confusion.

You can do it all at once, like this:

```
hapax_percentage <- chapter_hapax_v / chapter_lengths_m
```

This expression returns a new matrix containing the chapter names and the percentage of *hapax* in each chapter. These values can then be plotted, so that you can visualize the chapter-by-chapter *hapax richness* (Fig. 8.1).[2]

```
barplot(
  hapax_percentage,
  beside = TRUE,
  col = "grey",
  names.arg = seq(1:length(chapter_raws_l)),
  xlab = "Chapters",
  ylab = "Hapax Percentage"
  )
```

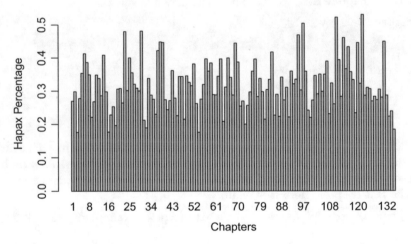

Fig. 8.1 *Hapax* percentage plot

Using the `cor` function, it is simple to calculate the extent of correlation between the number of *hapax* in a chapter and the length of the chapter:

```
cor(chapter_hapax_v, chapter_lengths_m)
##            [,1]
## [1,] 0.9677308
```

---

[2]When the "beside" argument is set to TRUE the columns are portrayed as juxtaposed bars; otherwise, they will be stacked. Enter "?barplot" in the console for details.

The correlation between the number of *hapax* in a chapter and the length of the chapter is extremely strong with an R-value of 0.9677308. As the chapters of *Moby Dick* get longer, not only do we observe the same words repeated more often, but we also see an increase in the number of new words being introduced.

8.5 Practice

1. Use `order` to rank the values in `hapax_percentage`. How does the rank of the cetology chapter compare to the others?

2. The correlation statistic found at the end of the chapter is not especially useful in and of itself. It becomes much more interesting when compared to another author's work, such as Jane Austen's *Sense and Sensibility* that you will find in the same folder as you found *Moby Dick*: `data/text`. First write the code necessary to get the chapter-by-chapter counts of the *hapax* in Austen's *Sense and Sensibility*. Save these in a list object titled `sense_raws_l`. From this object calculate the number of *hapax* and the chapter lengths for each chapter of *Sense and Sensibility*. Compute the correlation and describe how the correlation results for Melville and Austen compare and what they tell us about the two writers in terms of vocabulary usage habits.

3. Use what you learned in Chap. 6 to test the likelihood that these two correlation figures could have been the result of chance. To complete this exercise you will need to code separate randomization tests for both *Moby Dick* and *Sense and Sensibility*.

Chapter 9
Do It KWIC

Abstract In the last chapter a simple inline function was used within a call to the `sapply` function. In this chapter we explore user-defined functions more broadly and write a custom function for producing a Keyword in Context (KWIC) list.

9.1 Introduction

KWIC or *Keyword in Context* searches are a standard way of addressing Rupert Firth's observation that you will know a word's meaning, or sense, by looking at the other words around it, that is, by its context.[1] In this section (including the practice exercises), you will learn how to build a flexible KWIC tool in R. You will also be introduced to some R functionality that will allow you to access and analyze multiple texts at once.

Unlike previous chapters where you loaded a single file using `scan`, you are now going to access a collection of files in a directory. Begin by defining a variable that contains the relative path to the directory of text files.

```
input_dir <- "data/text"
```

You can now call R's `dir` function with this path variable as an argument to retrieve the names of all of the files in the directory. In addition to the path argument, which you have now stored in the `input_dir` object, the `dir` function can take an optional *search pattern string* written using a regular expression. Since you only want `dir` to return the files in the directory that have a *.txt* file extension, use an escaped period (\\.) followed by `txt` and the

---

[1] See Firth (1957).

© Springer Nature Switzerland AG 2020
M. L. Jockers, R. Thalken, *Text Analysis with R*, Quantitative Methods in the Humanities and Social Sciences,
https://doi.org/10.1007/978-3-030-39643-5_9

$ symbol (to mark the end of a string).[2] This creates a *pattern* (in regular expression speak) that will *match any string of characters that ends with* .txt. The expression looks like this:

```
files_v <- dir(input_dir, "\\.txt$")
files_v
## [1] "austen.txt"   "melville.txt"
```

Adding the full.names = TRUE argument, instructs the dir function to include the full directory path in its result.

```
files_v <- dir(input_dir, "\\.txt$", full.names = TRUE)
```

Having run this, you should now type files_v into R and return a vector of file paths; in this example, just two files will be returned.

```
files_v
## [1] "data/text/austen.txt"   "data/text/melville.txt"
```

9.2 Custom Functions

This console display of the content of the files_v vector is not very pretty or especially useful, and once you get a corpus containing many files, it can become difficult to read through this display. To better understand the idea of custom functions, you will write code to make the contents of the files_v vector display in a more organized and *reader-friendly* fashion.

Functions are, primarily, reusable chunks of code. You have already learned about many of R's built-in functions, and you have used and reused them many times. You can also create your own custom functions and call *them* over and over again. If you were baking a cake for a friend's birthday, you would buy some ingredients, pull out some pots and pans, and bake the cake. If you decided to go into the cake baking business, you would probably invest some time (and money) setting up a cake baking system that would take a certain set of ingredients and pump out a cake on the other end. That is what functions are; they are ingredient assembly systems.

In this section you will write a simple function called show_files that you can use for displaying file names. The specific purpose of the function in this example will be to display the contents of the files_v vector in an easy to read format that includes the index id of the each file in the vector. In R you begin a new function by giving it a name (show_files) and then using

---

[2]In regular expressions, the period is a special metacharacter. If you want to search for a literal period character, you need to escape it using two backslash characters. If you do not escape the period character, it will be treated as a wildcard that will match any character.

the `function`, *declaration* (which looks like you are calling the `function` *function*). Inside of parentheses, you will define the arguments (ingredients) that the function requires: in this case, two arguments: the path to a directory on your system (`directory_path`) and a regular expression (`pattern`).

Here is the basic outline of the function:

```
show_files  <- function(directory_path, pattern = "\\.txt$"){
  # some code goes here
}
```

Notice in the arguments to the function that we have predefined a default value for the `pattern` argument: `"\\.txt$"`. When you call this function, you can choose to use the default pattern or enter a different one. We will explore that option later.

The parenthetical arguments section of the declaration is followed by a set of opening and closing *curly braces* that surround the inner workings of the function. This inner section, inside the curly braces, is where the instructions (recipe) for what to do with the ingredients will be defined.

The objective of using this function is to provide an easy to read list of the files in the directory that you send in the `directory_path` argument. You learned above that you can use `dir` to generate a vector of files in a directory. You can add that code here inside the curly braces:

```
show_files  <- function(directory_path, pattern = "\\.txt$"){
  file_name_v <- dir(directory_path, pattern, full.names = TRUE)
    # some more code goes here
}
```

Next we want to iterate over the items in the `file_name_v` object, and for this we will use a `for` loop.

```
show_files  <- function(directory_path, pattern = "\\.txt$"){
  file_name_v <- dir(directory_path, pattern, full.names = TRUE)
  for(i in seq_along(file_name_v)){
    # some more code goes here
  }
}
```

The `for` loop will iterate over each of the items stored in the vector of file names (`file_name_v`), one item at a time. Notice, however, that instead of the familiar `for(i in 1:length(file_name_v))`, we have introduced a new function, `seq_along` or "sequence along" as an alternative to the `1:length` construction. The `seq_along` function is a "safer" version of `1:length(file_name_v)`. It is safer because it knows how to behave if it is accidentally sent a zero-length vector as an argument. Consider this example in which we create an empty numeric vector x with length zero.

```
x <- vector(mode = "numeric", length = 0)
```

If we now inspect this variable using **class** and **length**, we find that it is indeed a numeric vector with length of zero.

```
class(x)
## [1] "numeric"
length(x)
## [1] 0
```

However, if we use the `1:length(x)` convention, we get a very odd result, a vector containing two values, 0 and 1:

```
1:length(x)
## [1] 1 0
```

You can check this as follows:

```
y <- 1:length(x)
length(y)
## [1] 2
```

Even though **x** has zero length, the `1:length(x)` construction results in a vector with length 2. Though it seems unlikely that you would ever create a vector with length zero, you can avoid this little paradox by using **seq_along**:

```
y <- seq_along(x)
length(y)
## [1] 0
```

For printing lines into the R console (do not confuse this sense of the word *print* with *printing* on paper to your printer), R has several functions you can tap, but let us use the **cat** function here. **cat** is a function for concatenation (joining) and printing. Here you want to join the file name with the index of the file name in the vector and then add a *line return* (using the backslash escape character and an *n* to mean *newline*). To achieve this, you will be joining three items: the vector index *key*, the contents or *value* of the item in the vector at that index position, and a *newline* character. To join these pieces requires a bit of *glue*, so **cat** asks us to define a *separator* using the **sep** argument. You can use a space character for the *glue*, and the final function looks like this:

```
show_files <- function(directory_path, pattern = "\\.txt$"){
  file_name_v <- dir(directory_path, pattern, full.names = TRUE)
  for(i in seq_along(file_name_v)){
    cat(i, file_name_v[i], "\n", sep = " ")
  }
}
```

Before taking the function for a test drive (cake walk?), there is one more thing to do. Just as it is very easy to write complicated functions, it is also very easy to forget what they do! So add a brief comment to the function so that when you come back a week later you can be reminded of what it does:

```
# Function to print a vector of file paths and their index
# numbers in user-friendly format
show_files  <- function(directory_path, pattern = "\\.txt$"){
  file_name_v <- dir(directory_path, pattern, full.names = TRUE)
  for(i in seq_along(file_name_v)){
    cat(i, file_name_v[i], "\n", sep = " ")
  }
}
```

In RStudio, you can run a whole block of code by selecting it in the editing window and then hitting the **control + return** (for Mac) or **Ctrl + Enter** (for Windows) keys at the same time. Select the above lines in your R script and send them to the console using this shortcut. If you look in your "Environment" tab, you will now see **show_files** under the "Functions" section. Above that is the "Values" section where you should see both **files_v** and **input_dir** that you instantiated above.

With all of this done, you can now call the **show_files** function with any directory on your system and see the numbered result as output.

```
show_files(input_dir)
## 1 data/text/austen.txt
## 2 data/text/melville.txt
```

Mission accomplished, your first function!

9.3 A Tokenization Function

In previous chapters, you learned how to generate a tokenized vector of words from a text file. Since you are now an expert function maker, you will build a function that will do this task so that you can easily access the word data from any file in a directory on your system. This new function will take two arguments: a directory path and a tokenization pattern. It is always a good idea to give your functions names that make sense; call this one **make_token_v** and begin it with a comment:

```
# Function returns an ordered vector of words (tokens)
# from the file referenced in the file_path argument
make_token_v <- function(file_path, pattern){
  # more code needed here to:
```

```
# read in the text file from file_path
# convert text into a tokenized vector of words
# Use the pattern argument for tokenizing
# return vector of word tokens
}
```

Here we have entered a comment describing what we want this function to do and some "pseudo code" describing what we still need to write. Articulating an objective in advance can be a great way to guide your coding. The definition says that we want to return a **vector** object and that the code we still need to write should load a file and tokenize it. It turns out that everything required in that comment is code that you have already written in previous sections and/or exercises. By recycling code from your prior work you can produce the following:

```
# Function returns an ordered vector of words (tokens)
# from the file referenced in the file_path argument
make_token_v <- function(file_path, pattern = "\\W"){
  # read the file in (notice that it is here that we need
  # to know the input directory and the file id)
  text_v <- scan(file_path, what = "character", sep = "\n")
  # convert to single string
  text_v <- paste(text_v, collapse = " ")
  # lowercase
  text_lower_v  <- tolower(text_v)
  #  split text using regular expression from 'pattern' arg
  text_words_v <- strsplit(text_lower_v, pattern)
  # unlist the result
  text_words_v <- unlist(text_words_v)
  # remove the blanks
  text_words_v <-  text_words_v[which(text_words_v != "")]
  return(text_words_v) # return the resulting vector
}
```

The only thing that you have not seen yet is the last line where we call **return**. In R you do not always have to explicitly call **return** at the end of a function. By default R will return whatever object is returned in the last line of the function. Explicitly calling **return**, however, often makes it easier to read and debug your function code.

You now have two functions. The first function **show_files** takes an input directory argument and shows you the names of the files in that directory. The utility of the **show_files** function will become more apparent in the next chapter. The second function takes a path argument and creates and returns a tokenized vector of words from the file in the path. Assume that you have decided you want to tokenize the novel by Jane Austen, and that you have already run `show_files` and learned the location of that file is `data/text/austen.txt`. You would then tokenize the novel as follows:

```
austen_word_v <- make_token_v("data/text/austen.txt")
```

9.4 Finding Keywords and Their Contextual Neighbors

Now the fun begins. Consider that you have created an ordered vector of the words from a file. If you were to enter `austen_word_v[1:100]` you would get the first 100 words of Jane Austen's novel, one word at a time. At this point, we hope that you are already one step ahead of us and thinking to yourself, "hey, if I have all the words in order, I can find any word in the text and return its position in the text using a `which` statement." You already did this when you found the occurrences of *whale* in *Moby Dick*. Let us now find *anguish* in *Sense and Sensibility*.

```
positions_v <- which(austen_word_v == "anguish")
```

This expression will return the *position* of every instance of the word *anguish* in the austen_word_v vector. Go ahead and enter this now, and see what you get. The result should be something like this:

```
positions_v
## [1]   56584 108040
```

These are the positions of each separate occurrence of *anguish* in the file titled *austen.txt*. And if you can find the position of every occurrence of *anguish* in the word vector, you can find any other word (i.e., *whale* or *dog*). And, if you can find a word's position, you can also find the items that are next to it: before it and after it. You can do this by simply adding or subtracting values from the position of the *found* word. Deep breath.

To summarize, you have used the `which` statement to find all the instances of *anguish* and stored those positions in a new vector called `positions_v`. If you check the length of this `positions_v` vector, you will get a count of the number of times *anguish* occurs in the file:

```
length(positions_v)
## [1] 2
```

Let us say that you want to know the words that come just before and just after the first instance of *anguish* in this file (i.e., the context in which *anguish* appears). You might begin by specifically identifying the first instance:

```
first_instance <- positions_v[1]
```

Which is to say that you could put the value that is held in the first item in the `positions_v` vector into a new variable called `first_instance`. If you look at the full print out shown previously, you will see that the first value in the `positions_v` vector is 56584. The first instance of *anguish* is the 56584th word in the file. With this last R expression, you have put the number 56584 into the variable called `first_instance`.

If you want to check your work, just use that new variable in the original word vector, like this:

```
austen_word_v[first_instance]
## [1] "anguish"
```

Ta Da! Of course, since you already knew that *anguish* is the 56584th word in the file, you could have also done this:

```
austen_word_v[56584]
## [1] "anguish"
```

Ta Da! And, if you want to see the words just before and just after the 56584th word in the file, you could, of course, just do this:

```
austen_word_v[56583:56585]
## [1] "the"       "anguish" "of"
```

But consider that another way of getting access to the positions in the vector that are before and after the keyword is to add and subtract from the position of the keyword. Since 56584 is the value already stored in the `first_instance` variable you could subtract from (or add to) the value inside `first_instance`. With that in mind, you can use the following expression to achieve the same result as above, but without hard-coding any of the vector positions.

```
austen_word_v[(first_instance-1):(first_instance+1)]
## [1] "the"       "anguish" "of"
```

If you want to see the results *pretty printed*, just use `cat`:

```
cat(austen_word_v[(first_instance-1):(first_instance+1)])
## the anguish of
```

The practice exercise that follows will allow you to develop what you have learned here to create a simple KWIC list.

9.5 Practice

1. Using the functions described in this chapter and what you now know about vector indexing, write a script that will produce a *five-word* KWIC list for all occurrences of the word *dog* in both *Moby Dick* and *Sense and Sensibility*, separately.
2. For an even cleaner look, use your new knowledge of the `cat` function to format your output so that it looks something like this:

```
---------------------- 1 ----------------------
all over like a newfoundland [dog] just from the water and
---------------------- 2 ----------------------
a fellow that in the [dog] days will mow his two
---------------------- 3 ----------------------
was seen swimming like a [dog] throwing his long arms straight
---------------------- 4 ----------------------
filling one at last down [dog] and kennel starting at the
---------------------- 5 ----------------------
not tamely be called a [dog] sir then be called ten
---------------------- 6 ----------------------
t he call me a [dog] blazes he called me ten
---------------------- 7 ----------------------
sacrifice of the sacred white [dog] was by far the holiest
---------------------- 8 ----------------------
life that lives in a [dog] or a horse indeed in
---------------------- 9 ----------------------
the sagacious kindness of the [dog] the accursed shark alone can
---------------------- 10 ----------------------
boats the ungracious and ungrateful [dog] cried starbuck he mocks and
---------------------- 11 ----------------------
intense whisper give way greyhounds [dog] to it i tell ye
---------------------- 12 ----------------------
to the whale that a [dog] does to the elephant nevertheless
---------------------- 13 ----------------------
aries or the ram lecherous [dog] he begets us then taurus
---------------------- 14 ----------------------
is dr bunger bunger you [dog] laugh out why don t
------           --------- 15 ----------------------
to die in pickle you [dog] you should be preserved to
---------------------- 16 ----------------------
round ahab and like a [dog] strangely snuffing this man s
---------------------- 17 ----------------------
lad five feet high hang [dog] look and cowardly jumped from
```

```
---------------------- 18 ----------------------
as a sagacious ship s [dog] will in drawing nigh to
---------------------- 19 ----------------------
the compass and then the [dog] vane and then ascertaining the
```

Reference

Firth JR (1957) Studies in Linguistic Analysis. Blackwell

Chapter 10
Do It KWIC(er) (and Better)

Abstract This chapter expands upon the previous chapter in order to build an interactive and reusable Keyword in Context (KWIC) application that allows for quick and intuitive KWIC list building. Readers are introduced to interactive R functions including `readline` and functions for data type conversion.

10.1 Getting Organized

In the previous chapter, you learned how to find and access a series of index positions in a vector and then how to return values on either side of the found positions. In the practice exercise, you hard-coded a solution for finding occurrences of the word *dog* in *Sense and Sensibility* and *Moby Dick*. In this section you will learn how to abstract that code and how to create an interactive and reusable application that will allow you to repeatedly find keywords in context without having to hard-code the search terms.

If you have not already done so, now is the time to get organized. You will be dealing with more and more files as this book continues, and unless you keep your working spaces well-defined and organized things can get complicated. Within your "TAWR2" directory, you already have a sub-directory labeled "code." This is where you should be storing all of your .R files. Now is a good time to create a new sub-directory called "results." In the last exercise in this chapter, you will be generating a .csv file that you can save in your "results" directory and then open again in R or in a spreadsheet application such as Excel or Open Office.

© Springer Nature Switzerland AG 2020

M. L. Jockers, R. Thalken, *Text Analysis with R*, Quantitative Methods in the Humanities and Social Sciences,
https://doi.org/10.1007/978-3-030-39643-5_10

10.2 Separating Functions for Reuse

In the last chapter you created two functions, and in this chapter you will
create a third. Because you can reuse functions in separate projects, it is
convenient to keep them in a separate file so that you can access them from
different R scripts that you write for different projects. You should begin this
chapter, therefore, by copying your two functions from the last chapter into a
new file that you will title *corpus_functions.R*. Save this new file inside your
"code" sub-directory. Your functions file should include both `show_files` and
`make_token_v` from the last chapter. Here they are again, but without the
comments:

```
show_files  <- function(directory_path, pattern = "\\.txt$"){
  file_name_v <- dir(directory_path, pattern, full.names = TRUE)
  for(i in seq_along(file_name_v)){
    cat(i, file_name_v[i], "\n", sep = " ")
  }
}
make_token_v <- function(file_path, pattern = "\\W"){
  text_v <- scan(file_path, what = "character", sep = "\n")
  text_v <- paste(text_v, collapse = " ")
  text_lower_v  <- tolower(text_v)
  text_words_v <- strsplit(text_lower_v, pattern)
  text_words_v <- unlist(text_words_v)
  text_words_v[which(text_words_v != "")]
}
```

With your functions stored in a separate file, you can now *call* the *cor-
pus_functions.R* file as part of your working R script in order to load these
existing functions. Create a new R script (saved as "chapter10.R" in your
"code" directory) and enter the following expressions as the first two lines:

```
rm(list = ls())
source("code/corpus_functions.R")
```

The first line clears your workspace and the second line uses R's `source`
function to load the contents of your external functions file. When this script
is executed, R will load all of the functions that you create and save in the
corpus_functions.R file.

As in Chap. 9, you need to show R where to find your text files, so next you
will define an *input directory* with a relative path to the `data/plainText`
directory.

```
input_dir <- "data/text"
```

Since you also will be using R to create derivative data files that will need to be saved out to another directory, you will need to tell R where to write these files. Define an *output directory* variable, with the title "results," like this:

```
output_dir  <- "results"
```

The objective now is to write an interactive Keyword in Context (KWIC) function that will allow you to repeatedly enter different file paths and keywords and then return the hits for those terms along with some amount of context on either side of the key term.

10.3 User Interaction

R includes a set of built-in functions that, when invoked, require user feedback. Thus far we have been hard-coding file paths in R, but we could have been using R's `file.choose` function instead. If you enter `file.choose` at the R prompt, you will be prompted with a pop-up window that allows you to navigate your file system and locate a file. Here is an example that you can try on your system. Just enter the following expression at the R prompt in the console pane and then use your computer's windowing system to locate the file in the exercise directory called "melville.txt."

```
mytext <- scan(file.choose(), what = "character", sep = "\n")
```

If you did everything correctly, you should see the message:

```
Read 18172 items
```

You will now be able to enter

```
mytext
```

and see all the lines of *Moby Dick*.

10.4 `readline`

There are other functions in R that allow for user interaction as well, and one that we will use for this section is `readline`. `readline` is a function that will print information to the R console and then accept input entered into the console by the user. Enter this expression into the console and hit return:

```
myyear <- readline("What year was Moby Dick published? \n")
```

You will see the quoted question appear in the console and the blinking cursor prompt located after the question mark. At the cursor prompt, enter a number (e.g., 1851) and hit return. If you now type myyear at the R prompt and hit return, you will find that R has stored the value that you entered in the myyear variable. Here is how it should look:

```
> myyear <- readline("What year was Moby Dick published? \n")
What year was Moby Dick published? 1851
> myyear
[1] "1851"
```

10.5 Building a Better KWIC Function

Using the readline function, you can write a *KWIC* list function that asks the user (you) for a *file* to search, a *keyword* to find, and an amount of *context* to be returned on either side of the keyword. We will name this function doitKwic and call it in this fashion:

```
doitKwic(directory_path)
```

The only argument that you need to send this function is the location of (path to) a directory on your system. Open your *corpus_functions.R* file and begin writing this new function like this:

```
doitKwic <- function(directory_path){
    # instructions here will ask user for a file to search
    # a keyword to find and a "context" number for context
    # on either side of the of the keyword
}
```

Keep in mind that the argument name used inside the parentheses of the function does not have to be the same as the name used outside of the function. You already have an object called input_dir instantiated from above. This object contains the path expression "data/text" that is the location of two plain text files. So here we are defining a function that takes an argument called directory_path, and when we call this function, we will send it the information contained in the input_dir object.

You do not have to write your code this way (i.e., using different names when inside or outside of the function), but we find it useful to name our function arguments in a way that is descriptive of their content and a bit more abstract than the names we give to objects within the main script. We may decide to use this function on another project, and several months from now we may have forgotten what `input_dir` means. Using `directory_path` is a bit more descriptive, and it gives us some clues about what kind of data the function is expecting.

As the commented sections of the code suggest, we want the new function to ask the user for input. First it needs to ask which file in the directory to search in, then what keyword to search for, and finally how much context to display. For the first item, the function should display a list of the files that are found inside the directory located at `directory_path` and then ask the user to choose one. As it happens, we already have a function called `show_files` that does exactly this, and we can call the `show_files` function from inside the new `doitKwic` function! Remember that `show_files` is expecting to get a directory path as its argument. That information is passed to `show_files` in the `directory_path` argument. So as a next step, we might write the following:

```
doitKwic <- function(directory_path){
  show_files(directory_path)
  # more instructions here . . .
}
```

If `doitKwic` is called, it will successfully show the files found in the directory sent as the argument `directory_path`, but then it will do nothing else. In order to capture information from the user, we will need to wrap the call to `show_files` inside a call to `readline`:

```
doitKwic <- function(directory_path){
  readline(show_files(directory_path))
  # more instructions here . . .
}
```

This gets us a little bit closer, but we are not there quite yet. Recall that `show_files` presents us with both an id number and a path for each file. When you call `show_files` using `data/text` you get the following output:

```
## 1 data/text/austen.txt
## 2 data/text/melville.txt
```

Instead of having to copy or type in the entire file path that we want to search in, let us have our user just enter the index number of the file instead. We will capture that user input into a new object called `file_id`.

```
doitKwic <- function(directory_path){
  file_id <- readline(show_files(directory_path))
  # more instructions here . . .
}
```

There is now one more thing we have to fix. The `readline` function accepts input as *character* data, so if the user enters the number 2, to access the "melville.txt" file, that 2 is converted to the character "2." We must, therefore, convert, or recast, the character to a numeric value using `as.numeric`.

```
doitKwic <- function(directory_path){
  file_id <- as.numeric(readline(show_files(directory_path)))
  # more instructions here . . .
}
```

Now we can collect the other information we need: the keyword and the amount of context. We will add two more lines to our evolving function:

```
doitKwic <- function(directory_path){
  file_id <- as.numeric(readline(show_files(directory_path)))
  keyword <- readline("Enter a Keyword: ")
  context <- as.numeric(readline("How many words of context? "))
  # more instructions here . . .
}
```

Notice that we need to use `as.numeric` again in the last line to be sure the context the user enters is converted to a numeric value. With these three ingredients, we now have enough information to access, tokenize, and search for a keyword in a text file. The next thing to do is to take advantage of the function that we have already written for handling the tokenization: `make_token_v`. We will add a call to `make_token_v` to our function as follows:

```
doitKwic <- function(directory_path){
  file_id <- as.numeric(readline(show_files(directory_path)))
  keyword <- readline("Enter a Keyword: ")
  context <- as.numeric(readline("How many words of context? "))
  word_v <- make_token_v(
    dir(directory_path, full.names = TRUE)[file_id]
    )
  # more instructions here . . .
}
```

This last line is a bit complicated, so let us break it down. Recall that `make_token_v` takes a path argument. Here we have used the built-in `dir` function with the `full.names = TRUE` argument to return a file path using a combination of information that we have stored in the `directory_path` and `file_id` objects. Recall that calling `dir(directory_path, full.names = TRUE)` returns a vector object of file paths. We can access specific items in this vector using bracketed sub-setting, and the specific index of the item we want to access is now stored in the `file_id` object. Therefore, calling `dir(directory_path, full.names = TRUE)[file_id]` will return the precise path to a single file. That file is then sent to `make_token_v` where it is tokenized and returned into the `word_v` object.

All you need to do now is apply what you learned from the exercise in the last chapter. Using `which` you will identify the positions in the `word_v` object that match the user's keyword and store them in an object called `hits_v`. Then you will loop over the `hits_v` object using a `for` loop and along the way add and subtract the context values from the found positions in order to identify and display the user's keyword in context. The (almost) completed function looks like this:

```
doitKwic <- function(directory_path){
  file_id <- as.numeric(readline(show_files(directory_path)))
  keyword <- readline("Enter a Keyword: ")
  context <- as.numeric(readline("How many words of context? "))
  word_v <- make_token_v(
    file.path(directory_path, dir(directory_path)[file_id])
    )
  hits_v <- which(word_v == keyword)
  for(i in seq_along(hits_v)){
    start <- hits_v[i] - context
    end <- hits_v[i] + context
    before <- word_v[start:(start + context - 1)]
    after <- word_v[(start + context + 1):end]
    keyword <- word_v[start + context]
    cat("----------------------", i, "----------------------", "\n")
    cat(before,"[", keyword, "]", after, "\n")
  }
}
```

10.6 Fixing Some Problems

Unfortunately, this simple solution cannot handle all of the possible search scenarios that might occur, and we have left out some important arguments. Recall, for example, that by default, our `make_token_v` converts all characters to lowercase. If a user of our new `doitKwic` function were to enter a keyword containing a capital letter, nothing would be found. We can fix this very easily by altering the third line of the function to read `keyword <- tolower(readline("Enter a Keyword: "))`. This ensures that whatever the user enters will be converted to lowercase. But what if you *want* to search for a capitalized word? Right now that is not an option. And there is another more serious problem...

What if the very first word in the file you are searching in is a hit? In this case the first position in the `hits_v` vector would be 1 and that would cause `start` to be set to 1 - (minus) `context`: that is one minus whatever number the user entered for `context`. The result of that subtraction would be a negative

number and R would choke trying to access a value held at a negative vector
index! You cannot have that, so you need to add some code to deal with this
possibility. Here is one way to deal with the problem using an `if` conditional:

```
start <- hits_v[i] - context
if(start < 1){
  start <- 1
}
```

A similar problem exists on the other end of the vector. What if the last word
is a hit? Adding some amount of context after the last hit will result in R
trying to return a value that does not exist after the last word. We can deal
with this issue in a similar manner: if the value of **end** is greater than or equal
to the length of the entire vector, we can set **end** equal to the length of the
entire vector.

```
end <- hits_v[i] + context
if(end >= length(word_v)){
  end <- length(word_v)
}
```

We will deal with the lowercase issue and some other issues in the practice
exercises, but for now we at least have a function that will not break. Here
is the final version:

```
doitKwic <- function(directory_path){
  file_id <- as.numeric(readline(show_files(directory_path)))
  keyword <- readline("Enter a Keyword: ")
  context <- as.numeric(readline("How many words of context? "))
  word_v <- make_token_v(
    file.path(directory_path, dir(directory_path)[file_id])
    )
  hits_v <- which(word_v == keyword)
  for(i in seq_along(hits_v)){
    start <- hits_v[i] - context
    if(start < 1){
      start <- 1
    }
    end <- hits_v[i] + context
    if(end >= length(word_v)){
      end <- length(word_v)
    }
    output <- word_v[start:end]
    output[which(output == keyword)] <- paste(
      "[", keyword, "]", sep = ""
      )
```

```
    cat("------------------------", i, "------------------------", "\n")
    cat(output, "\n")
  }
}
```

Save this function to your *corpus_functions.R* file and then take it for a
test run using the following code:

```
source("code/corpus_functions.R")
input_dir <- "data/text"
doItKwic(input_dir)
```

10.7 Practice

1. In prior exercises and lessons, you have learned how to instantiate an empty
   object outside of a `for` loop and then how to add new data to that object
   during the loop. You have learned how to use `cbind` to add columns of data
   and `rbind` to add rows. You have also learned how to use `paste` with the
   `collapse` argument to glue together pieces in a vector of values and how
   to use `cat` to concatenate items in a vector. And you have used `colnames`
   to get and set the names of columns in a data frame. Using all of this
   knowledge, modify the function written in this chapter (`doItKwic`) so that
   the results of a KWIC search are put into a `data frame` object in which
   each row is a single KWIC result. Name this new function `doItKwicBetter`.
   Your resulting data frame should have four columns labeled as follows:
   position, left context, keyword, and *right context.* The *position* column will
   contain the index value showing where in the file the keyword was found.
   The *left* column will contain the words in the file vector that were found to
   the left of the keyword. The *keyword* column will contain the keyword, and
   the *right* column, the context that was found to the right of the keyword.
   Here is an example of results generated using the keyword *dog* with two
   words of context in the file "melville.txt."

	position	left	keyword	right
## 1	10643	like a newfoundland	dog	just from the
## 2	12464	that in the	dog	days will mow
## 3	23280	swimming like a	dog	throwing his long
## 4	47119	at last down	dog	and kennel starting
## 5	47195	be called a	dog	sir then be
## 6	47653	call me a	dog	blazes he called
## 7	70018	the sacred white	dog	was by far
## 8	103702	lives in a	dog	or a horse
## 9	103788	kindness of the	dog	the accursed shark
## 10	133135	ungracious and ungrateful	dog	cried starbuck he

```
## 11    133165    give way greyhounds    dog              to it i
## 12    143092        whale that a       dog           does to the
## 13    163384    the ram lecherous      dog           he begets us
## 14    166285    bunger bunger you      dog           laugh out why
## 15    166665       in pickle you       dog           you should be
## 16    167192         and like a        dog strangely snuffing this
## 17    199028       feet high hang      dog         look and cowardly
## 18    202985    sagacious ship s       dog          will in drawing
## 19    203037       and then the        dog           vane and then
```

2. Copy the function you created in the exercise above and modify it to
   include a feedback loop asking the user if the results should be saved as a
   .csv file. If the user answers "y" for "yes," generate a file name based on
   the existing user input (keyword, file name, context) and write that file to
   the **results** directory using a call to the **write.csv** function, as in this
   example below. Save this new function in your *corpus_functions.R* file as
   doItKwicStillBetter.

```
write.csv(results_df, file.path("results", some_file_name))
```

3. Neither of these "better" KWIC functions gives the user any options for
   tokenizing the texts. Right now both functions rely on the default behavior
   of the **make_token_v** function, which uses the regular expression "\\W". In
   order to give users flexibility to change the way files get tokenized, we need
   to alter the line of code that calls **make_token_v** to include a **pattern**
   argument, and we also need to add a new argument to the parameters
   of our KWIC function. Rewrite your **doItKwicStillBetter** function to
   achieve this objective and save it as **doItKwicBest**. After you save the
   function, you should be able to call it using the code shown below. Recall that [^A-Za-z0-9'] is a regular expression that retains apostrophes
   and possessives. If your function is correct, you will be able to search for
   instances of *ahab's*. After you have coded this new version, check your solution with the solution at the back of the book where you will find one
   more useful iteration of this function explained. Once you have finished
   the practice exercises for this chapter, save **doItKwic**, **doItKwicBetter**,
   doItKwicStillBetter, and **doItKwicBest** to your *corpus_functions.R*
   file so you can easily access them in the future.

```
doItKwicBest(input_dir, "[^A-Za-z0-9']")
```

Part II
Metadata

Chapter 11

Introduction to `dplyr`

Abstract This chapter introduces the `dplyr` suite of functions.

11.1 Start Up Code

The following is a block of code with which you are now quite familiar. You will begin this chapter by running this code and producing two lists: `chapter_raws_l` and `chapter_freqs_l`. Remember, `chapter_raws_l` and `chapter_freqs_l` respectively contain the raw and relative frequency of every token in *Moby Dick*, by chapter.

```
rm(list = ls())
text_v <- scan("data/text/melville.txt", what = "character", sep = "\n")
start_v <- which(text_v == "CHAPTER 1. Loomings.")
novel_lines_v <-  text_v[start_v:length(text_v)]
chap_positions_v <- grep("^CHAPTER \\d", novel_lines_v)
last_position_v <-  length(novel_lines_v)
chap_positions_v  <-  c(chap_positions_v , last_position_v)
chapter_raws_l <- list()
chapter_freqs_l <- list()
for(i in 1:length(chap_positions_v)){
  if(i != length(chap_positions_v)){
    chapter_title <- novel_lines_v[chap_positions_v[i]]
    start <- chap_positions_v[i] + 1
    end <- chap_positions_v[i + 1] - 1
    chapter_lines_v <- novel_lines_v[start:end]
    chapter_words_v <- tolower(paste(chapter_lines_v, collapse = " "))
    chapter_words_l <- strsplit(chapter_words_v, "\\W")
    chapter_word_v <- unlist(chapter_words_l)
    chapter_word_v <- chapter_word_v[which(chapter_word_v != "")]
```

© Springer Nature Switzerland AG 2020
M. L. Jockers, R. Thalken, *Text Analysis with R*, Quantitative Methods in the Humanities and Social Sciences,
https://doi.org/10.1007/978-3-030-39643-5_11

```
    chapter_freqs_t <- table(chapter_word_v)
    chapter_raws_l[[chapter_title]] <-  chapter_freqs_t
    chapter_freqs_t_rel <- 100*(chapter_freqs_t/sum(chapter_freqs_t))
    chapter_freqs_l[[chapter_title]] <- chapter_freqs_t_rel
  }
}
```

11.2 Using stack to Create a Data Frame

In earlier chapters, you learned how to use do.call and rbind to move the data contained inside a list object into a neater matrix of rows using the following R code:

```
mean_word_use_m <- do.call(rbind, lapply(chapter_raws_l, mean))
```

If, instead of the mean word use in a chapter, we wanted to know the length of each chapter in words, we could use the sum function instead of mean:

```
chapter_lengths_m <- do.call(rbind, lapply(chapter_raws_l, sum))
```

Another way of achieving a similar result is to use the stack function instead of do.call. The stack function combines, or "concatenates" data from several data structures into one:

```
chapter_lengths_df <- stack(lapply(chapter_raws_l, sum))
```

Notice, however, that stack returns a data frame object instead of a matrix.

```
class(chapter_lengths_m); class(chapter_lengths_df)
## [1] "matrix"
## [1] "data.frame"
```

If you examine the resulting data.frame (chapter_lengths_df), you will see that it has two columns and that the columns are labeled "values" and "ind."

```
head(chapter_lengths_df)
##    values                          ind
## 1    2244          CHAPTER 1. Loomings.
## 2    1453    CHAPTER 2. The Carpet-Bag.
## 3    6000   CHAPTER 3. The Spouter-Inn.
## 4    1674   CHAPTER 4. The Counterpane.
## 5     752         CHAPTER 5. Breakfast.
## 6     831        CHAPTER 6. The Street.
```

You can easily access the values column as a vector, using the $ shortcut.

```
chapter_lengths_df$values
##   [1] 2244 1453 6000 1674  752  831  948  968 3642 1567  732  890
##  [13] 1730  764 1215 5612 2345 1390 1258  934 1101 1677  371 1683
##  [25]  285 1230 1700 1419 1242  291  886 5206  982 2248 2632 2846
##  [37]  526  399  282 1641 3808 3655  318 2063 3573 1006  937 4041
##  [49]  845 1024 1525  726 1656 8101 1918 1320  965 1012  934 1492
##  [61] 1995  572  474 3080 1001  636  742 1209  443  894 2312 1676
##  [73] 2229 1660 1246  876  644 1672  948  913 4452 1161  789  815
##  [85] 2084 1861 4805 1195 1446 1062 2589  982 1647 1289  501 1842
##  [97]  246 1033 2527 2795 1790 1580  932 1441 1576  940 1066 1645
## [109]  930 2283  427  950 1261  653  904  522  478  911 2583  184
## [121]  649   49 1271 1223 1143 1425  742 1434  598 1727  434 1645
## [133] 3638 3393 4917
```

Recall what you learned about using sapply as a way of simplifying a list object. We found the number of *hapax legomena* in each chapter of *Moby Dick* using sapply with a user-defined function:

```
chapter_hapax_v <- sapply(chapter_raws_l, function(x) sum(x == 1))
```

A similar result can be achieved using lapply and stack, like this:

```
chap_haps_df_l <- lapply(chapter_raws_l, function(x) sum(x == 1))
chap_haps_df <- stack(chap_haps_df_l)
```

The big advantage of stack is that it returns a data frame which is easy to manipulate and essential as we begin exploring the benefits of dplyr and the so-called tidyverse.

Using stack we now have two data frames, one that holds the total number of words per chapter, chapter_lengths_df, and another that contains the count of *hapax* per chapter, chap_haps_df. These can be easily combined using the data.frame function:

```
a_data_frame <- data.frame(chapter_lengths_df, chap_haps_df)
```

Look at what has been achieved by simple combination:

```
head(a_data_frame)
##   values                        ind values.1
## 1   2244        CHAPTER 1. Loomings.      605
## 2   1453 CHAPTER 2. The Carpet-Bag.      433
## 3   6000 CHAPTER 3. The Spouter-Inn.    1054
## 4   1674 CHAPTER 4. The Counterpane.     465
## 5    752        CHAPTER 5. Breakfast.     266
## 6    831       CHAPTER 6. The Street.     343
##                          ind.1
## 1        CHAPTER 1. Loomings.
## 2 CHAPTER 2. The Carpet-Bag.
```

```
## 3 CHAPTER 3. The Spouter-Inn.
## 4 CHAPTER 4. The Counterpane.
## 5      CHAPTER 5. Breakfast.
## 6      CHAPTER 6. The Street.
```

We now have a data frame with repeated information in the form of all the chapter names. A better approach would be to take only what we need and relabel the columns at the same time. Remember, we can get the values of a column with $ and assign column names with = as arguments to `data.frame`.

```
hap_lens_df <- data.frame(
  chap_names = chapter_lengths_df$ind,
  chapter_lengths = chapter_lengths_df$value,
  num_hapax = chap_haps_df$values
  )
```

Now we have a very clean data structure containing only the data we need. Take a peek at it:

```
head(hap_lens_df)
##                      chap_names chapter_lengths num_hapax
## 1      CHAPTER 1. Loomings.           2244       605
## 2   CHAPTER 2. The Carpet-Bag.        1453       433
## 3 CHAPTER 3. The Spouter-Inn.        6000      1054
## 4 CHAPTER 4. The Counterpane.        1674       465
## 5      CHAPTER 5. Breakfast.          752       266
## 6      CHAPTER 6. The Street.         831       343
```

11.3 Installing and Loading `dplyr`

So far we have worked only with functions available in the base R installation. But there are many "libraries" that can be installed into R. These libraries, created by other R users, provide new functions. For this chapter you will install and learn to apply several functions from the `dplyr` package.

In RStudio it is easy to install packages by going to the "Tools" menu and selecting "Install Packages" from the drop-down menu. Under the "Install From" menu, choose "Repository (CRAN)." Now enter `dplyr` in the "packages" text field. Click the check-box to "Install Dependencies," and then click the Install button. Downloading the entire `dplyr` package with its functions is that easy.[1]

---

[1]While it is possible to download all of the available packages for R, doing so would certainly take a long time and would clog up your installation with way too many irrelevant

Now that the package is installed, you will need to "load" it. In R we load a package by going to the package "library." That is, we use the `library` function to check out and load the package.

```
library(dplyr)
```

With `dplyr` loaded, you have access to all the functions in the package. If you enter `?dplyr` in the console, you can see the help files for the package. You will notice that `dplyr` is described as a "grammar for data manipulation."

11.4 Using `mutate`, `filter`, `arrange`, and `select`

`dplyr` has a number of handy functions. Four of the most useful are `mutate`, `filter`, `arrange`, and `select`. All of these will be relatively familiar to you because they are functions for performing the same kinds of tasks you have already learned using `cbind`, `which`, `sort` and `$`.

11.4.1 Mutate

At its most simple, `mutate` is a way of "cbinding" new columns into a data frame. `mutate` allows you to create a new column in a data frame while performing some calculation or transformation based on data within existing columns. Consider the columns in our current object `hap_lens_df`. We have the length of each chapter in words and a count of the number of words in each chapter that are *hapax*. With `mutate` and a little division, we can easily calculate the percentage of each chapter that is composed of *hapax*. Let us do that using `mutate`.

---

features. The fact is that R is a multipurpose platform used in a huge range of disciplines including: bio-statistics, network analysis, economics, data-mining, geography, and hundreds of other disciplines and sub-disciplines. This diversity in the user community is one of the great advantages of R and of open-source software more generally. The diversity of options, however, can be daunting to the novice user, and, to make matters even more unnerving, the online R user community is notoriously specialized and *siloed* and can appear rather impatient when it comes to *newbies* asking simple questions. Having said that, the online community is also an incredible resource that you must not ignore. Because the packages developed for R are developed by programmers with at least some amount of *ad hoc* motivation behind their coding, the packages are frequently weak on documentation and generally assume some, if not extensive, familiarity with the academic discipline of the programmer (even if the package is one with applications that cross disciplinary boundaries).

```
new_df <- mutate(
  hap_lens_df,
  hap_percent = num_hapax/chapter_lengths
  )
```

Our call to the `mutate` function includes two arguments: the data frame object (`hap_lens_df`) and then the name of the new column we wish to create and the calculation to use for populating the cells of the new column. In this case, we create a new column titled "hap_percent" and we populate it with the results of dividing the data in the "num_hapax" column by the data in the "chapter_lengths" column. The `mutate` function understands that we want to perform this calculation on a row by row basis.

If you look at this new data frame, you will see that there is now a column called "hap_percent" and that it contains the values resulting from dividing each *hapax* count by the chapter length. This result can now be easily plotted (see Fig. 11.1):

```
barplot(
  new_df$hap_percent,
  names.arg = seq(1:length(chapter_raws_1)),
  xlab = "Chapter",
  ylab = "Percentage"
  )
```

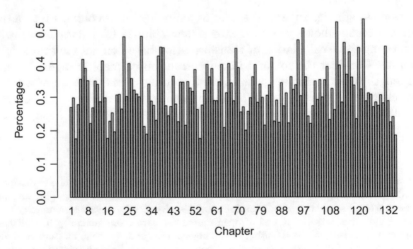

Fig. 11.1 Percentage of hapax

To create the "hap_percent" column, we used some simple mathematical division. Naturally, we can get more creative. Here is an example where we use `mutate` with `gsub` to create a new column of short chapter titles.

```
nice_df <- mutate(
  new_df,
  short_title = gsub("\\..*$", "", chap_names)
  )
head(nice_df)
##                      chap_names chapter_lengths num_hapax
## 1         CHAPTER 1. Loomings.            2244       605
## 2   CHAPTER 2. The Carpet-Bag.            1453       433
## 3  CHAPTER 3. The Spouter-Inn.            6000      1054
## 4 CHAPTER 4. The Counterpane.             1674       465
## 5         CHAPTER 5. Breakfast.            752       266
## 6        CHAPTER 6. The Street.            831       343
##   hap_percent short_title
## 1   0.2696078   CHAPTER 1
## 2   0.2980041   CHAPTER 2
## 3   0.1756667   CHAPTER 3
## 4   0.2777778   CHAPTER 4
## 5   0.3537234   CHAPTER 5
## 6   0.4127557   CHAPTER 6
```

The regular expression \\..*$ finds the first period in each chapter heading and replaces everything that follows it until the end of the string with nothing (""). The `mutate` function then takes the output and places it into a new column titled `short_title`. We put the output of this entire expression into a new data frame called `nice_df`.

Here are the column names:

```
colnames(nice_df)
## [1] "chap_names"     "chapter_lengths" "num_hapax"
## [4] "hap_percent"    "short_title"
```

11.4.2 filter

The `filter` function takes the place of `which`. It allows for the selection of items that meet a specific condition. The most common use of `filter` is to find rows in a data frame that match some condition. Here is an example of how you can use `filter` to identify the rows in `new_df` that have a percentage of *hapax* that is greater than some arbitrarily selected percentage, such as 0.5:

```
filter(nice_df, hap_percent > 0.5)
```

Here we employ `filter` to identify all the rows in which the value in the `hap_percent` column is greater than 0.5. Since we did not assign the output to a new variable, the result simply prints to the console showing that there were three chapters in *Moby Dick* that met the filter condition: chapters 97, 111, and 122.

11.4.3 select

What `filter` does for finding rows, `select` does for columns. We can use `select` to isolate a particular column in our data frame. Here is an example of how to use `select` to pull out all the *hapax* percentages from `nice_df`. Since the "hap_percent" column has 135 rows (for 135 chapters), we will just look at the first six rows, with help from the `head` function.

```
head(select(nice_df, hap_percent))
```

That is not a very exciting example, but you get the idea. Where `filter`, `select`, and the other functions in `dplyr` get interesting is when we begin to chain them together using a special operator that looks like this: `%>%` . This little beauty is called a "chain" operator, and it is typically pronounced "then." It works like a pipe ("|") in UNIX to chain together different operations. Say, for example, that we want to filter our `new_df` data frame to include certain rows and *then* we want to only show data from specific columns.

```
filter(nice_df, hap_percent > .5) %>%
  select(short_title, hap_percent)
##    short_title hap_percent
## 1   CHAPTER 97   0.5040650
## 2 CHAPTER 111   0.5222482
## 3 CHAPTER 122   0.5306122
```

The `%>%` operator allows us to get even more creative because we can chain together lots of different operations. Here is a more complex example in which we filter the data frame, *then* select a column, and *then* compute some simple summary statistics for the data:

```
filter(nice_df, hap_percent > .5) %>%
  select(hap_percent) %>%
  summary()
##   hap_percent
## Min.    :0.5041
## 1st Qu.:0.5132
## Median :0.5222
## Mean    :0.5190
```

```
##   3rd Qu.:0.5264
##   Max.   :0.5306
```

In the example above, we have only selected one column, but it is possible to select more than one column as well. In the next example, we summarize the data in two columns:

```
filter(nice_df, hap_percent > .5) %>%
  select(hap_percent, chapter_lengths) %>%
  summary()
##    hap_percent       chapter_lengths
##   Min.   :0.5041   Min.   : 49.0
##   1st Qu.:0.5132   1st Qu.:147.5
##   Median :0.5222   Median :246.0
##   Mean   :0.5190   Mean   :240.7
##   3rd Qu.:0.5264   3rd Qu.:336.5
##   Max.   :0.5306   Max.   :427.0
```

The results reveal that for these three chapters, the average length is just 240.7 words and the average percent of *hapax* is about 52%.

11.4.4 arrange

As you might suspect, arrange is similar to the sort function that we explored in previous chapters. Like sort, arrange can organize items in ascending or descending order. Let us filter nice_df to include only the rows with a hapax_percent greater than 40% (> .4) and then select the short_title and hapax_percent columns. We will then arrange the rows according to the percentage of *hapax*.

```
filter(nice_df, hap_percent > .4) %>%
  select(short_title, hap_percent) %>%
  arrange(hap_percent)
##      short_title hap_percent
## 1    CHAPTER 14   0.4083770
## 2    CHAPTER 6    0.4127557
## 3    CHAPTER 84   0.4171779
## 4    CHAPTER 37   0.4220532
## 5    CHAPTER 116  0.4329502
## 6    CHAPTER 69   0.4446953
## 7    CHAPTER 120  0.4456522
## 8    CHAPTER 39   0.4468085
## 9    CHAPTER 38   0.4486216
```

```
## 10  CHAPTER 131    0.4493088
## 11  CHAPTER 114    0.4609495
## 12   CHAPTER 95    0.4690619
## 13   CHAPTER 23    0.4797844
## 14   CHAPTER 30    0.4810997
## 15   CHAPTER 97    0.5040650
## 16  CHAPTER 111    0.5222482
## 17  CHAPTER 122    0.5306122
```

To reverse the order, we only need to change the last line to include the `desc` function, which organizes the values in descending order:

```
filter(nice_df, hap_percent > .4) %>%
  select(short_title, hap_percent) %>%
  arrange(desc(hap_percent))
##     short_title hap_percent
## 1   CHAPTER 122   0.5306122
## 2   CHAPTER 111   0.5222482
## 3    CHAPTER 97   0.5040650
## 4    CHAPTER 30   0.4810997
## 5    CHAPTER 23   0.4797844
## 6    CHAPTER 95   0.4690619
## 7   CHAPTER 114   0.4609495
## 8   CHAPTER 131   0.4493088
## 9    CHAPTER 38   0.4486216
## 10   CHAPTER 39   0.4468085
## 11  CHAPTER 120   0.4456522
## 12   CHAPTER 69   0.4446953
## 13  CHAPTER 116   0.4329502
## 14   CHAPTER 37   0.4220532
## 15   CHAPTER 84   0.4171779
## 16    CHAPTER 6   0.4127557
## 17   CHAPTER 14   0.4083770
```

We will continue to explore the power of `dplyr` functions in the chapters that follow. Complete the exercises in this chapter to develop a deeper familiarity with package.

11.5 Practice

1. What do the three chapters with *hapax* percentages greater than 0.5 all have in common? Use dplyr's `summary` function to verify your guess.

2. Modify the code to identify rows with a `hap_percent` less than 0.2. What do these chapters seem to have in common?

3. One of the chapters found in problem 2 is an outlier. What is odd about it?

4. Mutate `nice_df` into a new data frame called `repeat_df` that includes a new column called `repeat_words` that is calculated by subtracting the number of *hapax* in each chapter from the total number of words in each chapter. Use the `%>%` operator to `filter` the results such that only rows with `repeat_words` greater than 3000 are retained. Select the `short_title`, `chapter_lengths`, and `repeat_words` columns and arrange the resulting data from largest to smallest `repeat_words`. Everything you need is already in `nice_df`. Your result should look like this:

```
repeat_df
##     short_title chapter_lengths repeat_words
## 1    CHAPTER 54            8101         6677
## 2     CHAPTER 3            6000         4946
## 3    CHAPTER 16            5612         4620
## 4    CHAPTER 32            5206         4221
## 5   CHAPTER 135            4917         4013
## 6    CHAPTER 87            4805         3733
## 7    CHAPTER 81            4452         3495
## 8    CHAPTER 48            4041         3171
```

5. Mutate `repeat_df` again to include a new column that calculates the rate at which repeated words are repeated in each chapter and then arranges the result in descending order of repetition. Your result will look like this:

```
done_df
##     short_title chapter_lengths repeat_words repeat_rate
## 1    CHAPTER 87            4805         3733    1.287168
## 2    CHAPTER 48            4041         3171    1.274361
## 3    CHAPTER 81            4452         3495    1.273820
## 4    CHAPTER 32            5206         4221    1.233357
## 5   CHAPTER 135            4917         4013    1.225268
## 6    CHAPTER 16            5612         4620    1.214719
## 7    CHAPTER 54            8101         6677    1.213269
## 8     CHAPTER 3            6000         4946    1.213101
```

6. Start with the `nice_df` from above and use the `%>%` operator to do all of the following in one expression:

- Mutate `nice_df` to extract the chapter number from the `short_title` column as a new column called `chap_num`.
- Filter the data to keep chapters with word counts greater than 3000.

- Select all of the columns *except for* `chap_names` (HINT: there is an easy way to do this using the `minus` character).
- Mutate the `chap_num` column which is currently a character vector into a numeric vector using `mutate` and `as.numeric`.
- Arrange the result by descending chapter number.

Your result should look like this:

```
final_df
##      chapter_lengths num_hapax hap_percent short_title chap_num
## 1               4917       904   0.1838519 CHAPTER 135      135
## 2               3393       810   0.2387268 CHAPTER 134      134
## 3               3638       811   0.2229247 CHAPTER 133      133
## 4               4805      1072   0.2231009  CHAPTER 87       87
## 5               4452       957   0.2149596  CHAPTER 81       81
## 6               3080       642   0.2084416  CHAPTER 64       64
## 7               8101      1424   0.1757808  CHAPTER 54       54
## 8               4041       870   0.2152932  CHAPTER 48       48
## 9               3573       807   0.2258606  CHAPTER 45       45
## 10              3655       991   0.2711354  CHAPTER 42       42
## 11              3808       928   0.2436975  CHAPTER 41       41
## 12              5206       985   0.1892048  CHAPTER 32       32
## 13              5612       992   0.1767641  CHAPTER 16       16
## 14              3642       806   0.2213070   CHAPTER 9        9
## 15              6000      1054   0.1756667   CHAPTER 3        3
##      as_num
## 1       135
## 2       134
## 3       133
## 4        87
## 5        81
## 6        64
## 7        54
## 8        48
## 9        45
## 10       42
## 11       41
## 12       32
## 13       16
## 14        9
## 15        3
```

7. Why did we have to do the second mutation in problem 6?

Chapter 12
Parsing TEI XML

Abstract This chapter introduces readers to parsing XML in R with an emphasis on TEI encoded XML.

12.1 Introduction

If you have ever downloaded a digital text from the Internet, you already know that there is great variety when it comes to quality. Some digital texts are available in what is referred to as *dirty OCR*. This means that the texts have been scanned and run through an optical character recognition (OCR) process but not subsequently hand checked and corrected or cleaned up by a human editor (hence the term *dirty*). On the other end of the spectrum, there are digital texts that have been carefully created by double keying and human correction. Double keying involves the use of two typists who each key the entire text into a computer. Once the two versions are completed, they are compared to identify discrepancies. Double keying is not perfect, but it is one of the more reliable methods for deriving a high quality digital version of a text. Somewhere in between double keying and dirty OCR lies corrected OCR. In this case an original document is scanned and then cleaned by a human editor. While this method is still prone to errors, it is a significant step beyond dirty OCR and frequently good enough for processing and analysis tasks that involve generating global statistics, which is to say a big picture perspective where a single mis-keyed word will have little impact on the overall result.

Scholars working with digital text must at some point assess their corpus and form an opinion about its quality and in what ways the quality of the material will impact the analysis. Promising research by Maciej Eder (2013)

M. L. Jockers, R. Thalken, *Text Analysis with R*, Quantitative Methods in the Humanities and Social Sciences,
https://doi.org/10.1007/978-3-030-39643-5_12

has examined the extent to which OCR errors impact stylometric analysis. This research gives us hope of being able to quantify the margin of error caused by OCR problems. And, make no mistake, this is a very big problem. As the scanning efforts of Google continue and as projects such as the Internet Archive and HathiTrust continue to make more and more dirty OCR text available online, an algorithmic method for dealing with dirty OCR becomes more and more important. Some have argued that at the large scale these OCR issues become trivial. That is a hypothesis, however, and one born out of frustration with the reality of our digital corpora. If we want to mine the digital library as it exists today, we need to have a fairly high tolerance for error.

But alongside these large and messy archives there are a good number of digital collections that have been carefully curated, and, in some cases, enriched with detailed metadata. Two very fine examples are the *Chadwyck Healey* and *Alexander Street Press* collections. Both of these content providers offer carefully corrected, *XML* (or SGML) encoded digital texts. The high quality of these texts does, however, come at a price: access to these corpora is available for a fee, and the fee is beyond the budget of a typical scholar. If your institution does not subscribe to one of these collections, you are more or less out of luck.

Somewhere in between the high quality products of vendors such as *Chadwyck Healey* and *Alexander Street Press* and the dirty OCR of free resources such as *Google Books* and the *Internet Archive* is *Project Gutenberg*. The texts in *Project Gutenberg* tend to be of fairly high and fairly consistent quality. Having said that, they lack detailed metadata, and text provenance is often unclear. If your research does not demand the use of a particular edition, and if you can tolerate some degree of textual error, then *Project Gutenberg* may be a suitable source for digital texts. *Project Gutenberg* texts are frequently available in multiple formats: plain text, html, epub, etc. In many cases, it is possible to convert files in one format into another, and in our own work we have developed scripts for converting *Gutenberg's* plain text into TEI-XML.

12.2 The Text Encoding Initiative (TEI)

The Text Encoding Initiative (TEI) offers a document-encoding standard that is commonly used by humanities scholars. The TEI markup scheme provides a way of storing an original text file alongside an almost infinite amount of metadata. Since the files are extensible and editable, the amount of metadata available is only limited by the encoder's willingness to modify the documents. Say for example, you are collecting novels written by Irish- and German-American authors. For this project you might have a metadata field in your document where you can indicate the author's national origins. You may have another field where you indicate the author's gender, or birth date, or race, or sexual orientation. Once metadata of this sort is added to the XML files, it can be easily accessed by computer scripts and used, for example, as a sorting facet for a particular type of analysis.

In this chapter you will be working with texts that are encoded in TEI compliant XML. Unlike the plain text files (*Moby Dick* and *Sense and Sensibility*) that you have processed thus far, these TEI-XML files contain extra-textual information in the metadata of the <teiHeader> element. To proceed, you must be able to parse the XML and extract the metadata while also separating out the actual text of the book from the marked up *apparatus* around the book. You need to know how to parse XML in R.

12.3 Parsing XML with R Using the Xml2 Package

An in-depth discussion of XML and of the TEI standard is beyond the scope of this book. To understand the way that R parses XML, readers should be familiar with the basic construction of an XML document as an ordered hierarchy of content objects (OHCO) and should have some general familiarity with the structure of a TEI document: its primary divisions into <teiHeader>, <text>, <front>, <body>, and <back>.

In the last chapter, you learned how to install the dplyr package using the RStudio interface. You can also install packages using R's install.packages function at the R prompt. First be sure to clear your workspace and then install the xml2 package like this:

```
install.packages("xml2")
```

When you run this code in your console, you will see some console output referencing the URL where the package is located in the CRAN repository followed by a notice about the location on your computer of the "binary packages." Unless you see an error or a warning, you can assume that the package was successfully downloaded to your machine.

Once the xml2 package (or any package for that matter) is installed, you must call it into the active R session. For this you use the expression:

```
library(xml2)
```

Unlike the simple scan function that you used to read text files of *Moby Dick* and *Sense and Sensibility*, with XML files you will need a more sophisticated function that can understand the structure of XML. For this we will use the

read_xml function that is part of the xml2 package that you just loaded.
Begin by reading in the XML version of *Moby Dick* using read_xml[1]:

```
xml_doc <- read_xml("data/XML1/melville1.xml")
```

If you now enter class(xml_doc) into the console, you will see that the
object is a both an "xml_document" and an "xml_node." If you just enter
the object name (xml_doc) by itself, you will see a bit more information
about the TEI encoding and the two primary nodes, first the teiHeader and
then the text node.

Recall that when working with the plain text version of *Moby Dick*, you found
the chapter breaks using grep; finding the chapter breaks in this encoded
XML file is a lot easier because the chapters are all *marked up* in XML using a
<div1> element and a "chapter" attribute. You can gather the chapters using
the xml_find_all function. Here is how the call to xml_find_all starts, but
we still need to modify it due to some subtleties of XML and TEI.

```
# Not run
chapters_ns <- xml_find_all(
  xml_doc, xpath = "//div1[@type='chapter']"
  )
```

This code looks pretty complicated because along with the XML document
object (xml_doc), we also have to include an XPath argument. XPath is a
language for representing and selecting XML nodes, or *elements* in an XML
document. XPath uses forward slashes to represent the ordered hierarchy of
nodes in the document, much in the same way that R and UNIX and other
systems and languages use forward slashes to represent the structure of the di-
rectories (or folders) in your computer. To find the div1 elements that have a
chapter attribute, we use the XPath expression: //div1[@type='chapter'].
Effectively this tells the parser to read through the XML file and pull out all
the nodes (and their contents) that meet the condition of being inside a div1
element that has a type attribute with the value of "chapter." For example,
the first chapter of the *Moby Dick* XML document is contained inside the
following element: <div1 type="chapter" n="1" id="_75784">.

Because the XML file we have loaded is a TEI encoded file that references a
namespace,[2] we also have to use the ns argument to define the namespace.
This third argument, or parameter, is a bit tricky to understand because it
has to do with XML *namespaces*, which is not so much about R as it is about
XML. The xml_find_all function expects us to identify an XML namespace
as an item in a vector, so in what follows we have arbitrarily called that vector

---

[1]Notice the different path here. The XML version of *Moby Dick* is located in a different
sub-directory of the main "TAWR2."

[2]<TEI xmlns = "http://www.tei-c.org/ns/1.0">.

tei. After doing so, this new `tei` prefix must be used as a prefix in our XPath expression. The final call to the `xml_find_all` function, therefore, looks like this[3]:

```
chapters_ns <- xml_find_all(
  xml_doc, xpath = "//tei:div1[@type='chapter']",
  ns = c(tei = "http://www.tei-c.org/ns/1.0")
  )
```

If you enter `class(chapters_ns)`, you'll see that `chapters_ns` is an `xml_nodeset`. `chapters_ns` is a special kind of R list in which each item in the list is an XML node. This means that as you iterate over the list, you must employ XML-based functions to further refine the operations. For example, each chapter node encloses a `<head>` node as a child.[4] This `<head>` node is where the title of the chapter is stored. Enter the following expression to examine the contents of the first list item.

```
chapters_ns[[1]]
```

If you scroll up in the R console, you will see the beginning of the chapter:

```
## {xml_node}
## <div1 type="chapter" n="1" id="_75784">
## [1] <head>Loomings</head>
## [2] <p rend="fiction">Call me Ishmael. Some years ago-
## never mind how long precisely- having little or no money  ...
```

Notice that the chapter title, *Loomings*, is inside the `<head>` element. If you enter `class(chapters_ns[[1]])`, you will see that the first item of this R list is an `xml_node` that contains all the child nodes of the `<div1>` parent:

```
class(chapters_ns[[1]])
## [1] "xml_node"
```

Let us say that we want to pull out the titles of all the chapters in the book. We can use `xml_find_all` again with a slightly modified `xpath` expression.

```
titles_ns <- xml_find_all(
  xml_doc, "//tei:div1[@type='chapter']/tei:head",
  ns = c(tei = "http://www.tei-c.org/ns/1.0")
  )
```

To then access the textual content of these nodes, we call the `xml_text` function which returns the data in a character vector object.

---

[3]Notice that the `xpath` argument now includes the `tei` prefix.

[4]A node inside of another node is often referred to as a "child" node.

```
titles_v <- xml_text(titles_ns)
head(titles_v)
## [1] "Loomings"          "The Carpet-Bag"  "The Spouter-Inn"
## [4] "The Counterpane" "Breakfast"        "The Street"
```

With a little understanding of R lists from the first part of this book and
with some sense of how TEI-XML files are structured, you can put all of this
together and generate a chapter-by-chapter analysis of *Moby Dick* exactly as
you did previously using the `grep` function.

12.4 Accessing the Textual Content

The textual data of each chapter of *Moby Dick* is stored inside the `<p>` (paragraph) elements that are children of `div1[@type='chapter']`. This means
that for each chapter (`<div1>`) you want to extract both the title of the
chapter (found inside `<head>`) and the paragraphs (found inside `<p>`) as two
separate items. Ultimately it would be useful to store this data as a list object
in which each item in the list is named with the chapter title and the value of
the named list item is a table of words. This is exactly what you did with the
plain text files earlier in this book. From the XML file, you will now create
a list object identical to the one created from the plain text version of *Moby
Dick* in earlier chapters.

There are a variety of ways we could build this new object. In the earlier
chapter, we used a `for` loop and an empty `list` object that we filled with
data as we looped over the chapters. Here we will use a more efficient approach
that leverages `lapply` and our ability to create custom functions.

First we will write a custom function called `get_node_text` that takes three
arguments: an XML node object (`node`), an XPath expression (`xpath`), and a
namespace (`ns`). The `node` object will be an item sent from the `chapters_ns`
node list object. The later two arguments are familiar from what we just
covered above. The new function has three instructions to perform:

1. It needs to find all the child nodes in the `node` object that match the
   pattern in the `xpath` argument.
2. It needs to extract the textual content from those nodes.
3. It needs to paste together all those text nodes into a single character string
   that contains all the words from the chapter.

Here it is:

```
get_node_text <- function(node, xpath, ns){
  paragraph_nodes <- xml_find_all(node, xpath, ns)
```

```
    paragraph_v <- xml_text(paragraph_nodes)
    paste(paragraph_v, collapse = " ")
}
```

As written, this function will collect the text from each chapter. We can now use this function as an argument in `lapply`. Recall that `lapply` loops over list objects and applies the supplied function argument to each item in the list. Previously, we used `lapply` with the built in `mean` function. Instead of using one of R's built in functions, we can use our newly created `get_node_text` function.

```
# Do not run
text_l <- lapply(chapters_ns, get_node_text)
```

But before you try this, remember that the `get_node_text` function requires two more arguments. To complete our code, we need to define the `xpath` and `ns` values as additional arguments:

```
text_l <- lapply(
  chapters_ns,
  get_node_text,
  xpath = ".//tei:p",
  ns = c(tei = "http://www.tei-c.org/ns/1.0")
  )
```

Notice a slight change to the `xpath` expression used here. Since we are sending one node at a time from the `chapters_ns` node list, we do not need to use the longer `xpath`. By adding a period (`.`) in front of the two forward slashes (`//`), we indicate that we wish to work from the current node down. In this case, the current node will always be a chapter because we have already captured the chapters into the `chapters_ns` node list.

If you run the code above, you will now have a list object (`text_l`) with 134 items. Each of these items will contain the text of a chapter. If you wanted to read the first chapter, you could simply enter `text_l[[1]]` into the console.

If you were paying close attention in earlier chapters, you may remember that when we used grep to find chapters, we had a final list with 135 items. But here we only have 134? And if you remember, the last word of the last chapter of *Moby Dick* was *orphan*. But in this new list, generated from the XML file, the last word of the last chapter is *ago*. Why?

It turns out that our chapter finding algorithm in Chap. 5 did not understand that the novel actually contains an *Epilogue*, and it is the last word of the Epilogue that is *orphan*. This is a great example of where an XML encoded file can be more useful than a simple plain text file. Depending on the kind of analysis you are doing, you may or may not want to treat the Epilogue as a chapter. The editors of the TEI document we are using here made the decision that the Epilogue should not be considered a chapter![5]

12.5 Calculating the Word Frequencies

Now that we have the text of each chapter in a list, we can use `lapply` again, on this new list, to tokenize each chapter. For this we will write another useful function, called `tokenize`. Recall that we did something similar when we created a function called `make_token_v`. The function we write here will be even more versatile because it is more abstract, and it will have the added option of allowing us to choose to lowercase the words or not. Here is the function:

```
tokenize <- function(text_v, pattern = "[^A-Za-z0-9']", lower = TRUE){
  if(lower){
    text_v <- tolower(text_v)
  }
  word_v <- unlist(strsplit(text_v, pattern))
  word_v[which(word_v != "")]
}
```

Much of this should look familiar. The default `pattern` argument is the one we explored earlier that allows us to retain apostrophes. The `lower` argument is set to `TRUE` by default and, as a result, the condition of the `if` inside the function is `TRUE` and the text gets sent to the `tolower` function by default. We then split the string using the regular expression `pattern`, remove the blank values, and return the resulting vector. Save this function to your "*corpus_functions.R*" file and test it as follows:

```
source("code/corpus_functions.R")
tokenize("This is a test.")
## [1] "this" "is"   "a"    "test"
```

To apply this new function to all of the chapters, we just use `lapply` again to create yet another list object, but this time each item is the tokenized vector of words from each chapter:

---

[5]As long as we are on this subject, the editors also decided that the "Etymology" and "Extracts" that come before the famous "Call me Ishmael" should not be treated as chapters either. What those sections are, exactly, is something for scholars to debate.

```
word_tokens_l <- lapply(text_l, tokenize)
```

And now, for our final move, we can call on `lapply` again with R's built in `table` function.

```
word_tables_l <- lapply(word_tokens_l, table)
```

If we are interested in the raw counts of a particular word, such as *whale*, we can now use the exact same approach that we used in the beginning chapters of this book. The expression below will return a vector containing the raw counts of the word *whale* in each chapter.

```
unlist(lapply(word_tables_l, '[', 'whale'))
## whale whale whale  <NA>  <NA> whale whale  <NA> whale  <NA>
##     3     1     3    NA    NA     2     2    NA     7    NA
##  <NA>  <NA> whale  <NA>  <NA> whale  <NA> whale whale  <NA>
##    NA    NA     3    NA    NA     8    NA     5     1    NA
##  <NA> whale  <NA> whale  <NA> whale whale  <NA>  <NA> whale
##    NA     2    NA    20    NA     2     4    NA    NA     1
## whale whale whale whale whale whale  <NA> whale  <NA> whale
##     2   106     6     1    10    19    NA     2    NA     3
## whale whale  <NA> whale whale whale whale whale whale whale
##    41     3    NA    10    38     4     3     8     7     3
## whale whale whale whale whale whale whale whale whale whale
##     2     1     5    52    19     6     2     8    12    14
## whale whale whale whale whale whale whale whale whale whale
##     6     5    24     7     1     7    23     4     6    14
## whale whale whale whale whale whale whale whale whale whale
##    11    13    12    14     7     6     2    11     5    31
## whale whale whale whale whale whale whale whale whale whale
##    15    13     8    17    17    27     5    12    10    25
## whale whale whale whale whale  <NA> whale whale whale whale
##     6    10     5     1     2    NA     3     3    15    10
## whale whale whale whale whale whale  <NA>  <NA> whale whale
##    11     8    10    15     1     2    NA    NA     5     2
##  <NA> whale whale whale whale whale  <NA> whale  <NA>  <NA>
##    NA     2     1     4     4     2    NA     3    NA    NA
##  <NA>  <NA>  <NA>  <NA> whale  <NA> whale whale whale whale
##    NA    NA    NA    NA     1    NA     5     1     2     3
## whale whale whale whale
##     1    19    19    29
```

And, naturally, this data can be easily plotted (Fig. 12.1).

```
barplot(
  unlist(
    lapply(word_tables_l, '[', 'whale')
    ),
  names.arg = "Occurrences of Whale by Chapter"
  )
```

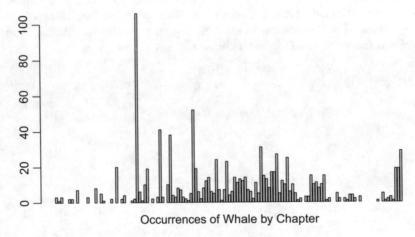

Fig. 12.1 Bar plot of whale frequency from XML file

And here's another little trick. If you want to collect and plot (Fig. 12.2) more
than one word, just send them to lapply as a vector using the c function:

```
barplot(
  unlist(
    lapply(word_tables_l, '[', c('whale', 'ahab'))
    ),
  names.arg = "Occurrence of Whale (blue) and Ahab (red)",
  col = c("blue", "red"),
  border = NA
  )
```

Before you try the practice exercises, do not forget to save your new function
tokenize to the *corpus_Functions.R* file in your **code** directory so you can
use it again in the future.

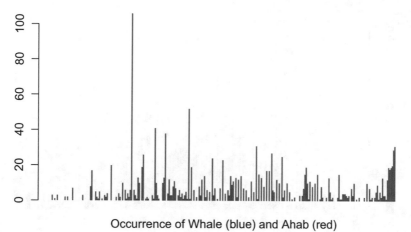

Occurrence of Whale (blue) and Ahab (red)

Fig. 12.2 Bar plot of whale and ahab frequency from XML file

12.6 Practice

1. Alter the code below to find the chapter titles, rather than the chapter text. Name the resulting list item `chapter_titles_l`.

```
text_l <- lapply(
  chapters_ns,
  get_node_text,
  xpath = ".//tei:p",
  ns = c(tei = "http://www.tei-c.org/ns/1.0")
)
```

2. Take these two list items (`text_l` and `chapter_titles_l`) and convert them into a data frame with two columns, one for the chapter title and another for the chapter text.

3. Write a custom function called `freq_table` to use instead of `table` that will return the relative frequencies instead of the raw counts. Here is how you will call the new function inside `lapply`

```
# Not run
word_tables_l <- lapply(word_tokens_l, freq_table)
```

Now use that function to create a new plot that charts the relative frequencies of *whale* and *ahab* instead of the raw counts. The resulting plot should look like this (Fig. 12.3).

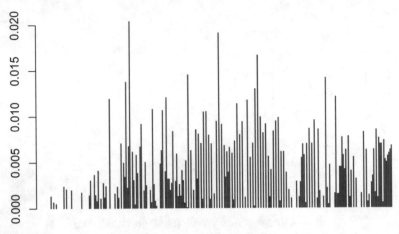

Fig. 12.3 Occurrences of "whale" (blue) and "ahab" (red)

Reference

Eder M (2013) Mind your corpus: systematic errors in authorship attribution. Digital Scholarship in the Humanities 28(4):603–614, URL https://doi.org/ 10.1093/llc/fqt039, https://doi.org/10.1093/llc/fqt039

Chapter 13
Parsing and Analyzing *Hamlet*

Abstract In this chapter, we leverage the rich metadata available in XML and the power of `dplyr` to explore the interaction of speakers in a classic drama.

13.1 Background

In Chap. 12 you learned about XML and gained some experience using the `xml2` package to parse a TEI encoded version of *Moby Dick*. In this chapter you will learn to do more with XML by parsing a version of Shakespeare's *Hamlet* that has been encoded to include information about both the speakers and receivers of the dialogue in the play. Our goal will be to understand a bit more about how the characters in the play interact and with whom.

The XML file you will be parsing has been encoded with "SPEAKER" and "RECEIVER" tags to indicate who is talking and who is being talked to. Each exchange between characters is encoded inside a "SPEECH" tag. Because each speech act is encoded in this manner, it is easy to compute who talks to whom most often, and because you know how to count and aggregate information about words, you can also study the content of the speeches. For example, you might wish to explore how Hamlet speaks to Claudius compared to Ophelia. Does Hamlet use a different vocabulary when speaking to different people?[1] Here is an example of the XML encoding you will find in the play:

```
## <SPEECH>
##     <SPEAKER>BERNARDO</SPEAKER>
```

---

[1] In his book *Computation into Criticism*, Burrows (1987) explores how the gender of characters in Jane Austen's novels are marked by certain habits of speech.

© Springer Nature Switzerland AG 2020   145
M. L. Jockers, R. Thalken, *Text Analysis with R*, Quantitative Methods in
the Humanities and Social Sciences,
https://doi.org/10.1007/978-3-030-39643-5_13

```
##    <RECEIVER>FRANCISCO</RECEIVER>
##    <LINE>Who's there?</LINE>
## </SPEECH>
## <SPEECH>
##    <SPEAKER>FRANCISCO</SPEAKER>
##    <RECEIVER>BERNARDO</RECEIVER>
##    <LINE>Nay, answer me: stand, and unfold yourself.</LINE>
## </SPEECH>
## <SPEECH>
##    <SPEAKER>BERNARDO</SPEAKER>
##    <RECEIVER>FRANCISCO</RECEIVER>
##    <LINE>Long live the king!</LINE>
## </SPEECH>
```

13.2 Collecting the Speakers

We begin, as we did in the previous chapter by loading the xml2 package and then calling the read_xml function with the location of the XML file. In this case, the file is located in the "drama" sub-directory of "data." The specific path is "data/drama/hamlet.xml." In addition to the xml2 package, we will also be utilizing functions from dplyr, so we will also load that package.

```
rm(list=ls())
library(xml2)
library(dplyr)
xml_doc <- read_xml("data/drama/hamlet.xml")
```

As seen above, each speaker's name is encoded inside a <SPEAKER> element. First we will use xml_find_all to collect all the speaker nodes:

```
speakers_ns <- xml_find_all(xml_doc, ".//SPEAKER")
length(speakers_ns)
## [1] 1248
```

Notice that we did not need to include a namespace (ns) argument to the xml_find_all function as we did in the previous chapter. This is because the XML file we are parsing now, "hamlet.xml," does not include a namespace declaration as an attribute of the root element. This is something to be aware of as you begin parsing files of your own. Encoding practices can vary wildly.

Calling length tells us that characters speak a total of 1248 times. If we want to know who the speakers are, the *dramatis personae* if you will, we could extract the text from these speaker nodes and use unique to show who they are.

```
speaker_names_v <- xml_text(speakers_ns)
unique(speaker_names_v)
##  [1] "BERNARDO"           "FRANCISCO"          "HORATIO"
##  [4] "MARCELLUS"          "KING CLAUDIUS"      "CORNELIUS"
##  [7] "VOLTIMAND"          "LAERTES"            "LORD POLONIUS"
## [10] "HAMLET"             "QUEEN GERTRUDE"     "All"
## [13] "OPHELIA"            "Ghost"              "REYNALDO"
## [16] "ROSENCRANTZ"        "GUILDENSTERN"       "First Player"
## [19] "Prologue"           "Player King"        "Player Queen"
## [22] "LUCIANUS"           "PRINCE FORTINBRAS"  "Captain"
## [25] "Gentleman"          "Danes"              "Servant"
## [28] "First Sailor"       "Messenger"          "First Clown"
## [31] "Second Clown"       "First Priest"       "OSRIC"
## [34] "Lord"               "First Ambassador"
```

If we want to know how many times each character speaks, then instead of using **unique** we could table the names in the **speaker_names_v** object instead. To see the speakers in order based on who speaks the most to the least, we just add a call to the **sort** function.

```
sort(table(speaker_names_v), decreasing = TRUE)
## speaker_names_v
##            HAMLET     KING CLAUDIUS             HORATIO
##               402               129                 116
##     LORD POLONIUS    QUEEN GERTRUDE             LAERTES
##                98                75                  65
##           OPHELIA       ROSENCRANTZ           MARCELLUS
##                58                49                  36
##       First Clown      GUILDENSTERN               OSRIC
##                35                33                  25
##          BERNARDO             Ghost            REYNALDO
##                23                14                  13
##      Second Clown         FRANCISCO        First Player
##                12                 9                   8
##           Captain PRINCE FORTINBRAS        Player Queen
##                 7                 6                   5
##               All       Player King               Danes
##                 4                 4                   3
##         Gentleman              Lord        First Priest
##                 3                 3                   2
##      First Sailor         Messenger           VOLTIMAND
##                 2                 2                   2
##         CORNELIUS  First Ambassador            LUCIANUS
##                 1                 1                   1
```

##	*Prologue*	*Servant*
##	1	1

No surprise, Hamlet is the most frequent speaker, and he is so by a long shot. Since it might be interesting to compare one play to another in terms of the dominance of one character versus many others, we might want to convert these raw counts to relative frequencies by dividing each character's raw count by the total number of speakers (Table 13.1).

Table 13.1 Partial table of top speakers

speaker_names_v	Freq
HAMLET	0.3221154
KING CLAUDIUS	0.1033654
HORATIO	0.0929487
LORD POLONIUS	0.0785256
QUEEN GERTRUDE	0.0600962
LAERTES	0.0520833
OPHELIA	0.0464744
ROSENCRANTZ	0.0392628
MARCELLUS	0.0288462
First Clown	0.0280449

```
sort(
  table(speaker_names_v)/length(speaker_names_v),
  decreasing = TRUE
  )
```

Doing so reveals that Hamlet accounts for 32.21% of the speech acts in the play. How do you think that compares to King Lear or Macbeth?

13.3 Collecting the Speeches

Which character talks the most often is one point of interest, but we might also be curious about to whom that character talks, and how often. For this we need to know not just who the speaker is, but also who is the receiver of the specific speech act.

As noted above, each speech act is encoded inside a <SPEECH> element. First we will use xml_find_all to collect all the speech nodes and length to get a count of how many speeches occur:

```
speeches_ns <- xml_find_all(xml_doc, ".//SPEECH")
length(speeches_ns)
## [1] 1236
```

Now that we have all the speeches in a nodeset list object (`speeches_ns`), we can iterate over the list extracting the speaker receiver pairs from each item. In the first speech act, for example, Bernardo speaks to Francisco and says: "Who's there?"[2] We might think of this as a type of relationship between two characters in a social network. In the language of social network analysis, or graph theory that studies the pairwise relationships between objects, we might say that Bernardo and Francisco are "nodes" and the speech that gets exchanged between them represents an "edge," or a "relationship." In this case the edge is directional in that the speech act flows from Bernardo to Francisco. We will get deeper into the dramatic network of characters in Hamlet as this chapter progresses, but for now let us just figure out who is talking to whom.

For each speech act, we need to extract both the speaker and the receiver as a specific pairing. For this we will utilize a custom function that we will name `get_pairing` along with `lapply` much in the same way that we did in the previous chapter. Here is the function:

```
get_pairing <- function(node){
  speaker_v <- xml_text(xml_find_all(node, "SPEAKER"))
  receiver_v <- xml_text(xml_find_all(node, "RECEIVER"))
  paste(speaker_v, " -> ", receiver_v)
}
```

First notice the single argument, `node`. Since we are going to use `lapply` to loop over the `speeches_ns` node list, each item sent to the function will be an individual speech node. Next we pull out the text from both the `SPEAKER` and `RECEIVER` elements and save them into new character vector objects called `speaker_v` and `receiver_v`. We then use `paste` to combine these two values along with a symbol (`->`) representing a directional arrow to show the relationship. The result for the first speech act will look like this:

```
## "BERNARDO  ->  FRANCISCO"
```

With the function ready, we can then call it inside of `lapply` and save the result into a new list object called `pairings_l`.

```
pairings_l <- lapply(speeches_ns, get_pairing)
```

If we now use `unlist` we can get a simple character vector containing all the pairs:

---

[2]Since `speeches_ns` is a type of list, you can access the contents of the first node by entering `speeches_ns[[1]]` at the console prompt.

```
pairs_v <- unlist(pairings_l)
```

This vector can then be sent to the `table` function in a manner similar to what we did above with the vector of speaker names. And if we want to have the results in a more useful form than a table, we can enclose it all inside a call to the `data.frame` function.

```
pairings_df <- data.frame(table(pairs_v))
```

This results in a data frame of 146 rows and 2 columns. The number of rows tell us how many distinct pairs there are in the play and the two columns contain the names of the pair and the number of times that pair appears. The first few rows are shown in Table 13.2.

From this we can see that the character *ALL* speaks to itself twice. On the other hand, *BERNARDO* speaks to *FRANCISCO* six times. And so on. Since we are likely interested in knowing who talks the most and to whom, we might

Table 13.2 Partial table of speaker receiver pairs

pairs_v	Freq
All -> All	2
All -> HAMLET	2
All -> LAERTES	1
BERNARDO -> FRANCISCO	6
BERNARDO -> HAMLET	4
BERNARDO -> HORATIO	9

Table 13.3 Partial table of frequent pairs

pairs_v	Freq
HAMLET -> HORATIO	98
HORATIO -> HAMLET	83
HAMLET -> ROSENCRANTZ	47
HAMLET -> GUILDENSTERN	39
ROSENCRANTZ -> HAMLET	36
HAMLET -> QUEEN GERTRUDE	35

invoke the `arrange` function from `dplyr` to sort the data in the `pairings_df` object:

```
arrange(pairings_df, desc(Freq))
```

Arranging the data in this way reveals that Hamlet speaks most often to Horatio and that the next most frequent pairing is of Horatio talking back to Hamlet (Table 13.3).

The `pairings_df` object is useful, but because we chose to represent the direction of the speech with the symbol ->, we actually limited our ability to do even more with this data. What if, for example, we are less interested in the direction of the speech and simply interested in which pairs of characters interact the most (regardless of the direction of the speech). In other words, we would like to know the total interaction between Hamlet and Horatio as opposed to the specific directions of the speech. And, perhaps even more interesting, what if we want to know how much speech was actually exchanged?

13.4 A Better Pairing

To give us more flexibility, and more data to explore, we will modify the `get_pairing` function to be a lot more powerful. First we will get rid of the line that involves pasting together the speaker and receiver with an arrow symbol. Instead we will save the speaker and receiver as separate items. Then we will pull out the text of the speech from the occurrences of the <LINE> element and `paste` them together using a space character as the glue with the `collapse` argument. Finally, we will put all of these collected data into a single vector using the `c` function to combine the items.

```
get_pairing <- function(node){
  speaker_v <- xml_text(xml_find_all(node, "SPEAKER"))
  receiver_v <- xml_text(xml_find_all(node, "RECEIVER"))
  lines_v <- paste(
    xml_text(xml_find_all(node, "LINE")),
    collapse = " "
    )
  c(speaker_v, receiver_v, lines_v)
}
```

After loading the function, we can test it by sending it just one node. In this example we send the first node in the `speeches_ns` object:

```
get_pairing(speeches_ns[[1]])
## [1] "BERNARDO"     "FRANCISCO"     "Who's there?"
```

It seems to be working as expected, but, unfortunately, there are still some problems that we need to resolve. Consider this case:

```
get_pairing(speeches_ns[[255]])
## [1] "HAMLET"
## [2] "HORATIO"
## [3] "MARCELLUS"
## [4] "Come on you hear this fellow in the cellarage Consent to swear."
```

Why do we see three characters? It turns out that Hamlet is talking to both Horatio and Marcellus! If you enter `speeches_ns[[255]]` you can see how this situation is encoded: there is one speaker and *two* receivers. There are a variety of ways that we might deal with this situation: we could, for example, consider this two separate speech acts and modify the function to return one vector for each act. Alternatively, we could conflate Horatio and Marcellus into a unified character. The second option is simpler, so we will implement that here by revising the third line of the function to do something similar to the fourth line.

```
get_pairing <- function(node){
  speaker_v <- xml_text(xml_find_all(node, "SPEAKER"))
  receiver_v <-  paste(
    xml_text(xml_find_all(node, "RECEIVER")),
    collapse = "/"
  )
  lines_v <- paste(
    xml_text(xml_find_all(node, "LINE")),
    collapse = " "
  )
  c(speaker_v, receiver_v, lines_v)
}
```

Now when we enter `get_pairing(speeches_ns[[255]])` the receiver field is populated with *HORATIO/MARCELLUS*. Since it might also be possible to have two speakers, speaking in unison, we might as well add the same code to the second line of the function, so that our final version is as follows:

```
get_pairing <- function(node){
  speaker_v <- paste(
    xml_text(xml_find_all(node, "SPEAKER")),
    collapse = "/"
  )
  receiver_v <-  paste(
    xml_text(xml_find_all(node, "RECEIVER")),
    collapse = "/"
  )
  lines_v <- paste(
    xml_text(xml_find_all(node, "LINE")),
    collapse = " "
  )
  c(speaker_v, receiver_v, lines_v)
}
```

Unfortunately, there is now another problem. If you study the XML file, you will see that there is an element <STAGEDIR> that sometimes appears as a child node of <LINE>. Here is an example:

```
speeches_ns[[74]]
## {xml_node}
## <SPEECH>
## [1] <SPEAKER>HAMLET</SPEAKER>
## [2] <RECEIVER>HAMLET</RECEIVER>
## [3] <LINE><STAGEDIR>Aside</STAGEDIR>A little more than kin, an ...
```

If you send this node to the `get_pairing` function, the word *Aside* is included as part of the speech. So we need a way to exclude stage directions that are embedded in lines of speech. While there are some convoluted ways that we might resolve this issue with R coding, the simplest way forward is to modify the `xpath` expression to exclude any `<STAGEDIR>` child nodes. We will not go into the details of `xpath` here other than to say that we can add some specific instructions ([not(self::STAGEDIR)]/text()) to the expression that will ignore the `<STAGEDIR>` child nodes of `<LINE>`. The final function is as follows:

```
get_pairing <- function(node){
  speaker_v <- paste(
    xml_text(xml_find_all(node, "SPEAKER")),
    collapse = "/"
    )
  receiver_v <-  paste(
    xml_text(xml_find_all(node, "RECEIVER")),
    collapse = "/"
    )
  lines_v <- paste(
    xml_text(xml_find_all(node, "LINE[not(self::STAGEDIR)]/text()")),
    collapse = " "
    )
  c(speaker_v, receiver_v, lines_v)
}
```

Now that we have a satisfactory function for extracting the data from an individual speech node, we should save it to the *corpus_functions.R* file and then reload that file by calling it via `source`. We can then use `lapply` to send every node to the function and return a new list object containing the data.

```
source("code/corpus_functions.R")
speech_data_l <- lapply(speeches_ns, get_pairing)
```

Each item in the resulting list is a vector containing three items. We can now combine all of these into a new data frame using the technique we explored earlier.

```
speech_data_df <- data.frame(
  do.call(rbind, speech_data_l),
  stringsAsFactors = FALSE
  )
```

The result is a data frame with 1236 rows and 3 columns. The first column contains the speaker, the second contains the receiver, and the third column contains all of the text that was passed from the speaker to the receiver. Presently, the columns are named with default values ("X1, X2, X3"), but we can reset them with the `colnames` function:

```
colnames(speech_data_df) <- c("Speaker", "Receiver", "Speech")
```

With this information in a data frame, we can now leverage the functions available in `dplyr` to perform some analysis. Let us begin by identifying all of the unique speakers and unique receivers:

```
speakers_df <- select(speech_data_df, Speaker) %>%
  unique() %>%
  arrange(Speaker)
```

If you now examine `speakers_df` you will see there are 39 distinct speakers, including a few dual speaker pairs—characters who spoke in unison according to the encoding in the XML file. Here are the first ten speakers in alphabetical order.

```
speakers_df[1:10,]
##   [1] "All"                "BERNARDO"
##   [3] "Captain"            "CORNELIUS/VOLTIMAND"
##   [5] "Danes"              "First Ambassador"
##   [7] "First Clown"        "First Player"
##   [9] "First Priest"       "First Sailor"
```

We can easily do the same thing to see who the receivers are

```
receivers_df <- select(speech_data_df, Receiver) %>%
  unique() %>%
  arrange(Receiver)
```

And if we are interested in the distinct pairings of speakers to receivers, we can find that quite easily as well using `mutate` to create a column containing data very similar to what we created at the beginning of this chapter:

```
pairings_df <- mutate(
  speech_data_df,
  pair = paste(Speaker, Receiver, sep = " -> ")
  ) %>%
  select(pair) %>%
  unique() %>%
  arrange(pair)
```

These are all interesting things to examine, but what about the text we have captured in that third column? Would not it be interesting to see who says the most (in words) and to whom? For this we will use `dplyr` along with a

modified version of the `tokenize` function that we wrote in the last chapter.
First we will edit the `tokenize` function so that it returns a count of the total
number of words in the input vector. We will rename it `get_token_count`
and, again, save it to *corpus_functions.R*:

```
get_token_count <- function(
  text_v,
  pattern = "[^A-Za-z0-9']",
  lower = TRUE
){
  if(lower){
    text_v <- tolower(text_v)
  }
  word_v <- unlist(strsplit(text_v, pattern))
  word_v <- word_v[which(word_v != "")]
  length(word_v)
}
```

Now we will integrate a call to this new function into our `dplyr` expression using the `rowwise` function to ensure that the operations of the
`get_token_count` function are applied to each row and not to the entire
column. First we will reload the newly revised version of *corpus_functions.R*
and then perform the operation[3]:

```
source("code/corpus_functions.R")
speech_data_counts_df <- rowwise(speech_data_df) %>%
  mutate(word_count = get_token_count(Speech))
```

If we sort this new data frame using `arrange` with the `desc` function, we
can quickly see who has the longer speeches and to whom those speeches are
directed:

```
sorted_speeches_df <- arrange(
  speech_data_counts_df,
  desc(word_count)
) %>%
  select(Speaker, Receiver, word_count)
```

Interestingly enough, at 460 words, the longest speech is Hamlet's soliloquy!

We know who has the longest speech, but it is also easy to use `dplyr`'s
`group_by` function, to see who has the most speech overall. In the next snippet
of code, we group the data by `Speaker` and then call `summarize` with the
`sum` function to add up all the word counts by each speaker.[4]

---

[3]If we omit the call to `rowwise`, we end up with the total word count of all words appearing
in every row.

[4]When you run the code below you will get a warning that "Grouping rowwise data frame
strips rowwise nature." Warnings in R, unlike errors, mean that your code still ran success-

```
group_by(sorted_speeches_df, Speaker) %>%
  summarize(Total = sum(word_count)) %>%
  arrange(desc(Total))
## # A tibble: 39 x 2
##    Speaker            Total
##    <chr>              <int>
##  1 HAMLET             11661
##  2 KING CLAUDIUS       4096
##  3 LORD POLONIUS       2682
##  4 HORATIO             2040
##  5 LAERTES             1440
##  6 OPHELIA             1186
##  7 QUEEN GERTRUDE      1056
##  8 First Clown          742
##  9 ROSENCRANTZ          691
## 10 Ghost                679
## # ... with 29 more rows
```

With 11,661 total words, Hamlet wins again! And Hamlet's total speech is more than double the next highest speaker, King Claudius. Naturally, we have to wonder where all of this speech is going? On whom is Hamlet expending all this breath? By adding another grouping column ("Receiver"), we can get this information very easily:

```
group_by(sorted_speeches_df, Speaker, Receiver) %>%
  filter(Speaker == "HAMLET") %>%
  summarize(Total = sum(word_count)) %>%
  arrange(desc(Total))
## # A tibble: 24 x 3
## # Groups:   Speaker [1]
##    Speaker Receiver                    Total
##    <chr>   <chr>                       <int>
##  1 HAMLET  HORATIO                      2771
##  2 HAMLET  HAMLET                       1848
##  3 HAMLET  QUEEN GERTRUDE               1393
##  4 HAMLET  ROSENCRANTZ/GUILDENSTERN      691
##  5 HAMLET  OPHELIA                       611
##  6 HAMLET  Players                       519
##  7 HAMLET  LORD POLONIUS                 476
##  8 HAMLET  ROSENCRANTZ                   465
##  9 HAMLET  LAERTES                       440
## 10 HAMLET  First Player                  357
## # ... with 14 more rows
```

fully. The warning is there to tell you that something unexpected might have happened. In this case, we can ignore the warning.

The only person Hamlet talks to more than himself is Horatio. Hamlet delivers 1848 words to himself and 2771 to Horatio.

13.5 Practice

1. In the first part of this chapter, we found that Hamlet accounts for 32.21% of the speech acts in the play. Use a similar method to discover who *receives* the greatest percentage of the speech acts.

2. Are there any characters who receive speech but do not speak? If so, who?

3. Use `dplyr` with `sorted_speeches_df` to calculate who hears the most words directed at them? What do you notice when you compare this result with to the result found in the first practice problem?

4. Using what you have learned here, and the `tokenize` function, find Hamlet's twenty most frequent words. Based on the top twenty words, what subject would you say Hamlet is obsessed with?

5. Compute the same information for *QUEEN GERTRUDE*. What subject appears to be of concern to the Queen? HINT: What word frequencies in the Queen's top twenty are higher than in Hamlet's?

Reference

Burrows JF (1987) Computation into Criticism: A Study of Jane Austen's Novels. Oxford University Press, Oxford

Chapter 14
Sentiment Analysis

Abstract This chapter describes how to perform sentiment analysis using the `syuzhet` package developed by Jockers. Readers will learn how to extract sentiment values from a text and compare and visualize the emotional arcs of two novels.

14.1 A Brief Overview

Novelist Kurt Vonnegut spurred our interest in sentiment analysis as a possible proxy for plot movement in fiction. Vonnegut argues that the highs and lows of the conflict and conflict resolution can be understood as deriving from the emotional highs and lows of the characters in the story. In his lecture "On The Shape of Stories," he even suggests that there is "no reason why the simple shapes of stories cannot be fed into computers."[1] Taking a cue from Vonnegut, Jockers (2015b) developed the `syuzhet` package for extracting and plotting the use of emotionally charged language ("sentiment") in stories. The tool is designed to help us study the use of positive and negative sentiment over the linear course of a narrative.

Studying sentiment from the beginning to the end of a narrative is similar to what we explored in Chaps. 4 and 5 when we found the occurrences of *whale* or *ahab* throughout *Moby Dick*. Instead of finding instances of a specific token, such as *whale*, sentiment analysis maps specific word tokens to specific sentiment values. These values, which are looked up in a sentiment dictionary

---

[1] You can watch the lecture on YouTube: https://www.youtube.com/watch?v=oP3c1h8 v2ZQ.

© Springer Nature Switzerland AG 2020

M. L. Jockers, R. Thalken, *Text Analysis with R*, Quantitative Methods in the Humanities and Social Sciences,
https://doi.org/10.1007/978-3-030-39643-5_14

(or "lexicon") range from positive to negative according to the specific design of the dictionary.[2]

To reveal and visualize the sentiment of novels, we will use the syuzhet package. syuzhet's style of sentiment analysis is suited for studying novels because it helps us consider the progression of sentiment from the beginning to the end of a text. This means that the focus is turned away from the actual *events* in the novel, and more toward the author's *presentation* or *organization* of the plot.[3]

14.2 Loading syuzhet

Like other packages you have used in this book, download syuzhet by going to RStudio's tools menu, and choosing "Tools" -> "Install Packages." Next, search for the syuzhet package, and begin the download process. To initialize syuzhet in your RStudio session, add the following code to the top of your new R script:

```
rm(list = ls())
library(syuzhet)
```

14.3 Loading a Text

In this chapter we will be exploring the sentiment arcs in both *Moby Dick* and *Sense and Sensibility*. To load these texts, we will use syuzhet's get_text_as_string. This function is similar to the scan function that we used earlier in this book. The get_text_as_string function takes a single file path argument.

```
moby_v <- get_text_as_string(path_to_file = "data/text/melville.txt")
sense_v <- get_text_as_string(path_to_file = "data/text/austen.txt")
```

The moby_v and sense_v objects contain the entire text of each novel as a single long string. No tokenization or other text manipulation has been done.

---

[2]In this chapter we explore a *lexicon-based approach* to sentiment analysis. There are other, more sophisticated, methods for performing sentiment analysis. These other methods employ machine learning algorithms. See, for example, Socher et al. (2013).

[3]The word *syuzhet* comes from the Russian formalist Vladimir Propp who divided narrative into the *fabula* and the *syuzhet*. The *fabula* are the specific elements of a plot, whereas the *syuzhet* is the manner in which those elements are organized in the linear movement of the narrative.

If you enter either of these objects at the R prompt, you will see the entire novel print to the console. If you want to know the overall sum of the sentiment in the entire novel, you can call the `get_sentiment` function with either one or both of these text vectors. The `get_sentiment` function tokenizes the text and then looks up every word in a sentiment lexicon assigning each word a sentiment value. The sum of these values is returned. In this example, both `moby_v` and `sense_v` are vectors of 1. If we send `get_sentiment` a vector of more than one item, a vector of sentences, for example, the function will return a new vector containing one sentiment value for each item in the input vector.

```
get_sentiment(moby_v); get_sentiment(sense_v)
## [1] -440.75
## [1] -38.3
```

These results for `moby_v` and `sense_v` indicate that there is far more negative than positive language in *Moby Dick* and that *Moby Dick* is, on the whole, more negative than *Sense and Sensibility*. If you have read the two novels, you will almost certainly agree with this assessment.[4]

14.4 Getting Sentiment Values

The syuzhet package gives us the option of tokenizing a text by word boundaries or by sentence boundaries. When we tokenize by sentences, the various sentiment values, both positive and negative, for the words in a given sentence will be summed in order to capture the overall sentiment of the sentence. Arguably, it is the sentence that is the fundamental unit of composition, so it makes sense to consider the overall sentiment of a sentence. Since we are curious about the *progression* of sentiment throughout the novels rather than learning about the overarching sentiment in each book, we will tokenize the two strings of text, `moby_v` and `sense_v` into vectors of sentences. For this we use syuzhet's `get_sentences` function:

```
moby_sentences_v <- get_sentences(moby_v)
sense_sentences_v <- get_sentences(sense_v)
```

`moby_sentences_v` now holds the text of *Moby Dick* as a vector of 9573 sentences, and `sense_sentences_v` contains the 4800 sentences in *Sense and*

---

[4]We say "almost certainly" because our research has shown that there is some degree of individual variation in how sentiment is assessed. See, for example, Jockers (2015a); Jockers (2016).

Sensibility.[5] get_sentences works differently from strsplit, which we used earlier to parse texts. strsplit used a regular expression (\\W) that split the string into vectors by *words* rather than *sentences.*[6] Even if you are not performing sentiment analysis, the get_sentences function may still come in handy for other types of text analysis.

Each index position in the two vectors, moby_sentences_v and sense_sentences_v, now contains a sentence of *Moby Dick* or *Sense and Sensibility*, respectively. For example, the first three index positions in moby_sentences_v, moby_sentences_v[1:3], are as follows:

```
moby_sentences_v[1:3]
## [1] "MOBY DICK; OR THE WHALE  By Herman Melville  CHAPTER 1."
## [2] "Loomings."
## [3] "Call me Ishmael."
```

The same, of course, can be done for *Sense and Sensibility*.

```
sense_sentences_v[1:3]
## [1] "SENSE AND SENSIBILITY  by Jane Austen  CHAPTER 1   The fa..."
## [2] "Their estate was large, and their residence was at Norlan..."
## [3] "The late owner of this estate was a single man, who lived..."
```

In this chapter we are not going to worry about removing the metadata at the beginning of the file or whether or not to include the chapter headings as "sentences." Here everything will be included as part of the text. You will notice right away that the first sentence of the text of *Sense and Sensibility* appears appended to the metadata and chapter heading from the novel. Keep in mind that the sentence tokenization is only as good as the text it is tokenizing. In this case, the file, "austen.txt," lacks the sort of punctuation required for a high quality parse. If you look a few sentences further down (i.e., sense_sentences_v[5:10]), however, you will find that the tokenizer is generally quite good at detecting sentence boundaries.

14.5 Accessing Sentiment

Now that you have parsed and prepped the novels, you are ready for some analysis! We will use syuzhet's get_sentiment function, which assigns a sentiment value to each item in an input vector. The get_sentiment function takes two arguments: a character vector (in this case, either

---

[5]That the novels have different lengths will be important to remember when we explore plotting them on the same graph.

[6]The get_sentences function implements a sentence splitting function from the textshape package.

moby_sentences_v or sense_sentences_v) and a *method* that determines which of syuzhet's built-in sentiment dictionaries to employ. The
default dictionary is called "syuzhet," but other possible methods are "bing,"
"afinn," "nrc," and "stanford."[7] Try using syuzhet's get_sentiment on
moby_sentences_v and sense_sentences_v, with the default "syuzhet"
method:

```
moby_sentiments_v <- get_sentiment(moby_sentences_v)
sense_sentiments_v <- get_sentiment(sense_sentences_v)
```

To understand what we have achieved here, take a look at the new object,
moby_sentiments_v, with the str function.

```
str(moby_sentiments_v)
## num [1:9573] 0 0 0 0.85 0 -1.6 -0.4 0.8 0 0.75 ...
```

Using str, we can see that moby_sentiments_v is a vector of numeric
values, of the same length as moby_sentences_v. As you might have
guessed, each value in moby_sentiments_v corresponds to a sentence in
moby_sentences_v, and each of its index positions contains a sentiment
value derived from the corresponding sentence.

Let us take a closer look by examining the actual values stored at the beginning of moby_sentiments_v.

```
head(moby_sentiments_v)
## [1]  0.00  0.00  0.00  0.85  0.00 -1.60
```

According to this vector of sentiment values, the most positive sentence of the
first six sentences in *Moby Dick* is the 4th sentence; the most negative is the
6th. We can look up the corresponding sentences in the moby_sentences_v
object:

```
moby_sentences_v[c(4,6)]
```

When reading through the second sentence, negative words immediately jump
out, words such as *grim, coffin, funeral,* etc.

> *Whenever I find myself growing grim about the mouth; whenever it is a damp,
> drizzly November in my soul; whenever I find myself involuntarily pausing before
> coffin warehouses, and bringing up the rear of every funeral I meet; and especially
> whenever my hypos get such an upper hand of me, that it requires a strong moral
> principle to prevent me from deliberately stepping into the street, and methodically
> knocking people's hats off–then, I account it high time to get to sea as soon as I
> can.*

---

[7]The syuzhet dictionary was developed in the Nebraska Literary Lab where it was tuned
specifically for fiction. The words and values in the default dictionary were extracted from
a collection of 165,000 human coded sentences taken from a small corpus of contemporary
novels.

In comparison, the sentiment in the first few sentences of *Sense and Sensibility* show much more variance. The first 6 sentiment scores for *Moby Dick* were 0, 0, 0, 0.85, 0, −1.6. Only two of the first few sentences had values that were above or below zero (neutral). In comparison, *Sense and Sensibility* begins with the following sentiment ratings:

```
head(sense_sentiments_v)
## [1]  0.80  2.90  1.00 -0.40  0.75  0.50
```

From these initial values, we could guess that the beginning of *Sense and Sensibility* is presented with a broader range of sentiment. If we wanted to compare the *central tendency* of sentence level sentiments in *Moby Dick* and *Sense and Sensibility*, we could look at the means:

```
mean(moby_sentiments_v); mean(sense_sentiments_v)
## [1] 0.02839758
## [1] 0.5121146
```

and at the standard deviations:

```
sd(moby_sentiments_v); sd(sense_sentiments_v)
## [1] 1.053748
## [1] 1.378005
```

Overall, *Moby Dick* is a bit more negative than *Sense and Sensibility*; its mean value of (0.0283976) is lower than *Sense and Sensibility*'s (0.5121146). The standard deviations suggest that *Sense and Sensibility* has more overall variance in sentiment values, and so we might expect a novel with more emotional twists and turns. Though this comparison is of too small a scale to derive any meaningful conclusions about *Moby Dick* and *Sense and Sensibility*, it is an interesting point of exploratory analysis that may lead to a variety of testable hypotheses, including the question of whether or not *Sense and Sensibility* does indeed have more emotional turns than *Moby Dick*.

14.6 Plotting

These measures of central tendency can be informative, even intriguing, but they tell us very little about how the narrative is structured and how the use of positive and negative language is deployed throughout the text. You may, therefore, find it useful to plot the values in a graph where the *x*-axis represents the passage of narrative time from the beginning to the end of the text, and the *y*-axis measures the degree of positive and negative sentiment in those narrative moments. Though looking at each integer value and its corresponding sentence might be valuable for targeting particular moments in a narrative, it is unlikely that the human mind can understand and retain the overall sentiment arc of a novel that contains thousands of sentences with fluctuating positive and negative values. A plot visualization that generalizes the highs and lows by smoothing the sentence to sentence fluctuations can usefully represent and convey the overall narrative arc.

Before we get to this smoothing, consider what a visualization of the data would look like if we simply plotted the raw sentiment values (Fig. 14.1). You can do this using the `plot` function:

```
plot(
        moby_sentiments_v,
        type = "l",
        xlab = "Novel Time",
        ylab = "Sentiment",
        main = "Raw Sentiment Values in Moby Dick"
        )
```

While this type of plotting could have been telling when plotting sentiment for a short text selection, in this graph there is too much visual information and "noise" to interpret the presentation of sentiment throughout the novel.

To reveal the overall trend in the data, the simple shape if you will, we can employ some form of *smoothing*. `simple_plot` is `syuzhet`'s out-of-the-box way to add smoothing and trend lines to the data. `simple_plot`'s output

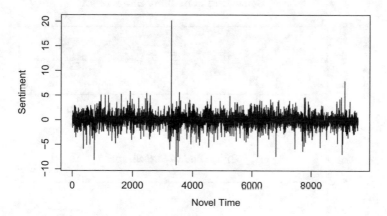

Fig. 14.1 Raw sentiment values in *Moby Dick*

uses and compares three different types of smoothing methods, including a moving average, *loess*, and a discrete cosine transformation (DCT). A call to `simple_plot` produces an image (Fig. 14.2) with two graphs for each text.

```
simple_plot(sense_sentiments_v,
            title = "Sense and Sensibility Simple Plot"
            )
```

The top graph includes three lines based on three different ways of smoothing the data. This allows for easy comparison and different levels of detail. The second graph shows only the DCT smoothed line, but does so on a normalized time axis. Notice that the x-axis in the top graph goes from zero to over 4000. These points correspond to the sentences in the text. Though the three lines do not have the exact same trajectory, their plot shapes follow similar patterns. According to the lower graph, *Sense and Sensibility*'s plot begins in positive territory, reaches a low point around midway, and then becomes more positive at the close of the novel.

14.7 Smoothing

Where `simple_plot` offers a quick and easy way to visualize a text's sentiment progression, it is not very flexible, and it is not useful if we wish to plot more than one novel on the same graph. One of the challenges of comparing the

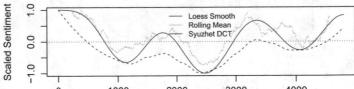

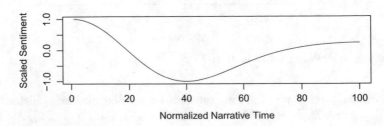

Fig. 14.2 Simple plot of *Sense and Sensibility*

sentiment trajectories from two different texts is that no two texts are the same length. As we saw above, *Moby Dick* has 9573 sentences and *Sense and Sensibility* has just 4800. Though these novels are different in the number of sentences, we could argue that they are the same in that both are narratives with beginnings, middles, and ends. They are both linear narratives meant to be read from beginning to end and both are meant to be complete, enclosed narratives. There is no perfect or even ideal number of sentences required for telling a good story. But if we want to understand how similar one plot shape is to another, we need a way of comparing them. One option is to graph their shapes and compare them visually (Figs. 14.3 and 14.4):

Though in the pages of this book the two images occupy the same width, you can see by looking at the x-axis that *Moby Dick* is twice as long as *Sense and Sensibility*. If we plotted these two sentiment trajectories on the same graph, we would get Fig. 14.5:

As we noted above, the length in sentences is not ultimately what matters in terms of our experience of the narrative as a linear progression from beginning to end. To see how these two novels shape up against each other, we need a way of normalizing narrative time.

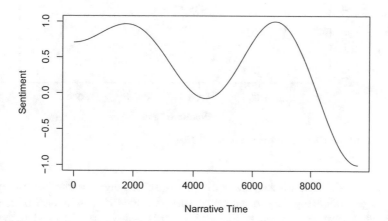

Fig. 14.3 The shape of Moby Dick

For purposes of plotting the two images, there is a simple solution. We can convert the values on the x-axis to percentages. The `rescale_x_2` function is designed for exactly this task of re-scaling values to a normalized x- and y-axis. Assume that we want to compare the shapes produced by applying a rolling mean to two different sentiment arcs. Having computed the raw sentiment values in *Moby Dick* and *Sense and Sensibility*, we can use the `rollmean` function from the `zoo` package. You will need to install and load the `zoo` package (as we have done with other packages elsewhere). Sometimes when you install a new package, that package includes other packages as

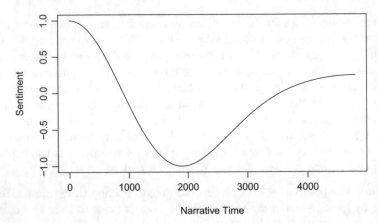

Fig. 14.4 The shape of sense and sensibility

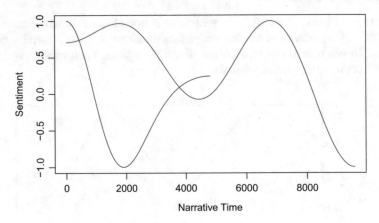

Fig. 14.5 Moby Dick and Sense and Sensibility

dependencies. If you already have one of those packages loaded, you may get a message indicating "one or more of the packages that will be updated by this installation are currently loaded." In this case, you will need to restart R and rerun your script from the beginning in order to take advantage of the updated packages.

```
install.packages("zoo")
library(zoo)
```

A rolling mean (sometimes called a moving average) is a calculation that summarizes a data set by creating a series of averages of different subsets of the data. The first value in the moving average is obtained by calculating the average of a subset of values inside a specified "window." The average is recorded and then the window is shifted to the right and a new average is calculated. The method proceeds in this manner until the window reaches the end of the series. For this exercise, we will set a window size that is equal to 10% of the length of the data series (number of sentences in each novel).

```
moby_window <- round(length(moby_sentiments_v)*.1)
moby_rolled <- rollmean(moby_sentiments_v, k = moby_window)
sense_window <- round(length(sense_sentiments_v)*.1)
sense_rolled <- rollmean(sense_sentiments_v, k = sense_window)
```

We now have two new objects, `moby_rolled` and `sense_rolled`, that contain the moving averages for the sentiments in the two novels. We can now send each of these to the `rescale_x_2` function:

```
moby_scaled <- rescale_x_2(moby_rolled)
sense_scaled <- rescale_x_2(sense_rolled)
```

If you consult the help files for `rescale_x_2` you will see that the function returns a list of three vectors (x, y, z). x is a vector of values from 0 to 1 that is equal in length to the input vector v. y is a scaled (from 0 to 1) vector of the input values equal in length to the input vector v. z is a scaled (from -1 to +1) vector of the input values equal in length to the input vector v. We can now use the data in the x and z vectors of the list objects to create a graphic (Fig. 14.6) that plots the two smoothed sentiment trajectories on the same plot with an x-axis that represents narrative time as a percentage rather than as a specific length.

```
plot(moby_scaled$x,
     moby_scaled$z,
     type="l",
     col="blue",
     xlab="Narrative Time",
     ylab="Emotional Valence",
     main = "Moby Dick and Sense and Sensibility with Rolling Means"
     )
lines(sense_scaled$x, sense_scaled$z, col="red")
```

14.8 Computing Plot Similarity

While this approach works well for plotting and visualizing the two shapes, because the two trajectories are still of different lengths, we do not have an easy way to compare them mathematically. Say, for example, we are interested in knowing whether or not the two shapes are highly correlated (and therefore highly similar.) Because `moby_scaled$z` has 8617 values and `sense_scaled$z` has 4321, we cannot compute their correlation using `cor(moby_scaled$z, sense_scaled$z)`. Consider a research situation in which you have *Moby Dick, Sense and Sensibility*, and 98 other novels. You want to figure out which of these novels has a sentiment arc most similar to *Moby Dick*. You can see from the plot (Fig. 14.6) that we just made that *Sense and Sensibility* does not seem very similar, but without looking at another 98 graphs, you cannot possibly know for sure.

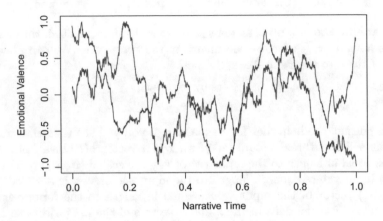

Fig. 14.6 Moby Dick and sense and sensibility with rolling means

Another problem with these rolling means is that there is a lot of data lost both at the beginning and at the end of each series. Consider that `moby_sentiments_v` has 9573 but `moby_rolled` has only 8617. With a rolling mean, we will always lose a number of values from the beginning and end of the series that is equal to the size of the window: half at the start of the series and half at the end.

All smoothing methods have difficulty dealing with the beginning and ends of a series, but some handle them better than others. If you go back and look at the output of the `simple_plot` function, you will notice that the blue and red lines, produced by using the `loess` and DCT smoothing functions, start at zero on the x-axis and go all the way to the end. Whereas the rolling mean starts late and ends early.

In the next example, we will use the `get_dct_transform` function to smooth the two data series. By default, `get_dct_transform` not only smooths the data, but also returns a result that is exactly 100 units long. We will set the `scale_range` argument to TRUE which will rescale the smoothed values to range from -1 to +1 on the y-axis. Setting `scale_range` to TRUE scales the values so that the most negative sentiment score in the novel is set to -1 and the most positive value is set to +1. All the values in between are scaled proportionally.

```
moby_dct <- get_dct_transform(
        moby_sentiments_v,
        scale_range = T
        )
plot(moby_dct,
     type="l",
     col="blue",
     xlab="Narrative Time",
     ylab="Emotional Valence",
     main = "Moby Dick with DCT smoothing and time normalization"
     )
```

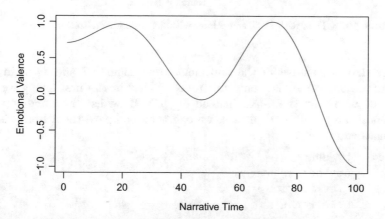

Fig. 14.7 Moby Dick with DCT smoothing and time normalization

As you can see in Fig. 14.7, the x-axis is 100 units. If we wanted to see the entire series, we could change the value of the x_reverse_len argument. In the next example, we set the x_reverse_len argument equal to the length of the original series.

```
moby_dct <- get_dct_transform(
        moby_sentiments_v,
        x_reverse_len = length(moby_sentiments_v),
        scale_range = T
        )
plot(moby_dct,
     type="l",
     col="blue",
     xlab="Narrative Time",
     ylab="Emotional Valence",
     main = "Moby Dick with DCT smoothing without time normalization"
     )
```

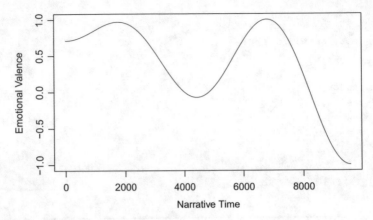

Fig. 14.8 Moby Dick with DCT smoothing without time normalization

Notice that the shapes of the sentiment arcs (Figs. 14.7 and 14.8) in both images are the same. The only difference is that in the first shape we have only 100 values on the x-axis instead of 9573. If we use the same approach to smooth and scale both novels, we can then compare them both visually and mathematically.

```
normed_moby_shape <- get_dct_transform(
      moby_sentiments_v,
      x_reverse_len = 100,
      scale_range = TRUE
      )
normed_sense_shape <- get_dct_transform(
      sense_sentiments_v,
      x_reverse_len = 100,
      scale_range = TRUE
      )
```

The length of both of these new vectors is now the same for each novel:

```
length(normed_moby_shape); length(normed_sense_shape)
## [1] 100
## [1] 100
```

So we can easily plot them together (Fig. 14.9):

```
plot(normed_moby_shape,
     type="l",
     col="blue",
     xlab="Narrative Time",
     ylab="Emotional Valence",
     main = "Two Novels with DCT Smoothing and Time Normalization"
     )
lines(normed_sense_shape, col="red")
```

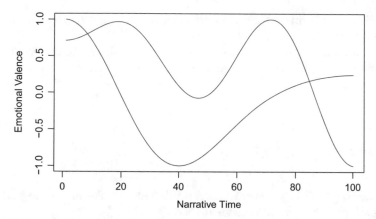

Fig. 14.9 Two novels with DCT smoothing and time normalization

And now we can also compare them mathematically:

```
cor(normed_moby_shape, normed_sense_shape)
## [1] 0.1456098
```

In this case, the correlation coefficient of 0.15 is very close to zero indicating that the two shapes are not very similar.[8]

14.9 Practice

1. Use the `summary` function on the two vectors of novel sentiment valences (`moby_sentiments_v` and `sense_sentiments_v`). How do the novels compare?
2. Combine the vectors for *Moby Dick*'s sentences and sentiment values into a data frame. One column should contain the sentences and the accompanying column should hold the sentiment value that the sentence was assigned. Label these columns "sentences" and "sentiment," respectively. Do not forget to ensure that all of the sentiment values are stored as numeric values.
3. Use your knowledge of `dplyr` to split this data frame into two new data frames; one for sentiment values above the mean sentiment (which you found in the first practice problem) and another for sentences with sentiment values below the mean. For each new data frame, also order the

---

[8]In this chapter we have only scratched the surface of the features available in the syuzhet package. If you would like to learn more about syuzhet's capabilities, enter `browseVignettes("syuzhet")` in the console and then click the link for the HTML version.

sentiment column so that the sentences with the most *extreme* sentiment are listed first.

4. Take a look at the most positive sentences in *Moby Dick*. Do you, as a human reader, identify these sentences as positive? How about the negative sentences?

References

Jockers ML (2015b) Syuzhet: Extract sentiment and plot arcs from text. URL https://github.com/mjockers/syuzhet

Socher R, Perelygin A, Wu J, Chuang J, Manning CD, Ng A, Potts C (2013) Recursive deep models for semantic compositionality over a sentiment tree-bank. URL https://www.aclweb.org/anthology/D13-1170

Jockers M (2015a) That Sentimental Feeling Matthew L. Jockers. URL http://www.matthewjockers.net/2015/12/20/that-sentimental-feeling/

Jockers M (2016) More syuzhet validation Matthew L. Jockers. URL http://www.matthewjockers.net/2016/08/11/more-syuzhet-validation/

Part III
Macroanalysis

Chapter 15
Clustering

Abstract This chapter moves readers from the analysis of one or two texts to a larger corpus. Machine clustering is introduced in the context of an authorship attribution problem, and we reuse some functions developed in previous chapters.

15.1 Introduction

This chapter introduces document clustering using a small corpus of 43 novels. It might be good to think about this experiment as a prototype, or model, for a much larger experiment. Many of the basic tasks will be the same, but instead of working with 4300 books you will develop your skills using just 43. Much of the processing done in this chapter will be familiar to you from previous parts of this book where we developed code to compare the vocabulary richness of *Moby Dick* on a chapter by chapter basis. Here, instead of chapters, you will have entire books to work with. The raw materials and the basic R objects will be the same.

15.2 Corpus Ingestion

The files you will use in this clustering experiment are all stored in the directory located at "data/XMLAuthorCorpus." The first thing you will require is a bit of R code that will go to this directory and survey its contents. To

© Springer Nature Switzerland AG 2020
M. L. Jockers, R. Thalken, *Text Analysis with R*, Quantitative Methods in
the Humanities and Social Sciences,
https://doi.org/10.1007/978-3-030-39643-5_15

keep things neat, put the path to this directory into an R object and call it
`input_dir`.

```
rm(list=ls())
input_dir <- "data/XMLAuthorCorpus"
```

You can now use the `dir` function to generate a vector containing the names
of all the files contained inside `input_dir`.

```
files_v <- dir(path = input_dir, pattern = ".*xml")
```

Notice how in addition to the path argument, we have added a *pattern* argument. This *pattern*, a regular expression, tells `dir` to return only those files
with names matching the regular expression.[1] The `files_v` variable now contains a vector of character strings that are the file names of the 43 XML files
found inside the **XMLAuthors** folder. Here they are

```
files_v
##   [1] "anonymous.xml"   "Carleton1.xml"   "Carleton10.xml"
##   [4] "Carleton11.xml"  "Carleton12.xml"  "Carleton13.xml"
##   [7] "Carleton14.xml"  "Carleton2.xml"   "Carleton3.xml"
##  [10] "Carleton4.xml"   "Carleton5.xml"   "Carleton6.xml"
##  [13] "Carleton7.xml"   "Carleton8.xml"   "Carleton9.xml"
##  [16] "Donovan1.xml"    "Donovan2.xml"    "Driscoll1.xml"
##  [19] "Driscoll2.xml"   "Driscoll3.xml"   "Edgeworth1.xml"
##  [22] "Jessop1.xml"     "Jessop2.xml"     "Jessop3.xml"
##  [25] "Kyne1.xml"       "Kyne2.xml"       "LeFanu1.xml"
##  [28] "LeFanu2.xml"     "LeFanu3.xml"     "LeFanu4.xml"
##  [31] "LeFanu5.xml"     "LeFanu6.xml"     "LeFanu7.xml"
##  [34] "Lewis.xml"       "McHenry1.xml"    "McHenry2.xml"
##  [37] "Norris1.xml"     "Norris2.xml"     "Norris3.xml"
##  [40] "Norris4.xml"     "Polidori1.xml"   "Quigley1.xml"
##  [43] "Quigley2.xml"
```

In this chapter, you will use text analysis and unsupervised clustering to
compare the word frequency *signal* of the anonymous novel to the signals
of the others, and then, based on that comparison, you will take a guess
at which author in the corpus is the most likely author of this anonymous
novel. Notice that the very first of these files in the `files_v` object is titled
anonymous.xml. This is the file whose authorship is uncertain.

With the file names stored in the `files_v` variable, you must now write code
to iterate over all of these file names and, at each name, pause to load and
process the text corresponding to the file name; for each file name in the
`files_v` vector, you want the script to perform some other bit of processing

---

[1] Enter **?regex** at the prompt to learn more about *regex* in R.

related to that file. This is very similar to code you developed in Chap. 12 and you will be able to reuse two functions you developed previously.

Begin with a `for` loop and a new variable called i (for integer):

```
# Not run
for (i in seq_along(files_v)){
  # Some code here
}
```

This expression tells R to begin by setting i equal to 1 and to iterate over (`seq_along`) all of the elements of the vector `files_v` and to stop only when it has finished with the 43rd item.

Remember from Chaps. 12 and 13 how you used the functions in the xml2 package to parse an XML file. Here we will use the same functions inside a `for` loop to parse all 43 files. So first, above the `for` loop in your script, you will need to load the package:

```
library(xml2)
```

Recall the way we used the `read_xml` function to load an XML file. This xml2 function requires a path argument that points to the location of the file on your computer. The first question you must address, therefore, is how to give the program the information it requires in order to figure out the file path to each of the files in the corpus directory.

You already know how to access one of the items in the `files_v` object via sub-setting, so now consider the following expression that uses the `file.path` function to join together the two objects you have instantiated:

```
file.path(input_dir, files_v)
```

Used in this way, `file.path` returns a series of file paths as a vector. Here we examine the first six file paths using the `head` function:

```
head(file.path(input_dir, files_v))
## [1] "data/XMLAuthorCorpus/anonymous.xml"
## [2] "data/XMLAuthorCorpus/Carleton1.xml"
## [3] "data/XMLAuthorCorpus/Carleton10.xml"
## [4] "data/XMLAuthorCorpus/Carleton11.xml"
## [5] "data/XMLAuthorCorpus/Carleton12.xml"
## [6] "data/XMLAuthorCorpus/Carleton13.xml"
```

Once wrapped inside a loop, you will be able to easily iterate over these file paths, loading each one in turn. Before you start looping, however, set the new variable i equal to 1. Doing so will allow you to do some prototyping and testing of the code without running the entire loop.

```
i <- 1
```

With i equal to 1, reenter the previous expression with the value i inside the
brackets of the files_v variable, like this:

```
file.path(input_dir, files_v[i])
## [1] "data/XMLAuthorCorpus/anonymous.xml"
```

Instead of returning the paths for all of the files, you get just the first file
(alphabetically) in the files_v object.

With the xml2 package loaded and this path name business sorted out, you
can now use the read_xml function to ingest, or load, the first XML file.
Rather than assigning the result of the file.path command to another variable, you can just embed one function inside the other, like this:

```
xml_doc <- read_xml(file.path(input_dir, files_v[i]))
```

If you enter this expression, and then type xml_doc at the R prompt, you
will see an abbreviated set of XML elements from the contents of the file
titled *anonymous.xml*. Success! You must now embed this expression within
your for loop so that you can iterate over all of the XML files in the files
directory. Do this as follows:

```
# Not run
for (i in seq_along(files_v)){
  xml_doc <- read_xml(file.path(input_dir, files_v[i]))
  # some more code goes here. . .
}
```

This code will consecutively load each of the XML files into an object called
xml_doc. Each time the program starts a new loop, the previous contents of
the xml_doc object will be overwritten by the new XML file. So, before the
next iteration begins, you need to process the contents of the xml_doc object
and store the results in some other variable that will persist beyond the loop.
For this, we will create an empty list called book_freqs_l and place it outside
of, and before, the for loop. This list will serve as a container for the results
that will be generated during the processing that takes place inside the loop.
Putting it all together, your code should now look like this:

```
# Not run
library(xml2)
input_dir <- "data/XMLAuthorCorpus"
files_v <- dir(path = input_dir, pattern = ".*xml")
book_freqs_l <- list()
for (i in seq_along(files_v)){
  xml_doc <- read_xml(file.path(input_dir, files_v[i]))
  #some more code goes here. . .
}
```

15.3 Custom Functions

Now that you have code for handling the iteration and loading of the XML files, you need to process the loaded files to extract the word frequencies. As luck would have it, you already built the two functions needed for this work and stored them in the *corpus_functions.R* file in the `code` directory. Here they are again as a reminder:

```
get_node_text <- function(node, xpath, ns){
  paragraph_nodes <- xml_find_all(node, xpath, ns)
  paragraph_v <- xml_text(paragraph_nodes)
  paste(paragraph_v, collapse = " ")
}


tokenize <- function(text_v, pattern = "[^A-Za-z0-9']", lower = TRUE){
  if(lower){
    text_v <- tolower(text_v)
  }
  word_v <- unlist(strsplit(text_v, pattern))
  word_v[which(word_v != "")]
}
```

These two functions need to be called at the top of your script so that they get loaded before the `for` loop. You can add a call to the `source` function to the top of your script:

```
# Not run
library(xml2)
source("code/corpus_functions.R") # Load the functions
input_dir <- "data/XMLAuthorCorpus"
files_v <- dir(path = input_dir, pattern = ".*xml")
book_freqs_l <- list()
for (i in seq_along(files_v)){
  xml_doc <- read_xml(file.path(input_dir, files_v[i]))
  # some more code goes here. . .
}
```

With the functions loaded, we must now finish the instructions inside the loop. We have an XML file loaded into the `xml_doc` object and need to extract out the contents of the text. Since these are TEI encoded XML files, the textual content is enclosed inside `<p>` elements that are child nodes of the `<body>` element. Recall that we did something similar when we extracted chapters from *Moby Dick*. Here, instead of chapters, we will extract all of the paragraphs. For this we will call our custom function `get_node_text` and store the result in a new variable called `para_text`.

```
# Not run
library(xml2)
source("code/corpus_functions.R") # Load the functions
input_dir <- "data/XMLAuthorCorpus"
files_v <- dir(path = input_dir, pattern = ".*xml")
book_freqs_l <- list()
for (i in seq_along(files_v)){
  xml_doc <- read_xml(file.path(input_dir, files_v[i]))
  para_text <- get_node_text(xml_doc,
    xpath = "/tei:TEI/tei:text/tei:body//tei:p",
    ns = c(tei = "http://www.tei-c.org/ns/1.0")
  )
  # some more code goes here. . .
}
```

Remember that `get_node_text` takes three arguments:

1. an `xml_document` object
2. an `xpath` expression that identifies the specific part(s) of the XML tree that we are interested in extracting
3. a namespace as the `ns` argument

In this case our document is stored in `xml_doc`; our `xpath` expression for finding the paragraph nodes that are the children of `<body>` that is a child of `<text>` is `/tei:TEI/tei:text/tei:body//tei:p`; and our namespace for the TEI declaration is `c(tei = "http://www.tei-c.org/ns/1.0")`. When `get_node_text` is called, it returns a character string of all the words found in the target nodes. This means that `para_text` will contain one long string of all the text from each novel. We can now send this text to the `tokenize` function in order to parse the long string into a vector of individual word tokens. We will store these in a new object called `word_v`.

```
# Not run
for (i in seq_along(files_v)){
  xml_doc <- read_xml(file.path(input_dir, files_v[i]))
  para_text <- get_node_text(xml_doc,
    xpath = "/tei:TEI/tei:text/tei:body//tei:p",
    ns = c(tei = "http://www.tei-c.org/ns/1.0")
  )
  word_v <- tokenize(para_text)
  # some more code goes here. . .
}
```

All we need now is to use `table` to count the occurrences of each word, and since we ultimately want the relative frequencies and not the raw counts, we can take advantage of recycling to divide each count by the length of the entire vector. We will store this result inside a new object called `freq_table`.

```
# Not run
for (i in seq_along(files_v)){
  xml_doc <- read_xml(file.path(input_dir, files_v[i]))
  para_text <- get_node_text(xml_doc,
    xpath = "/tei:TEI/tei:text/tei:body//tei:p",
    ns = c(tei = "http://www.tei-c.org/ns/1.0")
  )
  word_v <- tokenize(para_text)
  freq_table <- table(word_v)/length(word_v)
  # some more code goes here. . .
}
```

Next we want to insert this result into the list object (book_freqs_l) that
we created above the for loop. But before we do that, we will convert the
freq_table object from a table to the more flexible data frame type using
as.data.frame. And since it might be useful down the road to know which
file each frequency table was generated from, we will add the name of each
file as an index in the list object. The completed loop, which you can now
run, should look like this:

```
library(xml2)
source("code/corpus_functions.R") # Load the functions
input_dir <- "data/XMLAuthorCorpus"
files_v <- dir(path = input_dir, pattern = ".*xml")
book_freqs_l <- list()
for (i in seq_along(files_v)){
  xml_doc <- read_xml(file.path(input_dir, files_v[i]))
  para_text <- get_node_text(xml_doc,
    xpath = "/tei:TEI/tei:text/tei:body//tei:p",
    ns = c(tei = "http://www.tei-c.org/ns/1.0")
  )
  word_v <- tokenize(para_text)
  freq_table <- table(word_v)/length(word_v)
  book_freqs_l[[files_v[i]]] <- as.data.frame(
    freq_table, stringsAsFactors = FALSE
  )
}
```

When the entire script is run, it will take several seconds, the values returned
from processing each text are added to the book_freqs_l. The only thing
that might look odd here is the stringsAsFactors argument in the call to
the as.data.frame function. By default, the as.data.frame function will
treat strings as a special type of data called a factor. This can be useful in
certain cases, but right now we want the word tokens to be kept as character
strings and not treated as factors.

After processing, all of the data necessary for continuing the clustering experiment will be contained in the single list. Before you go on, however, you might want to inspect this new object. Try a few of these commands, and be sure that the results all make sense to you:

```
class(book_freqs_l)
names(book_freqs_l)
str(book_freqs_l)
```

You might also want to examine how the data in this list are stored. Remember that each list item is a data frame object with two columns. To peek at the first one, you can use `head(book_freqs_l[[1]])`. You will notice that the columns were automatically assigned the names `word_v` and `Freq`.

15.4 Unsupervised Clustering and the Euclidean Metric

Many years of authorship attribution research have taught us that the most effective way to distinguish between the text of one author and another is by comparing the different usages of high-frequency features in their writing. High-frequency features include words such as *the*, *of*, *and*, *to*, etc. as well as, in some studies, marks of punctuation and even common bigrams, such as *of the*. Here we will assume some familiarity with the concept of distinct stylistic *signals* and jump right into describing a process for comparing the word usage patterns of the writers in the sample corpus.[2]

The technique that we describe here involves a measurement known as *Euclidean distance*. Using the *Euclidean* metric, or what is sometimes called the *Pythagorean* metric, you can calculate each single book's *distance* from every other book in a corpus. Books with a closer distance will have more in common in terms of their feature usage habits, and books with a greater relative distance will be dissimilar. For the sake of illustration, assume that you have just three books and only two features for each book. Call the three books *a*, *b*, and *c*, and the two features *f1* and *f2*. Assume further that the measurements of the two features in each of the book are frequencies per 100 words, as follows:

```
my_m
##     f1 f2
## a 10   5
## b 11   6
## c  4  13
```

---

[2]For a brief overview of how this work is conducted, see Jockers (2013), pp. 63–67.

In book *a*, feature *f1* occurs 10 times per 100 words and feature *f2* occurs
5 times per hundred. In book *b* feature *f1* is found 11 times for every 100
words and so on. You can represent this information in an R matrix using
this code:

```
a <- c(10, 5)
b <- c(11, 6)
c <- c(4, 13)
my_m <- rbind(a, b, c)
colnames(my_m) <- c("f1", "f2")
```

These feature measurements can in turn be represented as x and y coordinate
values and plotted in a two-dimensional space, as in Fig. 15.1.

Once plotted, you can measure (as with a ruler) the distance on the grid
between the points. In this case, you would find that books *a* and *b* are
closest (least distant) to each other. Naturally, you do not want to actually
plot the points and then use a ruler, so instead you can employ the `dist`
function in R.

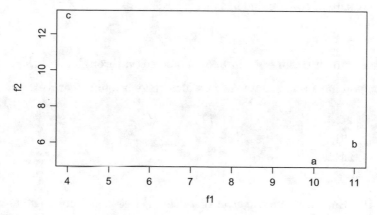

Fig. 15.1 Two-dimensional plotting

```
dm <- dist(my_m)
dm
##          a          b
## b  1.414214
## c 10.000000  9.899495
```

The result reveals that the *standard* or *ordinary* distance between points *a*
and *b* is 1.4142136, the distance between *a* and *c* is 10, and the distance between *b* and *c* is 9.8994949. These *distances* provide a way of describing the
relative nearness of the points, and, therefore, the similarity of the documents
from which these values were extracted. For convenience, you can think of

these distances as *meters*, *feet*, or *miles*; it does not ultimately matter since you are only concerned with the relative closeness of the points. In this example, using only two features (*f1* and *f2*) you would conclude that book *a* and book *b* are the most similar to each other within this closed set of three books.

When there are only two dimensions (or features) as in this example, the plotting and measuring is fairly simple and straightforward. It becomes more complex when thought of in terms of *fifty* or *five hundred* features and *twenty* or *forty* books. Nevertheless, the closeness of items in this high dimensional space can still be calculated using the Euclidean metric (which is the default method employed by R's `dist` function). The metric is expressed like this:

$$d(p, q) = \sqrt{(p_1 - q_1)^2 + (p_2 - q_2)^2 + \ldots + (p_i - q_i)^2 + (p_n - q_n)^2}$$

where d is the distance and p and q are the two books.

$$p_1$$

is the measure of feature one in book p and

$$q_1$$

is the measure of feature one in book q, and so on through all of the features.

Assume you have a new data set in which there are four features:

```
a <- c(10, 5, 3, 5)
b <- c(11, 6, 5, 7)
c <- c(4, 13, 2, 6)
my_m <- rbind(a, b, c)
colnames(my_m) <- c("f1", "f2", "f3", "f4")
```

Using the Euclidean metric, the distances d between books (*a*, *b*, *c*) are calculated as follows:

$$d(a, b) = \sqrt{(10 - 11)^2 + (5 - 6)^2 + (3 - 5)^2 + (5 - 7)^2} = 3.162278$$

$$d(a, c) = \sqrt{(10 - 4)^2 + (5 - 13)^2 + (3 - 2)^2 + (5 - 6)^2} = 10.09950$$

$$d(b, c) = \sqrt{(11 - 4)^2 + (6 - 13)^2 + (5 - 2)^2 + (7 - 6)^2} = 10.39230$$

To get the same results in R, you simply enter

```
dist(my_m)
##            a          b
## b   3.162278
## c  10.099505  10.392305
```

You can see that the distance between *a* and *b* (10) is much smaller than the distance between *a* and *c*. This indicates that *a* and *b* are more similar to each other in terms of these four features. With R it is a trivial matter to calculate the distances between every book and every other book in the example corpus. Everything you need for doing this calculation is already stored inside the `book_freqs_l` list object. You simply need to get that data out of the list and into a data matrix in which each row is a book and each column is one of the word features.

15.5 Converting an R List into a Data Matrix

Before we can apply the Euclidean metric to the authorship data, we need to get the word frequency information out of the `book_freqs_l` list and into a data matrix in which each row is a book and each column is a word feature. The cells in this matrix will contain the relative frequency values that were calculated inside the `for` loop. The first step in this process involves converting the `book_freqs_l` into an R data frame.

We learned earlier how to bind data from a list into rows of a data frame using the `do.call` function. We can do the same thing here to bind all 43 data frames from the list object into a single, and very long data frame.

```
freqs_df  <-  do.call(rbind, book_freqs_l)
```

If you now examine this data frame using `head(freqs_df)`, you will see that the names of the files (that we had stored in the list items) appear as `rownames`. You will also notice, however, that each file name now has a number appended to it. In order to transform this long form data frame into the wide form that we need for the clustering, we will first need to remove those appended numbers and move the file names into a column. First we will extract the row names and use the `gsub` (grep substitute) function to find and replace all the appended numbers:

```
text_names_v <- gsub(
  pattern = "\\.\\d+",
  replacement = "",
  x = rownames(freqs_df)
  )
```

`gsub` takes three arguments, a character `pattern` to search for, a `replacement` for the found pattern, and a character object to search in. You can think of the `pattern` as the "needle" and the character object as the "haystack." In this case our needle is a regular expression (\\.\\d+), which means "a period character followed by one or more digits." We will use this pattern to find and delete the appended numbers by setting the `replacement` argument to *nothing*, represented by the two quotation marks with nothing inside them. Examine the results of entering this expression:

```
head(text_names_v)
## [1] "anonymous.xml" "anonymous.xml" "anonymous.xml"
## [4] "anonymous.xml" "anonymous.xml" "anonymous.xml"
```

Now that we have the names of the files corrected, we need to bind this character vector with our `freq_df` data frame as a new column.

```
long_df <- data.frame(text_names_v, freqs_df)
```

And finally, to make things easier to read and understand, we will rename the columns:

```
colnames(long_df) <- c("file", "token", "freq")
```

With all this done, we can now reshape the data from `long form` to the `wide form` needed for clustering.

15.6 Reshaping from Long to Wide Format

There are several ways we can reshape a data frame and the `tidyr` and `reshape` packages both offer some options. But without having to load any additional packages, we can use the built-in `xtabs` function. "xtab" is short for "cross tabulation" and it works much like a pivot table in Excel. We need to tell the function what values we want to appear in the cells and how to conceive of the cross tabulation. In this case, we want the word frequencies to appear in the cells, and we want the cross tabulation to be based on the file names and the individual word tokens. To achieve this, `xtabs` expects a formula that looks like this: `freq ~ file + token`. In addition to this formula, we give `xtabs` a data argument—in this case the name of the long form data frame that we wish to cross tabulate.[3]

```
wide_t <- xtabs(formula = freq ~ file + token, data = long_df)
```

Notice that the output of calling `xtabs` is not a data frame (`class(wide_t)`). `wide_t` is a `xtabs table` object. For the clustering we will do in the next step, we need to convert this table into a `data.frame`. As with most things

---

[3]Using this formula, the file names become the first column in the resulting matrix and the tokens become the column headers. If, instead, we wanted to "transpose the matrix" and have the file names as the column headers, we would just change the formula to read `token + file` instead of `file + token`.

in R there are many ways to skin the cat. The simplest option here is to call the `as.data.frame.matrix` function:

```
wide_df <- as.data.frame.matrix(wide_t)
```

15.7 Preparing Data for Clustering

While it is certainly the case that you could apply the Euclidean metric to this large (i.e., 43 × 56674) data frame, doing so does not make a lot of sense in the case of authorship attribution. The goal is to figure out which of these texts is most *stylistically* similar to the anonymous text, and you do not want to bias the results by clustering the texts based on the similarity of their themes or content. Say, for example, that two of the books in this corpus were about horses. These two books would likely be drawn together in the clustering because they shared a similar *subject* and not necessarily because they shared a similar *style*. Therefore, before clustering it is useful to winnow the data to just those features that are extremely frequent.

There are many ways to do this winnowing; you could, for example, sort the data and keep only the 100 most frequent words in the corpus. We prefer to use a winnowing method based on setting a frequency threshold. In other words, we will limit the feature list to only those words that appear across the entire corpus with a mean relative frequency of some threshold. For this example, we will set the threshold to 0.01, or 1%.

First we will calculate the column means across the entire data frame (`colMeans`) and then we will check to see `which` of those means meets the condition of being greater than or equal to our threshold. The `colMeans` function returns a named vector of means.

```
token_means <- colMeans(wide_df)
head(token_means)
##                   '             ''              '''      ''americans       ''ansom
## 1.741339e-03 2.124454e-05 2.434679e-07 2.035591e-07 1.375302e-07
##          ''appen
## 5.501210e-07
```

If you look at the first few values using `head`, you will see some tokens made of apostrophe characters. Recall that our word tokenizing function specifically allowed the apostrophe as a "word character." What is important to see here is that this is a named vector. Because the vector has names, we can extract the names of the items in the vector that meet our threshold condition. For this we will use `which` to create a sub-setting condition inside square brackets. This we will enclose inside a call to the `names` function. We will call the result `keepers_v`

```
keepers_v <- names(token_means[which(token_means >= .01)])
head(keepers_v)
## [1] "a"    "and" "he"   "his" "i"    "in"
```

This `keepers_v` object can now be used to subset and select specific columns in the `wide_df` data frame. If you wanted to see all the data about these specific words in the first three files, you would just enter: `wide_df[1:3, keepers_v]`. Notice that you can access the columns of a data frame using the names of the columns. In this case the `keepers_v` object contains the names of those columns that met the mean frequency threshold.

With all this done, we can now cluster the data. First we will apply the Euclidean distance calculation by calling the `dist` function.

```
dist_m <- dist(wide_df[, keepers_v])
```

This produces a new matrix object that we have called `dist_m`. A distance matrix is a special type of table that reports the distance between pairs of objects. In this case the objects are the files. An object of type `dist` is difficult to inspect. You can use `str(dist_m)` to get some basic information, but to really peek inside, you may want to convert it to a simple matrix:

```
simple_dist_m <- as.matrix(dist_m)
```

Now you can apply some other function to really see what is going on:

```
dim(simple_dist_m)
## [1] 43 43
colnames(simple_dist_m)
##   [1] "anonymous.xml"   "Carleton1.xml"   "Carleton10.xml"
##   [4] "Carleton11.xml"  "Carleton12.xml"  "Carleton13.xml"
##   [7] "Carleton14.xml"  "Carleton2.xml"   "Carleton3.xml"
##  [10] "Carleton4.xml"   "Carleton5.xml"   "Carleton6.xml"
##  [13] "Carleton7.xml"   "Carleton8.xml"   "Carleton9.xml"
##  [16] "Donovan1.xml"    "Donovan2.xml"    "Driscoll1.xml"
##  [19] "Driscoll2.xml"   "Driscoll3.xml"   "Edgeworth1.xml"
##  [22] "Jessop1.xml"     "Jessop2.xml"     "Jessop3.xml"
##  [25] "Kyne1.xml"       "Kyne2.xml"       "LeFanu1.xml"
##  [28] "LeFanu2.xml"     "LeFanu3.xml"     "LeFanu4.xml"
##  [31] "LeFanu5.xml"     "LeFanu6.xml"     "LeFanu7.xml"
##  [34] "Lewis.xml"       "McHenry1.xml"    "McHenry2.xml"
##  [37] "Norris1.xml"     "Norris2.xml"     "Norris3.xml"
##  [40] "Norris4.xml"     "Polidori1.xml"   "Quigley1.xml"
##  [43] "Quigley2.xml"
rownames(simple_dist_m)
##   [1] "anonymous.xml"   "Carleton1.xml"   "Carleton10.xml"
##   [4] "Carleton11.xml"  "Carleton12.xml"  "Carleton13.xml"
```

```
##  [7] "Carleton14.xml"  "Carleton2.xml"   "Carleton3.xml"
## [10] "Carleton4.xml"   "Carleton5.xml"   "Carleton6.xml"
## [13] "Carleton7.xml"   "Carleton8.xml"   "Carleton9.xml"
## [16] "Donovan1.xml"    "Donovan2.xml"    "Driscoll1.xml"
## [19] "Driscoll2.xml"   "Driscoll3.xml"   "Edgeworth1.xml"
## [22] "Jessop1.xml"     "Jessop2.xml"     "Jessop3.xml"
## [25] "Kyne1.xml"       "Kyne2.xml"       "LeFanu1.xml"
## [28] "LeFanu2.xml"     "LeFanu3.xml"     "LeFanu4.xml"
## [31] "LeFanu5.xml"     "LeFanu6.xml"     "LeFanu7.xml"
## [34] "Lewis.xml"       "McHenry1.xml"    "McHenry2.xml"
## [37] "Norris1.xml"     "Norris2.xml"     "Norris3.xml"
## [40] "Norris4.xml"     "Polidori1.xml"   "Quigley1.xml"
## [43] "Quigley2.xml"
```

As you can see, the matrix has 43 rows and 43 columns, and the names of those rows and columns are the same. Let us look at just the first few rows and columns:

```
simple_dist_m[1:3, 1:3]
##                 anonymous.xml Carleton1.xml Carleton10.xml
## anonymous.xml    0.000000000   0.009972217    0.01387051
## Carleton1.xml    0.009972217   0.000000000    0.01144737
## Carleton10.xml   0.013870508   0.011447373    0.00000000
```

The values stored inside the cells are the calculated distances between the file in the row and the corresponding file in a column. So here you will see that the distance from the *anonymous.xml* file to the file called *Carleton1.xml* is 0.0099722. But notice too that the distance from any file and itself is always zero.

If you wanted to know which files were stylistically most similar to *Carleton1.xml*, you could select the *Carleton1.xml* column in the matrix and then sort the rows from smallest to largest:

```
sort(simple_dist_m[, "Carleton1.xml"])
##   Carleton1.xml Carleton11.xml   Carleton3.xml Carleton12.xml
##     0.000000000    0.006919052     0.008295471    0.008316020
##  Carleton14.xml   Carleton8.xml   Carleton7.xml        Kyne1.xml
##     0.008601454    0.008920331     0.009459768    0.009658346
##   anonymous.xml Carleton13.xml        Kyne2.xml   Carleton9.xml
##     0.009972217    0.010229984     0.010628076    0.011129111
##  Carleton10.xml    McHenry1.xml       Lewis.xml    McHenry2.xml
##     0.011447373    0.011909736     0.012000288    0.014090705
##   Carleton4.xml     LeFanu4.xml   Carleton5.xml     LeFanu2.xml
##     0.017162130    0.018493421     0.019913792    0.019961477
##   Donovan2.xml     Jessop2.xml     LeFanu7.xml       Norris1.xml
```

```
##      0.020676630      0.021075639      0.021272332      0.021300657
##    Driscoll1.xml    Carleton6.xml      Norris3.xml      LeFanu1.xml
##      0.021766826      0.022076064      0.022128428      0.022322383
##    Carleton2.xml      Norris4.xml    Donovan1.xml   Edgeworth1.xml
##      0.022746003      0.023061154      0.023349734      0.024765604
##    Driscoll3.xml      Jessop1.xml    Driscoll2.xml      Norris2.xml
##      0.024961006      0.024995979      0.025389137      0.025444092
##      LeFanu6.xml      Jessop3.xml      LeFanu5.xml    Polidori1.xml
##      0.027021386      0.028094894      0.028801653      0.032060653
##      LeFanu3.xml     Quigley2.xml     Quigley1.xml
##      0.036337114      0.048055239      0.049171042
```

As you would expect, the file most similar to *Carleton1.xml* is *Carleton1.xml*!
What is interesting to see is that most of Carleton's other books are highly
similar, which, of course, makes sense since the style in works by the same
author should be similar. From this result we can also see that the book that is
most dissimilar to *Carleton1.xml* is the book with the file name *Quigley1.xml*.
We could, of course, do the same thing for the *anonymous.xml* text, i.e.,
sort(simple_dist_m[, "anonymous.xml"]). But instead of doing that now,
let us use the hclust function to cluster all of the novels according to their
similarity and then produce a *dendrogram* plot of the clustering. In this way
we will be able to see all at once not only which books are most similar to the
anonymous book, but to each other as well. If years of research in authorship
attribution is valid, we should see books by the same authors clustering close
together.

15.8 Clustering the Data

Calling hclust produces a special "hclust" object that has a label attribute.
We can set the label names using the row names from the original data frame.

```
cluster <- hclust(dist_m)
cluster$labels <- rownames(wide_df)
```

From this we can produce a cluster dendrogram and visually inspect the
tree to identify the known authors and texts that are most similar to *anony-
mous.xml*.

```
plot(cluster)
```

Cluster Dendrogram

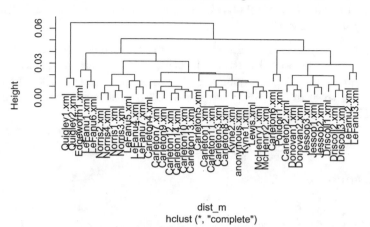

dist_m
hclust (*, "complete")

Fig. 15.2 Cluster dendrogram of 43 novels

If everything went well, you will have found *anonymous.xml* nestled comfortably between *Kyne1.xml* and *Kyne2.xml* (see Fig. 15.2). Peter B. Kyne is, in fact, the author of *anonymous.xml*! You will also observe that books by the same authors tend to cluster together. There is a big cluster of novels by Carleton, books by Norris form another independent cluster, Jessop and Driscoll both pull together independently.

Though this is a "canned" example corpus created for purposes of this chapter, we did not engineer the data to lead to this result. In fact the corpus was chosen based on just two criteria:

1. the works were out of copyright and could, therefore, be legally shared.
2. the works were clean and encoded in TEI compliant XML.

It is somewhat remarkable that the word frequencies from just 13 words can produce such a compelling result.[4]

15.9 Practice

1. Now that you have the correct answer, go back to the line of code in which you generated the `keepers_v` vector. Experiment with different threshold values. Examine how the attribution result changes, or does not, depending

---

[4]All these books are by Irish or Irish-American authors. They were digitized and encoded into TEI by Matthew Jockers as part of his work on the Irish-American West project at Stanford back in the early 2000s.

upon the number of features that you keep. What is the smallest number of word features you could use in this clustering experiment and still arrive at the same answer?

2. As a final experiment, write some code to see what happens if you select a random collection of features. In other words, instead of selecting from among the most high-frequency features, write code that uses the `sample` function to grab a random `sample` of 50 or 100 word features and then see if you still get accurate author clustering.

Reference

Jockers ML (2013) Macroanalysis: Digital Methods and Literary History, 1st edn. University of Illinois Press, Urbana

Chapter 16
Classification

Abstract This chapter introduces machine classification in the context of an authorship attribution problem. Various methods of text pre-processing are combined here to generate a corpus of 430 text samples. These samples are then used for training and testing a *support vector machines* supervised learning model.

16.1 Introduction

The clustering described in the last chapter is not ideally suited to authorship attribution problems. In fact, clustering is more often used in cases in which the classes are not already known in advance. Clustering is often employed in situations in which a researcher wishes to explore the data and see if there are naturally forming clusters. When the classes are known in advance (i.e., when there is a closed set of possible classes, or *authors* in this case) supervised classification offers a better approach. In addition to providing more information about feature level data, a supervised approach can also provide probabilistic data about the likelihood of a given document being written by one author versus another within the closed set of candidates. Though we will use an authorship attribution example here, consider that any category of metadata can be inserted into the place held by author. For example, if you wished to gauge the extent to which Irish style differs from British style, you could use *nationality* in place of *author* as the target class.

M. L. Jockers, R. Thalken, *Text Analysis with R*, Quantitative Methods in the Humanities and Social Sciences,
https://doi.org/10.1007/978-3-030-39643-5_16

16.2 A Small Authorship Experiment

For this chapter, you will use the same corpus of novels that was used in the clustering chapter, and you will be able to recycle much of the code and functions that you have already written. Begin by creating a new R script with the following code from the last chapter:

```
rm(list=ls())
library(xml2)
source("code/corpus_functions.R") # Load the functions
input_dir <- "data/XMLAuthorCorpus"
files_v <- dir(path = input_dir, pattern = ".*xml")
```

16.3 Text Segmentation

In the last chapter, you wrote a for loop to load a series of XML files and then send each XML document object to a set of custom functions that extracted the text from the XML nodes and then tokenized that text into a vector of words. In this chapter, instead of treating every novel as a single text, we will break each text into a series of smaller segments. Instead of having 43 texts for training and testing a classification model, we will create 430 texts by breaking each larger text into ten equally sized segments. Once a text has been tokenized into a vector of words, it is a fairly trivial matter to split that vector into a series of segments. For this we will use the aptly named split function in combination with the cut function.

For the sake of example, consider a vector v that contains the capital letters A–Z. Assume that we want to split this vector into thirteen equally sized chunks.[1] We first use the cut function to create a vector of integers that will be used as factors for the second argument of the split function.

```
# R has a small number of built-in constants.
# LETTERS is one of them
x <- LETTERS
groups_v <- cut(1:length(x), breaks = 13, labels = FALSE)
```

If you run the code above and then enter groups_v into the console you will see that the cut function has returned a vector of values. These values correspond to the "groups." The first two items in the vector contain the

---

[1]We know what you are thinking: there are 26 letters so what if you want an odd number of groups, like five? The cut function described here will optimize the size of the segments to be as close to equal as possible based on the length of the input vector.

number 1, for "group 1." The next two items contain the number 2 for group 2 and so on. We can now use this `groups` vector as the second argument in a call to the `split` function.

```
chunks_l <- split(x, groups_v)
```

The `split` function returns a `list` object. Inside each list item are the letters from the original vector x that compose each group. With that as the basic idea, we will apply this approach to segment each of the texts in our corpus. In the code at the beginning of this chapter you loaded a set of functions from your *corpus_functions.R* file and instantiated a new vector object called `files_v`. This vector contains the names of the files to load, tokenize, segment, and eventually use to build and test a classifier. The next step, then, is to iterate over these files and perform the necessary operations. For this, we will recycle some code from the last chapter and then add in our newly developed chunking code:

```
library(xml2)
source("code/corpus_functions.R") # Load the functions
input_dir <- "data/XMLAuthorCorpus"
# Not run
files_v <- dir(path = input_dir, pattern = ".*xml")
for (i in seq_along(files_v)){
  xml_doc <- read_xml(file.path(input_dir, files_v[i]))
  para_text <- get_node_text(xml_doc,
    xpath = "/tei:TEI/tei:text/tei:body//tei:p",
    ns = c(tei = "http://www.tei-c.org/ns/1.0")
  )
  word_v <- tokenize(para_text)
  # New code for chunking:
  groups <- cut(1:length(word_v), breaks = 10, labels = FALSE)
  chunks_l <- split(word_v, groups)
  # some new code goes here. . .
}
```

When you are developing code that involves loops, such as this `for` loop, it can be annoying and time consuming to test and debug if you run the entire loop. A useful way to test the code inside a loop, therefore, is to temporarily set the value of i equal to 1[2] and then execute the code in your loop one line at a time. Let us do that now to see how things are working. First we will set i equal to 1 and then we will execute the first two lines of code. We will then use **head** to peek at the first few values in the `word_v` object and **length** to see the size of the vector.

---

[2]Or some other number that is less than or equal to the length of the vector you are iterating over.

```
i <- 1
xml_doc <- read_xml(file.path(input_dir, files_v[i]))
  para_text <- get_node_text(xml_doc,
    xpath = "/tei:TEI/tei:text/tei:body//tei:p",
    ns = c(tei = "http://www.tei-c.org/ns/1.0")
  )
word_v <- tokenize(para_text)
head(word_v)
## [1] "in"      "the"     "summer" "of"      "1850"   "a"
length(word_v)
## [1] 99560
```

This appears as expected, so we will now execute the grouping and chunking
parts of the script and examine the contents of the resulting list object using
str:

```
groups <- cut(1:length(word_v), breaks = 10, labels = FALSE)
chunks_l <- split(word_v, groups)
str(chunks_l)
## List of 10
##  $ 1 : chr [1:9956] "in" "the" "summer" "of" ...
##  $ 2 : chr [1:9956] "timber" "at" "the" "edge" ...
##  $ 3 : chr [1:9956] "that" "i" "could" "stand" ...
##  $ 4 : chr [1:9956] "happy" "i'm" "delighted" "to" ...
##  $ 5 : chr [1:9956] "to" "hurry" "up" "lock" ...
##  $ 6 : chr [1:9956] "from" "cardigan" "a" "few" ...
##  $ 7 : chr [1:9956] "in" "the" "state" "timber" ...
##  $ 8 : chr [1:9956] "manager" "came" "on" "the" ...
##  $ 9 : chr [1:9956] "it" "poundstone" "looked" "up" ...
##  $ 10: chr [1:9956] "are" "won" "by" "the" ...
```

Calling str(chunks_l) reveals that the chunks_l object is a list of ten character vectors. These new character vectors are segments of the full word_v
object. Each of these can now be converted into a frequency table in the same
way that a table can be generated from the full vector.

As seen in previous chapters, the lapply function is well suited for use in
combination with the table function. You can now table each word vector
in the chunks_l list using a call to lapply.

```
chunk_table_l <- lapply(chunks_l, table)
```

Calling str(chunk_table_l) reveals a list of ten tables. These tables contain
the raw counts of each word token in each segment of the larger text. Since
there are multiple texts and, since the text segments across different novels
are not going to all be the same length, we must convert the raw counts to

relative frequencies. By now you should know that you can convert a single table of raw counts to relative frequencies using division:

```
chunk_table_l[[1]]/sum(chunk_table_l[[1]])
```

But since we do not want to convert each table in the list one at a time, having another function that we can use in a call to `lapply` is handy. Naturally R has just such a function: `prop.table`. So instead of dividing by `sum`, we will just call `prop.table` inside `lapply`.

```
chunk_frequencies_t_l  <- lapply(chunk_table_l, prop.table)
```

In the resulting `chunk_frequencies_l` object, you now have a list object containing the relative frequency data for 10 equally sized segments of the text. Here is how the loop portion of your script should look at this point.

```
# Not run
for (i in seq_along(files_v)){
  xml_doc <- read_xml(file.path(input_dir, files_v[i]))
  para_text <- get_node_text(xml_doc,
    xpath = "/tei:TEI/tei:text/tei:body//tei:p",
    ns = c(tei = "http://www.tei-c.org/ns/1.0")
  )
  word_v <- tokenize(para_text)
  # New code for chunking:
  groups <- cut(1:length(word_v), breaks = 10, labels = FALSE)
  chunks_l <- split(word_v, groups)
  chunk_table_l <- lapply(chunks_l, table)
  chunk_frequencies_t_l  <- lapply(chunk_table_l, prop.table)
  # some more code goes here. . .
}
```

It is useful to pause here and consider the final object that we will need for the classification experiment. Just as in the last chapter on clustering, we need to create a *wide form* data matrix in which each row is a text segment and each column is a word token or "feature." Recall from the previous chapter that we created the wide form matrix by transforming (reshaping) a long form matrix. We will use the same approach here, but now we also need to retain one additional piece of metadata. In addition to keeping track of which data comes from which books, we also need to keep track of which data comes from which *segment* of those texts. Consider the contents of the `chunk_frequencies_l` object as it exists right now. It is a list of 10 tables in which the names are the word tokens and the values are the calculated relative frequencies of those tokens in the given segment. Before we can take the next steps, we need to convert each of the tables in the list object to a data frame. Using `lapply` allows us to employ the `data.frame` function over each item in the list.

```
chunk_frequencies_df_l <- lapply(chunk_frequencies_t_l, data.frame)
```

If you examine the first part of the first item using:
`head(chunk_frequencies_df_l[[1]])`
you will see that each list item now contains a data frame with two columns labeled `Var1` and `Freq`. The next step is to bind all of the segments together just as we did in the last chapter using `do.call` and `rbind`.

```
segments_df <- do.call(rbind, chunk_frequencies_df_l)
```

When you add this line to the evolving script, it looks like this:

```
# Not run
for (i in seq_along(files_v)){
  xml_doc <- read_xml(file.path(input_dir, files_v[i]))
  para_text <- get_node_text(xml_doc,
    xpath = "/tei:TEI/tei:text/tei:body//tei:p",
    ns = c(tei = "http://www.tei-c.org/ns/1.0")
  )
  word_v <- tokenize(para_text)
  # New code for chunking:
  groups <- cut(1:length(word_v), breaks = 10, labels = FALSE)
  chunks_l <- split(word_v, groups)
  chunk_table_l <- lapply(chunks_l, table)
  chunk_frequencies_t_l  <- lapply(chunk_table_l, prop.table)
  chunk_frequencies_df_l <- lapply(chunk_frequencies_t_l, data.frame)
  # some more code goes here. . .
  segments_df <- do.call(rbind, chunk_frequencies_df_l)
}
```

When we did this in Chap. 15, we did not need to worry about capturing the segment metadata. As it happens, `do.call` automatically keeps track of this information and saves it in the `rownames` of the resulting data frame. If you enter `head(segments_df)` into the console, you will notice that each row contains a row name like this 1.1 1.2 1.3 1.4 1.5 1.6. . . The first number, before the decimal, is the chunk and the second number after the decimal is the row number. So in the first chunk, the token *'em* occurs with a frequency of 0.0005022097.

It turns out that we do not need to retain the row numbers, just the segment identifiers, but we also want to retain the name of the originating text files so that we know which segments belong to which books. Since we do not need to retain the row numbers, we can use `gsub` with a regular expression that removes the decimal and the information that comes after the decimal in the row names.

The approach is similar to what we did in Chap. 15, but with a different regular expression. The regular expression `"\\..*"` will find the period (`"."`)

character followed by any number of other characters.[3] We will replace the *regex* matches with nothing (""), and store the resulting strings in a new variable called `segment_ids_v`.

```
segment_ids_v <- gsub("\\..*", "", rownames(segments_df))
```

Since all of the segments in the current `segments_df` object come from the same book, it is easy to now add another "ID" column to the data frame that contains the value of the `files_v[i]` object concatenated with the segment identifiers using the `paste` function. The `paste` function *glues* each of these new strings to the corresponding segment/chunk reference value in a new column titled "ID." In this case, we will use an underscore (_) character as the *glue*.

```
book_df <- data.frame(
  ID = paste(
    files_v[i],
  segment_ids_v,
  sep="_"), segments_df
  )
```

If you examine the top of the new `book_df` object using `head`, you will see the column titled ID that contains a unique book and segment "key." At this point, you have everything you need extracted from this book. By setting i equal to 1, we were able to test and debug the code inside the loop one line at a time.

Before we run this loop, it is still necessary to create an empty container above the start of the `for` loop. This will allow us to bind each individual book's data into a single long data frame. We will add `long_df <- NULL` before the start of the loop, and then we will add `long_df <- rbind(long_df, book_df)` as the last line of code inside the loop.

When running big loops that do time consuming processing, we have found that it is also useful to add in one more line of code that reports out the progress of the script to the console, a little note to let us know things are progressing. The `cat` function is useful for this. `cat` will allow us to construct a brief message that appears in the console each time the loop completes processing of a file. In this way, we can easily monitor the progress of the script. The final `for` loop section of our script looks like this:

---

[3]In *regex* the *period* character is used as a special wild card. So in this expression the first period must be escaped using the double backslashes. This tells the *regex* engine to find the *literal* period. The second period in the expression is the period being used as a wild card metacharacter. The asterisk is another special character that is used as a multiplier. So here the asterisk repeats the wild card character indefinitely, until the end of the search string is reached.

```
long_df <- NULL
for (i in seq_along(files_v)){
  xml_doc <- read_xml(file.path(input_dir, files_v[i]))
  para_text <- get_node_text(xml_doc,
    xpath = "/tei:TEI/tei:text/tei:body//tei:p",
    ns = c(tei = "http://www.tei-c.org/ns/1.0")
  )
  word_v <- tokenize(para_text)
  # New code for chunking:
  groups <- cut(1:length(word_v), breaks = 10, labels = FALSE)
  chunks_l <- split(word_v, groups)
  chunk_table_l <- lapply(chunks_l, table)
  chunk_frequencies_t_l  <- lapply(chunk_table_l, prop.table)
  chunk_frequencies_df_l <- lapply(chunk_frequencies_t_l, data.frame)
  # some more code goes here. . .
  segments_df <- do.call(rbind, chunk_frequencies_df_l)
  segment_ids_v <- gsub("\\..*", "", rownames(segments_df))
  book_df <- data.frame(
    ID = paste(
      files_v[i],
      segment_ids_v, sep="_"
      ), segments_df
    )
  long_df <- rbind(long_df, book_df)
  cat(
    "Done Processing",
    files_v[i],
    "which is file",
    i,
    "of",
    length(files_v),
    "\r"
    )
}
```

Run the script now and monitor the processing in the console.

16.4 Reshaping from Long to Wide Format

We will now use exactly the same method used in the previous chapter to
cross tabulate long_df from a long form object to a wide form object. First
rename the columns, then use xtabs to do the reshaping. After that convert
the result to a data frame object. This will result in a new data frame with

430 rows, 10 rows for each of the 43 novels in the corpus. Note that when you run this code, the line calling xtabs may take half a minute or so to complete.[4] Here is the code:

```
colnames(long_df) <- c("file", "token", "freq")
wide_t <- xtabs(formula = freq ~ file + token, data = long_df)
wide_df <- as.data.frame.matrix(wide_t)
dim(wide_df)
## [1]    430 56674
```

Enter wide_df[1:4, 1:4] in the console to see the first four rows and the first four columns of data. You will notice that the new row names contain the unique identifiers. If you would like to examine the values for any specific word type, you can do that easily. Here is how to look at the frequencies for the words *of* and *the* in the first ten rows:

```
wide_df[1:10, c("of", "the")]
```

Before you can use any of this data in a classification test, however, you still have a bit more pre-processing to do. Since this is an authorship attribution experiment, you probably want to reduce the data frame to include only the very high-frequency features, and you will also need a way of keeping track of the metadata, specifically which texts belong to which authors.

16.5 Mapping the Data to the Metadata

First and foremost, you need a way of mapping the word frequency data contained in the rows to the specific authors, and not just to specific text samples (i.e., not just the specific segments). In this corpus you have multiple texts from multiple authors. In fact, excluding the anonymous book, there are twelve authors, forty-two books, and 420 book segments. What you need right away, therefore, is an *author* column. Because these files were named with the author's last name, you can extract the necessary metadata from what is now in the row names of the wide_df object.

Begin by deriving a new matrix object (metacols_m) by splitting the row names using that underscore character that was inserted during the paste command above.

```
metacols_m <- do.call(rbind, strsplit(rownames(wide_df), "_"))
head(metacols_m)
```

---

[4]We say "or so" because the time it takes to complete this operation is dependent on your computer's processor and the configuration of your system. On our MacBook Pro it took 14.19 s.

```
##        [,1]                    [,2]
## [1,]  "anonymous.xml"  "1"
## [2,]  "anonymous.xml"  "10"
## [3,]  "anonymous.xml"  "2"
## [4,]  "anonymous.xml"  "3"
## [5,]  "anonymous.xml"  "4"
## [6,]  "anonymous.xml"  "5"
```

To keep things organized and human readable, reset the column names to something that makes more sense:

```
colnames(metacols_m) <- c("sampletext", "samplechunk")
head(metacols_m)
##        sampletext        samplechunk
## [1,]  "anonymous.xml"  "1"
## [2,]  "anonymous.xml"  "10"
## [3,]  "anonymous.xml"  "2"
## [4,]  "anonymous.xml"  "3"
## [5,]  "anonymous.xml"  "4"
## [6,]  "anonymous.xml"  "5"
```

Using **head** you can inspect the first few rows, but remember that for some authors there are multiple books. If you want to see all of the unique values in the **sampletext** column, the **unique** function is handy:

```
unique(metacols_m[,"sampletext"])
##   [1] "anonymous.xml"   "Carleton1.xml"   "Carleton10.xml"
##   [4] "Carleton11.xml"  "Carleton12.xml"  "Carleton13.xml"
##   [7] "Carleton14.xml"  "Carleton2.xml"   "Carleton3.xml"
##  [10] "Carleton4.xml"   "Carleton5.xml"   "Carleton6.xml"
##  [13] "Carleton7.xml"   "Carleton8.xml"   "Carleton9.xml"
##  [16] "Donovan1.xml"    "Donovan2.xml"    "Driscoll1.xml"
##  [19] "Driscoll2.xml"   "Driscoll3.xml"   "Edgeworth1.xml"
##  [22] "Jessop1.xml"     "Jessop2.xml"     "Jessop3.xml"
##  [25] "Kyne1.xml"       "Kyne2.xml"       "LeFanu1.xml"
##  [28] "LeFanu2.xml"     "LeFanu3.xml"     "LeFanu4.xml"
##  [31] "LeFanu5.xml"     "LeFanu6.xml"     "LeFanu7.xml"
##  [34] "Lewis.xml"       "McHenry1.xml"    "McHenry2.xml"
##  [37] "Norris1.xml"     "Norris2.xml"     "Norris3.xml"
##  [40] "Norris4.xml"     "Polidori1.xml"   "Quigley1.xml"
##  [43] "Quigley2.xml"
```

As you can see, there are 43 unique texts. You can also see that some texts are by the same authors. You need a way to identify which books are by the same author, for example, "Quigley1.xml" and "Quigley2.xml" are by the same author. And you must do the same thing for the other authors from whom there are multiple samples. First remove all of the instances of the string ".xml" using gsub.

```
meta_names_v <- gsub("\\.xml$", "", metacols_m[,"sampletext"])
```

Now use gsub again, with another regular expression that will find instances of one or more *digits* (i.e., the 1 or 2 in *Quigley1* and *Quigley2*) followed by the end of string anchor metacharacter, which you indicate using the dollar ($) symbol. When a match is found, gsub will replace the matched string with nothing (""), which has the effect of deleting the digits. The result can be saved into a new object called author_v.

```
author_v <- gsub("\\d+$", "", meta_names_v)
```

You can then check your work using unique.

```
unique(author_v)
## [1] "anonymous" "Carleton"  "Donovan"   "Driscoll"  "Edgeworth"
## [6] "Jessop"    "Kyne"      "LeFanu"    "Lewis"     "McHenry"
## [11] "Norris"   "Polidori"  "Quigley"
```

With this new vector of author names, create a final data frame that binds this vector as a new column along with the two columns in the metacols_m variable to the existing final.df:

```
authorship_df <- data.frame(
  author_v,
  metacols_m,
  wide_df,
  stringsAsFactors = F
)
```

16.6 Reducing the Feature Set

At 430 by 56677, this new data frame contains way too many features for an authorship attribution test. You can reduce the number of columns to just those that contain the high-frequency features using the same approach we used in the last chapter. First calculate the feature means for each token and then set a retention threshold. For this example, we will use .005 for the minimum threshold. Remember though, that the first three columns in authorship_df are *metadata* (containing the author and text information), so we only want to calculate the means for the columns containing the token frequency data. To access only these columns, you can use bracketed subsetting and a sequence vector running from 4 through the number of columns in the authorship_df object. To determine that end point, use ncol (number of columns), another R function that is similar to `length` but specific to data frames and matrices.

```
token_means <- colMeans(authorship_df[,4:ncol(authorship_df)])
keepers_v <- names(token_means[which(token_means >= .005)])
```

Since only a handful of words will meet this criteria of having a mean frequency at or above .005, we can inspect the entire vector of "keepers."

```
keepers_v
##  [1] "a"     "and"  "as"   "at"   "be"   "but"  "for." "had"
##  [9] "he"    "her"  "him"  "his"  "i"    "in."  "is"   "it"
## [17] "not"   "of"   "on"   "she"  "that" "the"  "to"   "was"
## [25] "with"  "you"
```

We can now use these names to identify the subset of columns in the `authorship_df` object that we want to retain for analysis:

```
"# not run"
smaller_df <- authorship_df[, names(keepers_v)]
```

Since this line of code does not also retain the metadata columns about the authors and texts that we were so careful to preserve and organize, we still need to add those in. While you *could* just `cbind` those meta columns back in to the new `smaller_df` like this,

```
"# not run"
smaller_df <- cbind(author_v, metacols_m, smaller_df)
```

a simpler solution is to identify the columns right from the start by combining the names from the `keeper_v` vector with the column names of the first three columns in the main `authorship_df` data frame.

```
smaller_df <- authorship_df[, c(names(authorship_df)[1:3], keepers_v)]
```

16.7 Performing the Classification with SVM

With all of the data preparation done, you are finally ready to perform the classification analysis and see if you can figure out who wrote that anonymous book! Begin by identifying the rows in the new data frame belonging to the anonymous author.

```
anon_v <- which(smaller_df$author_v == "anonymous")
```

Next identify the data that will be used to train the model by telling R to use only the rows of `smaller.df` that do *not* include those identified in the

anon_v vector. This negation of specific rows is achieved using the "-" operator before the object name. The *minus* sign has the effect of communicating
"all the rows except for these" or "less these." For this classification, you also
do not want to include the first three columns where the metadata is stored,
so use 4:ncol(smaller.df) to grab only the 4th through last columns.

```
train  <-  smaller_df[-anon_v, 4:ncol(smaller_df)]
```

Next you need to identify a *class* column that the classifier will use to organize
the data. That is, you need to give the classifier a set of values for the classes
that are already known. In this case, the true author names are stored in
the column headed *author_v*. This new object needs to be a factor, which
is a special R data type. Factors are very similar to vectors except that in
addition to storing the vector data, in this case a set of character strings
referring to authors, the factor also stores *levels*. Factors provide an efficient
way of storing repetitive character data because the unique character values
are actually only stored once and the data itself is stored as a vector of
integers that refer back to the single character strings. To achieve this, use
the as.factor function:

```
class_f  <-  as.factor(smaller_df[-anon_v, "author_v"])
```

With the classes identified, you now need to pick a classifier and run the classification.[5] To keep things simple and to avoid having to load a lot of complex
classification packages, we will use a comparatively familiar algorithm, SVM
or *Support Vector Machines* which is part of the e1071 package.

```
install.packages("e1071")
library(e1071)
```

At this point, you can generate a model using the svm classifier function and
the data contained in the train and class_f objects:

```
model_svm <- svm(train, class_f)
```

Once the model is generated, it is possible to examine the details using the
summary function.

```
summary(model_svm)
```

To test the accuracy of the model, use the predict function with the
model.svm and the training data in the train object.

---

[5]There are many good classification algorithms that can be used for authorship attribution
testing, see, for example, Jockers and Witten (2010). In this paper, Jockers and Witten
conclude that the Nearest Shrunken Centroids is especially good for authorship attribution
problems, but frankly, the others methods tested also performed quite well. Interested readers might also look at the work of Jan Rybicki and Maciej Eder found at the Computational
Stylistics Group website: https://sites.google.com/site/computationalstylistics/.

```
pred_svm  <-  predict(model_svm, train)
```

The `pred_svm` object will now contain a vector of text labels and the machine's guesses. Examine the contents of `pred_svm` as follows:

```
as.data.frame(pred_svm)
```

You should see a few misattributions, but for the most part, you will notice that the model has done very well. To print out a summary in the form of a confusion matrix you can use `table`:

```
table(pred_svm, class_f)
```

When you look at the *Carleton* column in the results, you will note that 139 of the *Carleton* samples were assigned correctly to *Carleton*. You will see that 20 of the *Donovan* samples were correctly assigned to *Donovan*, and so on. This model has performed very well in terms of accurately classifying the known authors.

Based on this validation of the model's accuracy in classifying the known authors, you can classify the anonymous text with a good deal of confidence. First isolate the test data:

```
testdata  <-  smaller_df[anon_v,4:ncol(smaller_df)]
```

Send the test data to the model for prediction, and view the results using `as.data.frame`.

```
final_result <- predict (model_svm, testdata)
as.data.frame(final_result)
##                        final_result
## anonymous.xml_1            Kyne
## anonymous.xml_10           Kyne
## anonymous.xml_2            Kyne
## anonymous.xml_3            Kyne
## anonymous.xml_4            Kyne
## anonymous.xml_5            Kyne
## anonymous.xml_6            Kyne
## anonymous.xml_7            Kyne
## anonymous.xml_8            Kyne
## anonymous.xml_9            Kyne
```

The results of this `svm` classification confirm what was observed in the clustering test in Chap. 15; Kyne has been identified as the most likely author of every single segment of the anonymous book!

16.8 Practice

1. Now that you know the author and have seen how the classifier correctly guesses the author of each of the ten samples, increase the number of features the model uses by decreasing the feature `mean` used to determine the number of features retained in the `keepers_v` object. In the example in this chapter, 26 high-frequency features were retained using a mean relative frequency threshold of .005. Decrease this number in order to observe how the attributions change with the addition of context sensitive words. When using the 681 highest frequency word features, for example, the classifier gets every single attribution wrong. Why?

2. For the example in this chapter, we used a corpus wide mean relative frequency threshold to select the high-frequency features to keep for the analysis. In the previous exercise you saw how increasing the number of features can lead to incorrect results because author style gets lost in context. Another winnowing method involves choosing features based on the restriction that every selected feature must appear at least once in the work of every author. Write code that will implement such winnowing in order to generate a new set of values for the `keepers_v` object. Here is some sample code for you to consider. Notice that feature `f1` is not found in either of the samples from author `C` and feature `f5` is not found in any of the samples from author `A`. Features `f1` and `f5` should, therefore, be removed from the analysis.

```
authors <- c("A","A","B","B","C", "C")
f1 <- c(0, 1, 2, 3, 0,0)
f2 <- c(0, 1, 2, 3, 0,1)
f3 <- c(3, 2, 1, 2, 1,1)
f4 <- c(3, 2, 1, 2, 1,1)
f5 <- c(0, 0, 1, 2, 1,1)
author_df <- data.frame(authors, f1,f2,f3,f4, f5)
author_df # Show the original data frame
##    authors f1 f2 f3 f4 f5
## 1       A  0  0  3  3  0
## 2       A  1  1  2  2  0
## 3       B  2  2  1  1  1
## 4       B  3  3  2  2  2
## 5       C  0  0  1  1  1
## 6       C  0  1  1  1  1
```

Reference

Jockers ML, Witten DM (2010) A comparative study of machine learning methods for authorship attribution. Digital Scholarship in the Humanities 25(2):215–223, https://doi.org/10.1093/llc/fqq001

Chapter 17
Topic Modeling

Abstract This chapter introduces topic modeling using the `mallet` package and topic-based word cloud visualization using the `wordcloud` package. (In this chapter we assume that readers are already familiar with the basic idea behind topic modeling. Readers who are not familiar may consult Appendix B for a general overview and some suggestions for further reading.)

17.1 Introduction

Topic modeling is a statistical method for identifying words in a corpus of documents that tend to co-occur together and as a result share some sort of semantic relationship. The words *ship*, *ocean*, and *captain* are semantically related to each other and might be described as words that we would expect to appear in a topic called "seafaring." Latent Dirichlet Allocation (LDA) is one example of a topic modeling algorithm. LDA is the most popular topic modeling approach, and though the mathematics involved is quite complicated, the basic idea is fairly straightforward. The LDA algorithm treats every text as a *bag of words*[1] and attempts to identify collections of words that co-occur together in each text but also co-occur in other texts throughout the corpus. As you might imagine, any single document is likely to be "about" more than one thing, and so the LDA model assumes that every document is a collection of topics in different proportions. Likewise, the model assumes that the entire corpus is a collection of topics in different proportions. Key here, however,

---

[1] This means that the order of the words in the text do not matter.

© Springer Nature Switzerland AG 2020

M. L. Jockers, R. Thalken, *Text Analysis with R*, Quantitative Methods in the Humanities and Social Sciences,
https://doi.org/10.1007/978-3-030-39643-5_17

is that the model also assumes that there is a finite number of possible topics. One of the subtle and sometimes difficult decisions that you will have to make involves how to set the number of topics to be harvested in the topic modeling process.

17.2 R and Topic Modeling

At the time of this writing there are at least three topic modeling packages for R. These include `topicmodels` from Bettina Grün and Kurt Hornik, `lda` by Johnathan Chang, and `mallet` by David Mimno.[2] Though the `mallet` package for R is a relative newcomer, the `Java` package upon which it is based is not. We have chosen to use the `mallet` package here because Mimno's implementation of topic modeling in the `MALLET JAVA` package is the *de facto* tool used by literary researchers.[3] In short, `MALLET` is the most familiar topic modeling package in the humanities, and it makes the most sense to work with it here.[4]

17.3 Text Segmentation and Preparation

Topic modeling treats each document as a *bag of words* in which word order is disregarded. Since the topic model works by identifying words that tend to co-occur, the bigger the bag, the more words that will tend to be found together in the same bag. If novels, such as those we will analyze here, tended to be constrained to only a very small number of topics, or themes, then treating each entire novel as one bag might be fruitful. In reality, though, novels tend to have some themes that run throughout their entirety and others that appear at specific points and then disappear. In order to capture these transient themes, it is useful to divide novels and other large documents into *chunks*

---

[2]The `topicmodels` package provides an implementation of (or interface to) the C code developed by LDA pioneer David Blei. See Blei et al. (2003). Johnathan Chang is a researcher at Facebook who has worked with Blei and with whom he has co-authored several papers including the influential topic modeling paper: Chang et al. (2009). David Mimno, a professor at Cornell, is the developer and maintainer of the Java implementation of LDA in the popular *MAchine Learning for LanguagE Toolkit* (*MALLET*) developed at the University of Massachusetts under the direction of Andrew McCallum: McCallum, Andrew Kachites. See McCallum (2002).

[3]Mimno released (to CRAN) his R "wrapper" for the `MALLET` topic modeling package on August 9, 2013. See Mimno (2013).

[4]We have used all three of these packages to good effect. Each one has its advantages and disadvantages in terms of ease of use, but functionally they are all comparable.

or *segments*, somewhat like we did in Chap. 16, and then run the model over those segments instead of over the entire text.[5] You must, therefore, begin by pre-processing the novels in the corpus into segments.

Unlike the previous chapter where we segmented texts based on percentage (i.e., each book was chunked into 10 equal sized portions), here we will write a function that allows for chunking based on a set number of words. That is, you will be able to set a specific chunk size, such as 1000 words, and then divide each text into some number of word segments that are 1000, or roughly 1000, words long.

Begin by loading the `xml2` package, referencing the corpus directory, and then generating a vector of file names. This should be familiar from previous chapters.

```
rm(list=ls())
library(xml2)
input_dir <- "data/XMLAuthorCorpus"
files_v <- dir(path = input_dir, pattern = ".*xml")
```

As in the last chapter, here too you will be able to recycle functions you have already written by calling your *corpus_functions.R* file with the `source` function.

```
source("code/corpus_functions.R") # Load the functions
```

Ultimately, the script written in this chapter is going to involve a `for` loop that will iterate over the files stored in the `files_v` object. For testing purposes, let us temporarily avoid dealing with the `for` loop and set i equal to 1 and recycle some code and custom functions (`get_node_text` and `tokenize`) from the previous chapters to tokenize the XML document.

```
i <- 1
xml_doc <- read_xml(file.path(input_dir, files_v[i]))
  para_text <- get_node_text(xml_doc,
    xpath = "/tei:TEI/tei:text/tei:body//tei:p",
    ns = c(tei = "http://www.tei-c.org/ns/1.0")
  )
word_v <- tokenize(para_text)
```

Now create and set a variable called `chunk_size`.

```
chunk_size <- 1000 # number of words per chunk
```

---

[5]There appears to be no conventional wisdom regarding ideal text-segmentation parameters. David Mimno reports in email correspondence that he frequently chunks texts down to the level of individual paragraphs. Until new research provides an algorithmic alternative, trial and experimentation augmented by domain expertise appear to be the best guides in setting segmentation parameters.

Here, the goal is to divide the text into an unknown number of segments that are *equal in length* to the value set in the `chunk_size` variable. Recall from the last chapter how we set the value of the `breaks` parameter of the `cut` function to 10 in order to generate ten segments. To segment a text based on the length of the segments, we will need to use a slightly different approach. Your first thought might be to divide the length of the `word_v` by the `chunk_size` and then use the resulting value as the value for the `breaks` argument in the `cut` function. For example:

```
# Not run
num_breaks <- length(word_v)/chunk_size
```

But notice that the value of `num_breaks`, 99.56, is not an even number. There are 99 full segments of 1000 words each and then one segment at the end that is only about half the size we want. When chunking a file using percentages, as in the last chapter, each chunk is *almost* exactly the same size. When we split a text into 500 or 1000 word chunks, however, the last chunk will always be something smaller than the desired chunk size you have set. Thus, you need a way of dealing with this "remainder" chunk.

Instead of using `cut`, we will use `seq_along` and a new function `ceiling` along with the `split` function used for similar purposes in the last chapter.

```
x <- seq_along(word_v)
chunks_l <- split(word_v, ceiling(x/chunk_size))
```

The value of `x` in the code shown above is a simple vector of numbers that corresponds to the indices of the `word_v` vector. We have seen how the `seq_along` function works in previous chapters. What is interesting here is the way that we use `x` in combination with some division and the `ceiling` function.

To understand what is going on in this code, let us look at a simple example. Instead of using the very long `x` by computing a sequence along the length of `word_v`, we will just get a short sequence of 100 values.

```
some_vector <- 1:100
x <- seq_along(some_vector)
some_chunk_size <- 9
chunks_l <- split(some_vector, ceiling(x/some_chunk_size))
```

Run this code now and examine the contents of `chunks_l`. You will find a list of 12 items. The first 11 each contains 9 values (9 is the chunk size we set in `some_chunk_size`). The last list item, however, only includes 1 value. That is because 100/9 = 11.11111. In other words, since 100 is not evenly divisible by 9, there was some remainder.

OK, but what about `ceiling`? The `ceiling` function performs a type of rounding. First consider what happens when we divide `x` by the value of `some_chunk_size` (which is 9 in this example). Due to vector recycling, each

value in x is divided by 9. When we wrap this result inside the `ceiling`
function, each of these resulting values is rounded up to the nearest whole
number. If you want to see this in action, just enter the following code:

```
x/some_chunk_size
ceiling(x/some_chunk_size)
```

What this second line of code effectively does is return the factor vector
that we can then use in the `split` function to identify the members of each
segment. So here again is the code that we need to create our text segments:

```
x <- seq_along(word_v)
chunks_l <- split(word_v, ceiling(x/chunk_size))
```

After running this code, you can check to see if the results match your expec-
tations in two ways. First, you may want to inspect one element of the list.
For example, to see values held in the first list item, enter `chunks_l[[1]]`.
You should see a character vector of words from the first novel in the `files_v`
vector. Now enter `length(chunks_l[[1]])` to return the length of the first
vector. It should be 1000. Now use `lapply` with the `length` function to return the length of all of the vectors: `lapply(chunks_l, length)`. What you
will observe is that there are 99 items containing 1000 words and a 100th
item containing only 560 words!

A simple way to deal with this situation is to add the final "remainder" chunk
onto the second-to-last chunk, but you might not always want to do this. Say,
for example, that the `chunk_size` variable is set to 1000 words, and the last
chunk ends up being 950 words long. Would you really want to add those
950 words to the previous chunk resulting in a chunk of 1950 words? The
answer is, of course, a subjective one, but a chunk of 950 words is probably
close enough to 1000 to warrant full "chunk" status; i.e., it should remain a
chunk of its own. But what if the last chunk were just 500 words, or 100
words; those samples are getting comparatively small. Since you must pick a
cutoff value, it is convenient to set a condition such that the last chunk must
be at least *one-half* the size of the value set in the `chunk_size` variable. You
can code this exception easily using the `length` function and some simple
division wrapped up inside another `if` conditional, like this:

```
if(length(chunks_l[[length(chunks_l)]]) <= chunk_size/2){
  chunks_l[[length(chunks_l)-1]] <- c(
    chunks_l[[length(chunks_l)-1]],
    chunks_l[[length(chunks_l)]]
    )
  chunks_l[[length(chunks_l)]] <- NULL
}
```

This conditional expression begins by getting the `length` of the word vector
held in the last item of the `chunks_l` list and then checks to see if it is

less than or equal to (<=) one-half of `chunk_size`. If the condition is met (i.e., `TRUE`), then the words in the last chunk are added to the words in the second-to-last chunk and the last chunk is then removed by setting it to `NULL`

In this case, since the length of the last vector is 560, the last segment will be allowed to stay as a full chunk. Let us now put all of this code together:

```
i <- 1
xml_doc <- read_xml(file.path(input_dir, files_v[i]))
  para_text <- get_node_text(xml_doc,
    xpath = "/tei:TEI/tei:text/tei:body//tei:p",
    ns = c(tei = "http://www.tei-c.org/ns/1.0")
  )
word_v <- tokenize(para_text)
chunk_size <- 1000
x <- seq_along(word_v)
chunks_l <- split(word_v, ceiling(x/chunk_size))
if(length(chunks_l[[length(chunks_l)]]) <= chunk_size/2){
  chunks_l[[length(chunks_l)-1]] <- c(
    chunks_l[[length(chunks_l)-1]],
    chunks_l[[length(chunks_l)]]
    )
  chunks_l[[length(chunks_l)]] <- NULL
}
```

Because the topic modeling algorithm does its own built in tokenization, we now need to reassemble all the word vectors in each item of the `chunks_l` list back into strings. This is accomplished using `lapply` to apply the `paste` function to each list item (`chunk_strings_l <- lapply(chunks_l, paste, collapse=" ")`). The resulting list can then be morphed into a data frame object using `do.call` and `rbind` (`chunks_df <- do.call(rbind, chunk_strings_l)`). The entire script now looks like this:

```
i <- 1
xml_doc <- read_xml(file.path(input_dir, files_v[i]))
  para_text <- get_node_text(xml_doc,
    xpath = "/tei:TEI/tei:text/tei:body//tei:p",
    ns = c(tei = "http://www.tei-c.org/ns/1.0")
  )
word_v <- tokenize(para_text)
chunk_size <- 1000
x <- seq_along(word_v)
chunks_l <- split(word_v, ceiling(x/chunk_size))
if(length(chunks_l[[length(chunks_l)]]) <= chunk_size/2){
  chunks_l[[length(chunks_l)-1]] <- c(
    chunks_l[[length(chunks_l)-1]],
    chunks_l[[length(chunks_l)]]
```

```
  )
  chunks_l[[length(chunks_l)]] <- NULL
}
chunk_strings_l <- lapply(chunks_l, paste, collapse=" ")
chunks_df <- do.call(rbind, chunk_strings_l)
```

With the basic code written and tested using the hard-coded value for i, all
we need now is to remove the hard-coded i and replace it with a for loop
that will send all of the files in the files_v variable through this process and
then bind all the results into a master data frame that we will call corpus_df.
Naturally, however, there is one complicating factor. In addition to keeping
track of the file names, you also need to keep track of the segment numbers.
Eventually you will want to be able to move from the topic model and return
to the original texts and the specific text segments. So you need to retain
this metadata in some form or another.

You did something similar in the previous chapter. First we will capture the
original file names from the files_v and *massage* them a bit using gsub to
remove the file extensions:

```
textname_v <- gsub("\\..*", "", files_v[i])
```

With the unique file names in hand, we can label the segments numerically
by generating a sequence of numbers from 1 to the total number of chunks,
which in this case is the same as the number of rows (found using the nrow
function) in the chunks_df variable: i.e., 1:nrow(chunk_df). We will call
these the chunk_ids_v: as in chunk_ids_v <- 1:nrow(chunks_df). The file
names and the chunk IDs can then be pasted together in order to create a
unique segment ID: chunk_names_v <- paste(textname_v, chunk_ids_v,
sep="_"). Finally, we combine the unique segment ID values with the segments together into a new data frame that we will call file_df.

```
i <- 1
xml_doc <- read_xml(file.path(input_dir, files_v[i]))
  para_text <- get_node_text(xml_doc,
    xpath = "/tei:TEI/tei:text/tei:body//tei:p",
    ns = c(tei = "http://www.tei-c.org/ns/1.0")
  )
word_v <- tokenize(para_text)
chunk_size <- 1000
x <- seq_along(word_v)
chunks_l <- split(word_v, ceiling(x/chunk_size))
if(length(chunks_l[[length(chunks_l)]]) <= chunk_size/2){
  chunks_l[[length(chunks_l)-1]] <- c(
    chunks_l[[length(chunks_l)-1]],
    chunks_l[[length(chunks_l)]]
```

```
  )
  chunks_l[[length(chunks_l)]] <- NULL
}
chunk_strings_l <- lapply(chunks_l, paste, collapse=" ")
chunks_df <- do.call(rbind, chunk_strings_l)
textname_v <- gsub("\\..*","", files_v[i])
chunk_ids_v <- 1:nrow(chunks_df)
chunk_names_v <- paste(textname_v, chunk_ids_v, sep="_")
file_df <- data.frame(
  id = chunk_names_v,
  text = chunks_df,
  stringsAsFactors = FALSE
  )
```

Note that we have added the `stringsAsFactors = F` argument to this call to `data.frame`. By default, `data.frame` treats character strings as factors, and since we most definitely want strings and not factors, we need to explicitly set this argument to `FALSE`.

Now remove the hard-coded value for `i` and wrap all of this code inside a `for` loop. Just before the loop we will instantiate an empty data frame object (`documents_df`) into which we will collect each of the resulting `file_df` objects. Here is the final script with the loop. Run this code now and then inspect the results using the `dim` and `str` functions.

```
library(xml2)
input_dir <- "data/XMLAuthorCorpus"
files_v <- dir(path = input_dir, pattern = ".*xml")
source("code/corpus_functions.R") # Load the functions

documents_df <- NULL
chunk_size <- 1000

for (i in seq_along(files_v)){
  xml_doc <- read_xml(file.path(input_dir, files_v[i]))
  para_text <- get_node_text(
    xml_doc,
    xpath = "/tei:TEI/tei:text/tei:body//tei:p",
    ns = c(tei = "http://www.tei-c.org/ns/1.0")
  )
  word_v <- tokenize(para_text)
  x <- seq_along(word_v)
  chunks_l <- split(word_v, ceiling(x/chunk_size))
  if(length(chunks_l[[length(chunks_l)]]) <= chunk_size/2){
    chunks_l[[length(chunks_l)-1]] <- c(
      chunks_l[[length(chunks_l)-1]],
```

```
      chunks_l[[length(chunks_l)]]
      )
    chunks_l[[length(chunks_l)]] <- NULL
  }
  chunk_strings_l <- lapply(chunks_l, paste, collapse=" ")
  chunks_df <- do.call(rbind, chunk_strings_l)
  textname_v <- gsub("\\..*","", files_v[i])
  chunk_ids_v <- 1:nrow(chunks_df)
  chunk_names_v <- paste(textname_v, chunk_ids_v, sep="_")
  file_df <- data.frame(
    id = chunk_names_v,
    text = chunks_df,
    stringsAsFactors = FALSE
    )
  documents_df <- rbind(documents_df, file_df)
}
```

If everything worked correctly you will have a new data frame with 3504 rows
and 2 columns labeled "id" and "text." Mission accomplished; now let us do
some topic modeling!

17.4 The R Mallet Package

The first and most important thing to know about the mallet package is
that it is not a complete wrapper for the entire MALLET toolkit. As the documentation for the package notes: "Mallet has many functions, this wrapper
focuses on the topic modeling sub-package written by David Mimno." So, do
not look to this R wrapper if you want to access any of MALLET's other functions, such as document classification or hidden Markov models for sequence
tagging. This package is strictly for topic modeling. mallet is installed like
any other package in R and you will want to be sure to include any package
dependencies. Once installed it is invoked using the usual library(mallet)
expression.

```
library(mallet)
```

You will notice that mallet relies on the rJava package, which allows R to
create Java objects and call Java methods.[6] Recall that MALLET is written in
Java, not R. When you first try to run mallet, it is possible you will get an
error related to rJava not being able to load:

---

[6] *Methods* in Java are more or less synonymous with *functions* in R.

```
Error: package or namespace load failed for 'rJava':. . .
```

If you get this error on a Mac, you can usually resolve it by opening your computer's terminal and issuing the following command: sudo R CMD javareconf. To access your terminal from within RStudio, start at the "Tools" drop-down menu, "Tools" —> "Terminal" —> "New Terminal."[7] On Windows, simply installing Java should resolve the issue (See https://www.java.com/en/download/windows-64bit.jsp)

17.5 Simple Topic Modeling with a Standard Stop List

In the stylistic analysis that was covered in prior chapters, high-frequency words were retained and used as markers of individual authorial style. In topic modeling you will typically want to remove or *stop-out* high-frequency words such as *the, of, and, a, an,* etc., because these words carry little weight in terms of thematic or topical value. If you do not remove these common function words, your topic model will generate topics (weighted word distributions) that are less about shared semantic sense, that is, less about topics or themes, and more about syntactical conventions. Here is an example showing the top seven words from 20 "topics" that we derived from the exercise corpus without using a stop list:

```
## 0 0.04674     the to a of and don in
## 1     0.06203 the to and of a bryce in
## 2     0.1085  of the and in a is to
## 3     0.14428 the of to and they their in
## 4     0.29792 the and of a in to was
## 5     0.16571 the a to of and was i
## 6     0.45213 you i to it a and that
## 7     0.24112 the of and a in by with
## 8     0.35832 i you to my and is me
## 9     0.55731 the of to and in that which
## 10    0.59945 a to of he was his had
## 11    0.13994 the to you an a that it
## 12    0.03846 hycy ye bryan an o a the
## 13    0.10359 the and a to of in susan
## 14    0.50041 the of and a in was which
## 15    0.07111 and the a of in with
## 16    0.18016 the a and of his sir is
## 17    0.39585 her she and the to was a
## 18    0.12091  and i a the in my
## 19    0.58441 he the his and was to him
```

---

[7]For more information, take a look at https://github.com/rstudio/rstudio/issues/2254.

As you can see, these are semantically meaningless.

In the `data` directory, we have included a stop list (*stoplist.csv*) containing 606 high-frequency words. In your own work you may want to add to or cut this list to suit your research objectives, but this list will be sufficient for our purposes here.

The first step in generating a topic model with the `mallet` package is to invoke the `mallet.import` function. This function takes five arguments:

1. `id.array`
2. `text.array`
3. `stoplist.file`
4. `preserve.case`
5. `token.regexp`

The first argument (`id.array`) is an array, or vector, of document IDs. You have this information stored in the first column of the `documents_df` data frame object that you created above. The second argument (`text.array`) is a vector of text strings, and you have this data in the second column of the `documents_df` data frame object. Next is the stop list file which will be referenced using a relative path to its location on your computer; in this case the path will be `data/stoplist.csv`. The next argument, `preserve.case`, is irrelevant in this example because you have already elected to lowercase all of the words as part of the `tokenize` function. Had you not already done this, `mallet` would allow you to choose to do so or not at this point.[8] The final argument, `token.regexp`, allows you to define a specific regular expression for tokenizing the text strings. The default expression is one that keeps any sequence of *one or more Unicode characters*. Because you have gone to a lot of trouble to retain apostrophes, you will need to give `mallet.import` a new value to replace the default `token.regexp` argument. To keep those apostrophes, the default expression (`[\\\\p\{L\}]+`) should be replaced with `[\\\\p\{L\}']+`. The complete expression, with the slightly modified regular expression, is as follows:

```
mallet_instances <- mallet.import(documents_df$id,
  documents_df$text,
  "data/stoplist.csv",
  FALSE,
  token.regexp="[\\p{L}']+")
```

The `mallet_instances` object created here is a Java object that is called a *Mallet instance list*. This is not an R object and must be accessed using other Java methods. The `mallet` package provides other functions as a gateway or bridge to those methods.

---

[8] `mallet`'s default behavior is to convert to lowercase.

The next step is to create a *topic model trainer object*, which, for the moment, can be thought of as a kind of place holder object that you will fill with data in the next few steps. Notice that it is at this stage that the number of topics that the model will contain is set.[9] For the sake of this tutorial, we are setting the number of topics equal to the number of novels in the corpus. The reasons for this choice are purely pedagogical and will make more sense as we work through the rest of this chapter.

```
topic_model <- MalletLDA(num.topics = 43)
```

Because the `mallet` package is simply providing a bridge to the Java application, this might feel a bit obtuse, and it can be a bit disconcerting when you are unable to employ R functions, such as `class` and `str`, to explore the makeup of these objects. If you try, you will see references to the `rJava` package.

```
class(topic_model)
## [1] "jobjRef"
## attr(,"package")
## [1] "rJava"
```

In this case, `jobjRef` is a *reference* (or pointer) to a Java object that has been created and masked behind the scenes. Unless you are willing to dig into the actual source, that is, leave the world of R and go study the `MALLET` Java application, then you will have to accept a bit of obscurity.[10]

With the trainer object (`topic_model`) instantiated, you must now fill it with the textual data. For this you will call the `loadDocuments` method with the `mallet_instances` object that was created a moment ago as an argument.

```
topic_model$loadDocuments(mallet_instances)
```

---

[9]How to set the number of topics is a matter of significant discussion in the topic modeling literature, and there is no obvious way of knowing in advance exactly where this number should be set. In the documentation for the `MALLET` program, Mimno writes: "The best number depends on what you are looking for in the model. The default (10) will provide a broad overview of the contents of the corpus. The number of topics should depend to some degree on the size of the collection, but 200–400 will produce reasonably fine-grained results." Readers interested in more nuanced solutions may wish to consult chapter 8 of Jockers (2013), or visit http://www.matthewjockers.net/2013/04/12/secret-recipe-for-topic-modeling-themes/ for Jockers's "Secret" Recipe for Topic Modeling Themes.

[10]The `MALLET` program is not terribly difficult to run outside of R and there are many good tutorials available online. A few of these are specifically written with humanities applications of topic modeling in mind. Perhaps the best place to start is with Shawn Graham, Scott Weingart, and Ian Milligan's online tutorial titled "Getting Started with Topic Modeling and MALLET." See http://programminghistorian.org/lessons/topic-modeling-and-mallet.

When invoked, some initial processing of the documents occurs as `mallet` prepares the data for modeling. Among other things, `mallet` will output to the R console some information about the number of tokens found in the entire corpus after stop word removal (*total tokens*) and about the length of the longest individual document after stop word removal (*max tokens*). At this point, if you wish to access a list of the entire vocabulary of the corpus, you can invoke the `getVocabulary` method to return a character vector containing all the words:

```
vocabulary <- topic_model$getVocabulary()
```

You can then inspect this character vector using typical R functions:

```
class(vocabulary)
## [1] "character"
length(vocabulary)
## [1] 55347
head(vocabulary)
## [1] "summer"   "topsail"   "schooner" "slipped"   "cove"
## [6] "trinidad"
vocabulary[1:50]
##  [1] "summer"      "topsail"      "schooner"   "slipped"
##  [5] "cove"        "trinidad"     "head"       "dropped"
##  [9] "anchor"      "edge"         "kelp"       "fields"
## [13] "fifteen"     "minutes"      "small"      "boat"
## [17] "deposited"   "beach"        "man"        "armed"
## [21] "long"        "squirrel"     "rifle"      "axe"
## [25] "carrying"    "food"         "clothing"   "brown"
## [29] "canvas"      "pack"         "watched"    "return"
## [33] "weigh"       "stand"        "sea"        "northwest"
## [37] "trades"      "disappeared"  "ken"        "swung"
## [41] "broad"       "powerful"     "back"       "strode"
## [45] "resolutely"  "timber"       "mouth"      "river"
## [49] "john"        "cardigan"
```

At this point, you can also access some basic information about the frequency of words in the corpus and in the various documents of the corpus using the R mallet method (function) `mallet.word.freqs`.

```
word_freqs <- mallet.word.freqs(topic_model)
```

Calling this function will return a data frame containing a row for each unique word type in the corpus. The data frame will have three columns:

1. words
2. term.freq
3. doc.freq

The word types are in the words column; term.freq provides a count of the total number of tokens of that given word type in the corpus; and, finally, doc.freq provides a count of the total number of documents that contain that word at least once. You can look at the first few rows in the data frame using R's head function:

```
head(word_freqs)
##        words term.freq doc.freq
## 1     summer        69       54
## 2    topsail         1        1
## 3   schooner        16       10
## 4    slipped       130      120
## 5       cove         7        7
## 6   trinidad        17        9
```

Invoking head reveals that the word type *summer* occurs 69 times in the corpus in 54 different documents. The word *topsail*, on the other hand, occurs just once in one document.[11]

With the documents pre-processed, you are now ready to run the actual training process. Before that, however, you have the opportunity to *tweak* the *optimization hyperparameters*! Though this step is not required (if you skip it the default values of 200 burn-in iterations and 50 iterations between optimization will be implemented), it is worth knowing that you can control the *optimization interval* and the *burn-in* using the following expression[12]:

```
# Not run
topic_model$setAlphaOptimization(40, 80)
```

Because hyperparameter optimization is on by default, you can skip this step and go directly to the training of the model. The key argument that must now be set is the number of iterations to use in training. This argument determines the number of sampling iterations. In theory, as you increase the number of iterations the quality of the model will improve, but model quality is a rather subjective measure based on human evaluation of the resulting topic word clusters. In our own tests, we have observed that as one increases the number of iterations, topic quality increases only to a certain point and then levels off. That is, after you reach a certain number of iterations, the

---

[11]Do not forget that prior to modeling you have chunked each novel from the example corpus into 1000 word segments.

[12]The ramifications of resetting these values is beyond the scope of this chapter, but interested readers may wish to consult Hanna Wallach, David Mimno, and Andrew McCallum. "Rethinking LDA: Why Priors Matter." In proceedings of *Advances in Neural Information Processing Systems (NIPS)*, Vancouver, BC, Canada, 2009.

composition and quality of the resulting topics does not change much.[13] For now, set the number of iterations to 400. In your own work, you may wish to experiment with different values and examine how topic composition changes with different values.

```
topic_model$train(400)
```

When you run this command, a great deal of output (which we have not shown here) will be sent to your R console. After every 50 iterations, R will spit out a set of the seven top words in each topic. Here is a small snippet of that output:

```
## INFO:
## 0      0.11628 sir reilly replied man mr woodward robert
## 1      0.11628 bejabers camp timber d'arcy men gold happy
## 2      0.11628 wid replied good night man ould ha
## 3      0.11628 man sir mr darby poor honor people
## 4      0.11628 man hand knew heard read told business
## 5      0.11628 man time black made eye stood appearance
## 6      0.11628 mrs doctor aunt dr face good half
## . . .
```

R will also provide probabilistic information about how likely the data are given the model as it exists at a specific moment in the process. This figure is represented as a log-likelihood and appears as `INFO: <190> LL/token: -9.3141` in the output. Although the meaning of the log-likelihood number is beyond the scope of this book, numbers closer to zero generally indicate better fitting models.[14]

17.6 Unpacking the Model

With the model run, you can inspect the results and begin to see what is revealed about the corpus in terms of its thematic content. Start by exploring the composition and coherence of the 43 topics you instructed `mallet` to identify. For extracting this information from the model, `mallet` provides two functions that return R objects: `mallet.topic.words` and `mallet.top.words`. Use the first of these to generate a matrix in which each row is a topic and each column a unique word type in the corpus. Once run, you can examine the size of the resulting matrix using `dim`:

---

[13]Our anecdotal experience seems consistent with more scientific studies, and interested readers may wish to consult Griffiths and Steyvers (2004).

[14]David Mimno's "Topic Modeling Bibliography" provides a comprehensive list of resources for those wishing to go beyond this text. See http://www.cs.princeton.edu/~mimno/topics. html.

```
topic_words_m <- mallet.topic.words(topic_model,
  smoothed=TRUE,
  normalized=TRUE)
```

The values that appear in the cells of this matrix vary depending upon how you set the `normalized` and `smoothed` arguments. In this example we have set both `normalized` and `smoothed` to `TRUE`. When normalization is set to `TRUE` the values in each topic (row) are converted to percentages that sum to one. This can be checked with the `rowSums` function:

```
rowSums(topic_words_m)
```

When set to `FALSE`, the value in any given cell will be an integer representing the count of the occurrences of that word type that were assigned to a particular topic (row) during processing. If you want to explore this matrix further, you can use bracketed sub-setting to access the values, for example[15]:

```
topic_words_m[1:3, 1:3]
```

These results are not terribly informative because there is no column header to show which word types are associated with each column of values. You can, however, retrieve that information from the model and then add the column headers yourself using the `colnames` function.

```
vocabulary <- topic_model$getVocabulary()
colnames(topic_words_m) <- vocabulary
topic_words_m[1:3, 1:3]
##              summer       topsail      schooner
## [1,] 1.327843e-06 1.327843e-06 1.327843e-06
## [2,] 3.315951e-07 3.315951e-07 3.315951e-07
## [3,] 8.043322e-07 8.043322e-07 8.043322e-07
```

Having set the column values, you can compare the relative weight of specific word types (as a percentage of each topic). In this example, we use R's `c` function to create a vector of key words and then use that vector as a way to select named columns from the matrix:

```
keywords <- c("california", "ireland")
topic_words_m[, keywords]
##           california        ireland
## [1,] 1.327843e-06 1.566520e-02
## [2,] 3.315951e-07 3.315951e-07
## [3,] 8.043322e-07 5.553145e-04
## [4,] 9.570549e-07 3.813123e-03
## [5,] 5.176236e-07 5.176236e-07
```

---

[15]Keep in mind that due to random sampling your values will not always match the values shown in this book.

```
##   [6,]  3.104906e-07  3.104906e-07
##   [7,]  2.321853e-07  2.899271e-03
##   [8,]  6.463212e-07  6.463212e-07
##   [9,]  6.805181e-07  6.805181e-07
##  [10,]  3.996122e-07  1.408482e-03
##  [11,]  5.218863e-07  5.218863e-07
##  [12,]  4.046535e-07  4.046535e-07
##  [13,]  9.352515e-07  9.352515e-07
##  [14,]  2.805931e-07  2.805931e-07
##  [15,]  1.894476e-07  1.894476e-07
##  [16,]  9.718746e-07  9.718746e-07
##  [17,]  1.500295e-07  1.500295e-07
##  [18,]  4.134300e-03  4.183471e-07
##  [19,]  6.640075e-07  6.640075e-07
##  [20,]  3.173902e-07  3.173902e-07
##  [21,]  1.143779e-03  1.065560e-06
##  [22,]  3.799342e-07  3.799342e-07
##  [23,]  1.502870e-06  1.502870e-06
##  [24,]  9.507115e-08  9.507115e-08
##  [25,]  5.710602e-07  5.710602e-07
##  [26,]  8.605327e-07  8.605327e-07
##  [27,]  4.034031e-07  4.034031e-07
##  [28,]  2.596278e-07  2.596278e-07
##  [29,]  4.874167e-07  4.874167e-07
##  [30,]  1.046529e-04  6.786784e-07
##  [31,]  1.126814e-06  1.126814e-06
##  [32,]  4.974650e-07  4.974650e-07
##  [33,]  8.536676e-07  8.536676e-07
##  [34,]  1.083956e-02  5.076536e-03
##  [35,]  1.525652e-03  8.294236e-07
##  [36,]  1.888693e-07  1.888693e-07
##  [37,]  2.919902e-07  2.919902e-07
##  [38,]  4.829628e-07  4.829628e-07
##  [39,]  1.650274e-07  1.650274e-07
##  [40,]  2.147678e-06  2.147678e-06
##  [41,]  5.317065e-07  5.317065e-07
##  [42,]  7.359953e-07  7.359953e-07
##  [43,]  1.304953e-03  8.107258e-07
```

You can calculate which of the topic rows has the highest concentration of these key terms using R's rowSums and max functions inside a call to which. Save that row number in a new variable called imp_row. Keep in mind that if you are copying and executing this code as you read along, your row values and weights are likely to be different from what is shown here because the topic model employs a process that begins with a random distribution of words across topics. Though the topics you generate from this corpus will be generally similar, they may not be exactly the same as those that appear in this text.

```
imp_row <- which(
  rowSums(topic_words_m[, keywords]) ==
  max(rowSums(topic_words_m[, keywords]))
  )
```

Examining these results shows that the topic in row 34 has the highest incidence of these keywords in our model.[16] While exploring the `topic_words_m` object in this manner can be fruitful, we are usually less interested in specific words and more interested in examining the *top* or most heavily weighted words in each topic.

For this ranked sorting of topic words, `mallet` offers another function: `mallet.top.words`. This function takes three arguments:

1. `topic_model`
2. `word.weights`
3. `num.top.words`

The first of these is the model itself, the second is a row from the matrix of word weights that you have already created and stored in the `topic_words_m` object, and finally a third argument stipulating a user-defined number of "top words" to display. Assuming you wish to see the top 10 words from topic 34 (the row number you saved in the `imp_row` variable), you would enter:

```
mallet.top.words(topic_model, topic_words_m[imp_row,], 10)
##                   words      weights
## irish             irish 0.017365889
## men                 men 0.012404349
## san                 san 0.012022692
## california   california 0.010839555
## city               city 0.009083933
## state             state 0.008473282
## mr                   mr 0.007748134
## native           native 0.007748134
## people           people 0.007709968
## francisco     francisco 0.007595471
```

---

[16]It must be noted here that in the MALLET Java program, topics are indexed starting at zero. Java, like many programming languages, begins indexing with 0. R, however, begins with 1. Were we to run this same topic modeling exercise in the Java application, the topics would be labeled with the numbers 0-42. In R they are 1-43.

The most heavily weighted word in this topic is the word `irish`. Were you to assign a label to this topic, you might, after examining all these top words, choose *Irish California* or *Irish-American West* as a general descriptor.[17]

17.7 Topic Visualization

Looking only at the top ten words in a topic can be a bit misleading. Bear in mind that each topic in this model consists of values for all of the word types! Generally you will want to examine more than just the top ten words when making a decision about how to label/interpret the topical or thematic essence of a topic. It can, therefore, be useful to visualize a larger number of the top words in the topic using a word cloud visualization. Thanks to Ian Fellows, R has a package for generating word cloud images from exactly the type of data returned by the `mallet.top.words` function.

Begin by installing and then loading the `wordcloud` package:

```
library(wordcloud)
```

Now employ the `mallet.top.words` function again to grab 100 of the top words and their associated weights from the model. Instead of simply printing the results to the R console, save the output into a new variable called `topic_top_words`.

```
topic_top_words <- mallet.top.words(topic_model,
   topic_words_m[imp_row,], 100)
```

You can now call the `wordcloud` function providing a vector of words and a vector of word weights from the `topic_top_words` object as the first two arguments. To these we have added three more arguments that control the aesthetic look of the final word cloud (Fig. 17.1).[18]

```
wordcloud(topic_top_words$words,
          topic_top_words$weights,
          c(2, .4), rot.per=0, random.order=F)
```

---

[17]For those who may not have intuited as much, the corpus of texts used in this book is composed of novels written entirely by Irish and Irish-American authors.

[18]To see how to control the look of the visualization, consult the help documentation for the `wordcloud` function using `?wordcloud`.

Fig. 17.1 Word cloud of topic 34

17.8 Topic Coherence and Topic Probability

Because we are familiar with this corpus, we know that choosing the words *california* and *irish* will prove useful in identifying a topic that deals with the Irish presence in California and San Francisco, a topic found prominently in several books in this corpus. Often, however, you will be dealing with larger corpora and you will have to inspect the makeup of each topic in order to determine if the topics are *coherent*. You need to inspect them to see if they are *topical* or *thematic* in nature. If you complete the first chapter exercise right now, you will be able to examine 43 different word clouds. During that inspection, you will inevitably notice a high number of character names in many of the topics. Depending on your research goals, the presence of character names could be a significant problem.

Let us assume that you are hoping to track thematic change throughout a corpus. If that is the case, then the presence of character names is going to skew your results rather dramatically. There is a topic, for example, where the words *nell*, *tim*, and *sheila* are prominent. Without even doing the calculations, we can tell you that this topic is going to be dominant in one book in the corpus (Josephine Donovan's novel *Black Soil*). This same topic will be comparatively absent from the other novels. We can also predict, based on our knowledge of this corpus, that there will be another topic featuring *gerald* from a book titled *Gerald Ffrench's Friends* and still another topic with *john* and *big* and *flurry*. These will be dominant in the book *Kansas Irish* where *Big Flurry* is the nickname of the main character, *Florence Driscoll*.

As noted previously, we intentionally picked 43 topics in order to highlight this problem (as you will recall, there are 43 books in the corpus). Even if we had not rigged the system, we would have had a way of exploring the extent to which certain topics were more probable or *present* in certain documents. `mallet` provides a function (`mallet.doc.topics`) for inspecting the probability of each topic appearing in each document. Or in more simple terms, `mallet` provides a function for assessing the *proportion* of a document that is *about* each topic.

```
doc_topics_m <- mallet.doc.topics(topic_model,
  smoothed = TRUE,
  normalized = TRUE)
```

Calling this function returns a matrix object in which each column is a topic and each row is a document from the corpus. The values in the cells of the matrix are the corresponding probabilities of a given topic (column) in a given document (row).

When the `normalized` argument is set to `TRUE` (as it is here) then the values in each row will sum to one. In other words, summing the 43 topic probability measurements for each document will return 1. This makes it easy to think about the values as percentages or proportions of the document. In topic modeling, we assume that documents are composed of topics in different proportions. In truth, though, that is a bit of an oversimplification because this is a closed system and the model is only able to assign proportions for the 43 topics in this particular configuration. So, what we are really assuming is that documents are composed of *these* 43 topics in differing proportions. It would not be entirely fair to say that the book *Gerald Ffrench's Friends* is 36% about *topic 8* (even though .36 is the mean proportion of this topic across all the segments from this book). A slightly better way to express this proportion might be to explicitly say: "of the 43 topics in this particular model that could be assigned to *Gerald Ffrench's Friends*, `topic` 8 is assigned with the highest probability, a probability of 0.36."

Let us now write some code to explore the proportions of each topic in each document and see if there are documents in the corpus that are dominated by specific topics. If you discover that a particular topic is more or less unique to one particular text, then you might have grounds to suspect a problem. Of course it is perfectly reasonable to imagine a situation in which there is one outlier book in the corpus, perhaps one book about vampires in a corpus of books about faeries. Here, however, you will find that there is a problem and that it is most certainly associated with character names.

Recall that every book in this corpus was split into segments before modeling. You now want to look at the books as a whole again and calculate the `mean` topical values across the segments as a way of assessing the general saturation of topics in books. You begin with the `doc_topics_m` object, a matrix of dimension 3504 × 43. You know that these 3504 rows correspond to the segments from all of the novels, and you still have a data frame object called `documents_df` instantiated in the work space where these document *ids* are stored. You can put those values into a new vector called `file_ids_v`.

```
file_ids_v <- documents_df[,1]
head(file_ids_v)
## [1] "anonymous_1" "anonymous_2" "anonymous_3" "anonymous_4"
## [5] "anonymous_5" "anonymous_6"
```

Now you must massage the names in this vector so that the chunk identifier is split off into a separate vector from the main file name. You can use the `strsplit` function to break these character strings on the *underscore* character and return a list object. You can then use `lapply` and `do.call`, as you have done before, to convert these values into a two column matrix.

```
file_id_l <- strsplit(file_ids_v, "_")
file_chunk_id_l <- lapply(file_id_l, rbind)
file_chunk_id_m <- do.call(rbind, file_chunk_id_l)
head(file_chunk_id_m)
##          [,1]         [,2]
## [1,] "anonymous"  "1"
## [2,] "anonymous"  "2"
## [3,] "anonymous"  "3"
## [4,] "anonymous"  "4"
## [5,] "anonymous"  "5"
## [6,] "anonymous"  "6"
```

The first column provides a way of identifying which rows in the `doc_topics_m` object correspond to which text files. With that information, you can then use `dplyr`'s `summarize` function to calculate the topical mean for each topic in each document. First save a copy of `doc_topics_m` as a data frame because you will need an object that allows both character data and numerical values.

```
doc_topics_df <- as.data.frame(doc_topics_m)
```

Now use `data.frame` to bind the character data values in the first column of `file_chunk_id_m` to the topical values in `doc.topics.df`:

```
doc_topics_df <- data.frame(
  file = file_chunk_id_m[,1],
  doc_topics_df,
  stringsAsFactors = F
  )
```

We can now use `dplyr`'s `group_by` and `summarize_all` functions to calculate the mean usage of each topic across the segments of each document.

```
library(dplyr)
doc_topic_means_df <- group_by(doc_topics_df, file) %>%
  summarize_all(mean)
```

The `doc_topic_means_df` object is a new data frame of 43 rows by 44 columns. There is now one row for each of the 43 texts and there is one column for each of the 43 topics. Then there is one more column (the first) with the file name, or *group*. With this data in one place, you have several options for how to assess the `mean` values. Since you only have 43 documents in the corpus, you can visualize the document means for any specific topic using a simple bar plot. Here we show the means for topic number 18. But notice that the column names in the `doc_topic_means_df` are each prefixed with a "V" as in "V1" through "V43." When you call `barplot`, you can use the `$` column reference shortcut along with the column name to send data for all the rows and only the column you want. In this example (Fig. 17.2), we will plot the `values` from column V18.[19]

```
barplot(
  doc_topic_means_df$V18,
  names.arg = c(1:43),
  main = paste("Topic", key_topic),
  xlab = "Books",
  ylab = "Topic Mean"
  )
```

Notice that for this topic, in our model, there is one outlier document, document 26. This is the document in row 26 of the `doc_topic_means_df` data frame. Your model will be different, but you can identify the names of specific files by retrieving the value held in the `file` column of the `doc_topic_means_df` object. Say we are interested in the name of the file in the 12th row. We would retrieve that information with simple bracketed sub-setting:

```
# Not run
doc_topic_means_df[12, "file"] # Just using 12 for example.
```

---

[19]Remember that your plots will not look the same since each run of the topic model is slightly different.

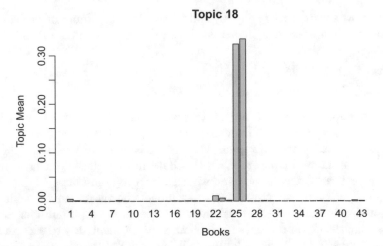

Fig. 17.2 Bar plot of topic means in 43 documents

In our model, the file at row 25 is titled *Kyne2*. The code below shows you how to get the top ten words for topic 12.

```
top_words <- mallet.top.words(
  topic_model, topic_words_m[12,],
  10
  )
```

Not surprisingly, the top words in this topic indicate that this is a largely character-driven topic, which is why it is an outlier topic and only prominent in one text. The top ten words in this topic are *don, d'arcy, bejabers, parker, farrel, horse, pablo, man, father, miguel*. Seven of these ten are the names of characters in Peter B. Kyne's novel, *The Pride of Palomar*. If you look at the barplot and the data again, you will find that the book with the next highest use of this topic is another book by the same author. The novel with the file name "Kyne2" is titled *Tide of Empire* and like *The Pride of Palomar* it is a novel in the western genre. So words such as "ranch" that appear in this topic are prominent in *The Pride of Palomar* and also appear with some regularity in *Tide of Empire*. Though topics are not necessarily a marker of authorship, in this case we have found a topic that, at least in this corpus, is primarily used by only one of the authors.

While this is interesting, if we ultimately want to understand the themes and topics in a corpus of novels, we probably do not want to harvest a lot of topics that are dominated by the names of characters in particular books. If you use the approach described above to look at the top words in some of the other topics, you will find that there are many among the 43 that have characters as prominent words.

One way to deal with the character name problem is to add these names to the stop list. You will have the opportunity to do this and to compare your results in one of the exercises below. Another, slightly more complicated, way of dealing with character names and some related problems of topic coherence involves pre-processing the corpus with a part-of-speech tagger and then culling out words of different grammatical classes. This is the subject of the next chapter.

17.9 Practice

1. Write a script that uses a `for` loop to iterate over all of the topics data in order to produce a word cloud for each.

2. In the `data` directory you will find an expanded stop word list that includes common names and high-frequency words: `stoplist-exp.csv`. Replace the reference to `stoplist.csv` in the example code of this chapter with `stoplist-exp.csv` and generate a new model with a new set of topics and document proportions. Plot the means as you did in this chapter, and then assess the extent to which these new topics are distributed across the corpus. Make word clouds for each topic and consider how the new ones compare to those that included character names.

References

Blei DM, Ng AY, Jordan MI (2003) Latent Dirichlet allocation. Journal of Machine Learning Research 3(Jan):993–1022

Chang J, Gerrish S, Wang C, Boyd-Graber JL, Blei DM (2009) Reading tea leaves: How humans interpret topic models. In: Advances in neural information processing systems, pp 288–296

Griffiths TL, Steyvers M (2004) Finding scientific topics. Proceedings of the National academy of Sciences 101(suppl 1):5228–5235

Jockers ML (2013) Macroanalysis: Digital Methods and Literary History, 1st edn. University of Illinois Press, Urbana

McCallum AK (2002) Mallet: A machine learning for language toolkit. http// mallet.cs.umass.edu

Mimno D (2013) mallet: A wrapper around the Java machine learning tool mallet. https://CRAN.R-project.org/package=mallet, r package version 1.0

Chapter 18
Part of Speech Tagging and Named Entity Recognition

Abstract In this chapter we explore Part of Speech (POS) tagging using the
openNLP library. openNLP is an interface to the Apache's Natural Language
Processing toolkit of the same name. Apache OpenNLP is a JAVA based
machine learning toolkit for the processing of natural language text. Much in
the way that the mallet package for R is an interface to MALLET, the openNLP
package in R provides and R-based interface to the Apache library.

18.1 Pre-processing Text with a Part-of-Speech Tagger

In the research for Chap. 8 of *Macroanalysis*, Jockers discovered that by "stop-
ping out" (removing) all but the nouns in his corpus of novels, he could generate highly coherent and highly thematic topics.[1] In order to do this kind of
modeling, the novels in the corpus were pre-processed using a part-of-speech
(POS) tagger.

There are several R packages available today that perform a wide variety of
natural language processing tasks. Two that we have used are spacyr and
openNLP. The former is a "wrapper" to the spacy NLP package that is written
in the programming language Python. The latter is, similarly, a wrapper, for
the Apache openNLP library written in JAVA. We like the spacyr package a
great deal, but because of some idiosyncrasies associated with its installation,
we find it easy to introduce Part of Speech (POS) tagging and named entity
recognition (NER) using the openNLP library.

---

[1] All 500 of them can be viewed at http://www.matthewjockers.net/macroanalysisbook/
macro-themes/.

© Springer Nature Switzerland AG 2020
M. L. Jockers, R. Thalken, *Text Analysis with R*, Quantitative Methods in
the Humanities and Social Sciences,
https://doi.org/10.1007/978-3-030-39643-5_18

Begin by installing the openNLP package. When you do so, the rJava and NLP packages will also be installed since openNLP depends on functionality in both. Though you do not have to specifically load the rJava library, you will need to load both openNLP and NLP:

```
rm(list = ls())
install.packages("openNLP")
library(openNLP)
library(NLP)
```

In the first part of this chapter, we will explore a very simple tagging task. In the second half we will apply this learning to create a new topic model based only on the nouns in the corpus documents. Begin by loading the libraries and creating a simple "text" string to use for practice. Keep in mind that POS tagging and NER are processor intensive. Depending on your computer's specifications, it can take anywhere from a few seconds to several minutes to tag a long text. Developing your code with a very short example will save you a lot of headaches as you test and debug your code.

```
sample_text_s <- as.String(
  'This is a test.  This sentence was written by Matthew Jockers
  on October 4, 2019.  The idea is to create an example that will
  include a few "challenges." Such challenges might include words
  inside quote marks, different types of names, including place
  names. We wrote this sentence in "Washington state." Named
  entity recognition is not perfect.  This sentence was actually
  written by Rosamond Thalken. This sentence is worth $1.50 on
  the open market.  Microsoft and Apple both offered us 30% of
  the market value.'
)
```

Notice that we have introduced a new function here: as.String from the NLP package. This function creates a string object from a character vector and ensures that it is encoded in UTF-8 and that any lines separated by a newline character are concatenated. This string object is also special because it includes a useful sub-setting method that takes as indices the location of characters in the string. So, for example, if we wanted to access the first word in the sample text, we could enter sample_text_s[1,4] in the console. Doing so returns the first four characters in the string, 1 through 4. This sub-setting ability will be useful down the road.

After ensuring that we have a string object, we need to instantiate three "annotators" from the openNLP library: The first is a sentence annotator, the second is a word annotator, and the third is a POS tag annotator. These Annotator objects become part of a text analysis "pipeline" as parameters or arguments referenced in a call to the annotate function. The pipeline is organized so that an input text string is first tokenized into sentences and then into words and then annotated with the part of speech tags corresponding to the individual words. The **annotate** function computes the annotations for the input text by iteratively calling each of the given annotators. The output from calling **annotate** is an **Annotation** object which contains a set of lists.

```
sent_token_annotator <- Maxent_Sent_Token_Annotator()
word_token_annotator <- Maxent_Word_Token_Annotator()
pos_tag_annotator <- Maxent_POS_Tag_Annotator()
annotated_string <- annotate(sample_text_s, list(sent_token_annotator,
  word_token_annotator, pos_tag_annotator))
```

If you wish to inspect the content of this **Annotation** object you can do so using **str** or, since it is a type of list, by bracketed sub-setting, such as **annotated_string[[1]]** which will reveal some information about the contents of the first list item. If you examine the contents in depth, you will see that the first four items in the list have a **type** attribute with the value **sentence**. These four items correspond to the four sentences from the input string, and each of them is *annotated* with information about their position in the overall string. The first sentence, for example, has a **start** value of 1 and an **end** value of 15. If you look at the input string, you will see that these numbers mark the position, from start to end, of the first sentence if you counted one character at a time from left to right. If you now examine the fifth item (**annotated_string[[5]]**), you will see that it provides the annotations for the first **word** type. Notice, however, that we now also have **POS=DT** as an annotated "feature." "DT" is the POS tag for "determiner," which is the correct class of the first word (*This*) in the input string.[2]

With the text annotated in this way, we can use the **subset** function to select only those list items meeting the condition where the **type** is "word."

```
word_pos <- subset(annotated_string, type == "word")
```

The new **word_pos** object remains an **Annotation** list type object, so we can use one of the **apply** family of functions to extract the contents. In this case we will use **sapply** which effectively combines the functionality of **lapply** and **unlist** in one function.

```
tags_v <- sapply(word_pos$features, "[[", "POS")
```

This new tags_v object is a vector of all the POS tags from the annotation process. The corresponding words can be found by using the **word_pos** object as the indices for accessing the contents of the **string** object held inside **sample_text_s**:

```
words_v <- sample_text_s[word_pos]
```

---

[2]**openNLP** uses the treebank tag set from the Penn treebank Project. You can find the full list of tags here: https://www.ling.upenn.edu/courses/Fall_2003/ling001/penn_treebank_pos.html.

We can now bind these two vectors into a data frame:

```
word_pos_df <- data.frame(
  Token = words_v,
  POS = tags_v,
  stringsAsFactors = FALSE
)
```

With the results in a data frame object, it is a trivial matter to `filter` the contents to retain only words that match a certain POS type:

```
library(dplyr)
nouns_df <- filter(word_pos_df, POS == "NN") %>%
  select(Token) %>%
  mutate(Token = tolower(Token))
```

If we now wish to use these nouns as the material for a new noun-based topic model, we can paste them together into a single string and then create a data frame similar to the one created in the last chapter.

```
text_v <- paste(nouns_df$Token, collapse = " ")
documents_df <- data.frame(
  id = "some_filename",
  text = text_v,
  stringsAsFactors = FALSE
)
```

To run this POS tagging process over the entire corpus, we need to modify the code from the last chapter to include the new tagging process and a slight alteration to the chunking part of the script. Below we show the complete script, but be advised that running this script is processor intensive; it could take a while and could even crash your machine.[3] If you have problems running this code, or if you would prefer to move on with the chapter without doing the tagging yourself, just enter `load("data/documents_nouns_only_df_copy.Rdata")` in the console to load the tagged version of `documents_df` that we included with the text book materials. In the next section, we explain how to `save` and `load` `.Rdata` files.

```
library(xml2)
library(dplyr)
library(openNLP)
library(NLP)
```

---

[3]On our MacBook Pro, running this loop took 60 min to complete. Though there are some things we could change in this script to better optimize the processing, ideally large jobs such as this are done on a compute cluster where each text can be simultaneously processed on a different node. Setting up and running a process like this on a cluster for *parallel processing* is beyond the scope of this book.

```
input_dir <- "data/XMLAuthorCorpus"
files_v <- dir(path = input_dir, pattern = ".*xml")
source("code/corpus_functions.R") # Load the functions

sent_token_annotator <- Maxent_Sent_Token_Annotator()
word_token_annotator <- Maxent_Word_Token_Annotator()
pos_tag_annotator <- Maxent_POS_Tag_Annotator()

documents_df <- NULL
chunk_size <- 1000

for (i in seq_along(files_v)){
  xml_doc <- read_xml(file.path(input_dir, files_v[i]))
  para_text <- get_node_text(xml_doc,
    xpath = "/tei:TEI/tei:text/tei:body//tei:p",
    ns = c(tei = "http://www.tei-c.org/ns/1.0")
  )
  text_s <- as.String(para_text)
  annotated_string <- annotate(text_s, list(sent_token_annotator,
  word_token_annotator, pos_tag_annotator))
  word_pos <- subset(annotated_string, type == "word")
  tags_v <- sapply(word_pos$features, `[[`, "POS")
  words_v <- text_s[word_pos]
  word_pos_df <- data.frame(
    Token = words_v,
    POS = tags_v,
    stringsAsFactors = FALSE
  )

  nouns_df <- filter(word_pos_df, POS == "NN") %>%
    select(Token) %>%
    mutate(Token = tolower(Token))

  word_v <- nouns_df$Token
  x <- seq_along(word_v)
  chunks_l <- split(word_v, ceiling(x/chunk_size))
  if(length(chunks_l[[length(chunks_l)]]) <= chunk_size/2){
    chunks_l[[length(chunks_l)-1]] <- c(
      chunks_l[[length(chunks_l)-1]],
      chunks_l[[length(chunks_l)]]
    )
    chunks_l[[length(chunks_l)]] <- NULL
  }
  chunk_strings_l <- lapply(chunks_l, paste, collapse=" ")
  chunks_df <- do.call(rbind, chunk_strings_l)
  textname_v <- gsub("\\..*", "", files_v[i])
```

```
chunk_ids_v <- 1:nrow(chunks_df)
chunk_names_v <- paste(textname_v, chunk_ids_v, sep="_")
file_df <- data.frame(
  id = chunk_names_v,
  text = chunks_df,
  stringsAsFactors = FALSE
  )
documents_df <- rbind(documents_df, file_df)
cat("Done with", files_v[i], "\r")
}
```

18.2 Saving and Loading .Rdata Files

After running this loop, you can use the data inside the `documents_df` object exactly as you did in the previous chapter. But since it took a good deal of time to produce this data, it would be a good idea to **save** the output into an `.Rdata` file so that you do not have to run this whole POS tagging and text chunking script again. Here we will save the file as `documents_nouns_only_df.Rdata` into the **data** sub-directory of the project.

```
save(documents_df, file = "data/documents_nouns_only_df.Rdata")
```

Once the file has been saved, you can load it at any time using the **load** function:

```
load("data/documents_nouns_only_df.Rdata")
```

18.3 Topic Modeling the Noun Data

You can use the same code from the last chapter to build a new topic model from the nouns-only text files. Here we will finish by creating a word cloud (Fig. 18.1) of the eleventh topic.

```
library(mallet)
library(wordcloud)
mallet_instances <- mallet.import(documents_df$id,
  documents_df$text,
  "data/stoplist.csv",
  FALSE,
  token.regexp="[\\p{L}']+")
```

```
topic_model <- MalletLDA(num.topics=43)
topic_model$loadDocuments(mallet_instances)
word_freqs <- mallet.word.freqs(topic_model)
topic_model$train(400)
topic_words_m <- mallet.topic.words(topic_model,
  smoothed=TRUE,
  normalized=TRUE)
vocabulary <- topic_model$getVocabulary()
colnames(topic_words_m) <- vocabulary
topic_top_words <- mallet.top.words(topic_model,
  topic_words_m[11,], 100)
wordcloud(topic_top_words$words,
  topic_top_words$weights,
  c(3, .5), rot.per = 0, random.order = F)
```

Fig. 18.1 Word cloud of noun based topic 11

18.4 Named Entity Recognition

Named entity recognition (NER) using openNLP works very much like POS tagging. Let us go back to our example sentence from the beginning of this chapter. Notice that it has several names in it. To annotate for named entities, we will need to add the Maxent_Entity_Annotator, and we will no longer need the `Maxent_POS_Tag_Annotator` annotator. Before running this code, though, you will need to install the **openNLP** model. Unfortunately, this cannot be installed directly from the **CRAN** repository, as you have done with other **R** packages. Nevertheless, it is easy to acquire the model file from the Institute for Statistics and Mathematics Resource Homepage using the following code (note that this will take several minutes to download):

```
install.packages(
  "openNLPmodels.en",
  repos = "http://datacube.wu.ac.at/",
  type = "source"
  )
```

Once the model files are installed, you will be able to run the following code to annotate the person entities:

```
sample_text_s <- as.String(
  'This is a test.  This sentence was written by Matthew Jockers
  on October 4, 2019.  The idea is to create an example that will
  include a few "challenges." Such challenges might include words
  inside quote marks, different types of names, including place
  names. We wrote this sentence in "Washington state." Named
  entity recognition is not perfect.  This sentence was actually
  written by Rosamond Thalken. This sentence is worth $1.50 on
  the open market.  Microsoft and Apple both offered us 30% of
  the market value.'
  )
sent_token_annotator <- Maxent_Sent_Token_Annotator()
word_token_annotator <- Maxent_Word_Token_Annotator()
entity_tag_annotator <- Maxent_Entity_Annotator(kind = "person")
annotated_string <- annotate(sample_text_s, list(sent_token_annotator,
  word_token_annotator, entity_tag_annotator))
```

If you inspect the `type` column of the resulting `annotated_string` object, you will see that in addition to `sentence` and `word` "types" there are now also `entity` types.

```
entities <- subset(annotated_string, type == "entity")
sample_text_s[entities]
## [1] "Matthew Jockers"  "Rosamond Thalken"
```

Notice that when we called the `Maxent_Entity_Annotator` we included a `kind` argument. This tells the annotator what `kind` of entities to detect. If we want to find the place names, we have to be explicit and set `kind` equal to "location."

```
entity_tag_annotator <- Maxent_Entity_Annotator(kind = "location")
annotated_string <- annotate(sample_text_s, list(sent_token_annotator,
  word_token_annotator, entity_tag_annotator))
```

```
entities <- subset(annotated_string, type == "entity")
sample_text_s[entities]
## Washington
```

Other options for the kind argument include "date," "location," "money," "organization," "percentage," "person," and "misc".

18.5 Practice

1. Revise the code at the end of the chapter to extract the following entities:

- October 4
- "Microsoft" "Apple"
- $1.50
- 30%

Appendix A: Variable Scope Example

This is an example of scope within functions. First create a variable outside of a function.

```
my_var_to_process <- 10
```

Now create a function that uses the same name for an argument as an existing variable.

```
my_func <- function(my_var_to_process){
  # overwrite the value in my.var.to.process
  # with a new value that adds ten
  my_var_to_process <- my_var_to_process + 10 # add ten
  # return the new value
  return(my_var_to_process)
}
```

The value returned by calling `my_func` is 20.

```
my_func(my_var_to_process)
## [1] 20
```

But the value in the original variable is still 10 even though the same name was used inside the function.

```
my_var_to_process
## [1] 10
```

© Springer Nature Switzerland AG 2020
M. L. Jockers, R. Thalken, *Text Analysis with R*, Quantitative Methods in the Humanities and Social Sciences,
https://doi.org/10.1007/978-3-030-39643-5

Appendix B: The LDA Buffet

A version of what follows was originally posted to http://www.matthewjockers. net/macroanalysisbook/lda/ on August 12, 2012.

> ... imagine a quaint town, somewhere in New England perhaps. The town is a writers' retreat, a place they come in the summer months to seek inspiration. Melville is there, Hemingway, Joyce, and Jane Austen just fresh from across the pond. In this mythical town there is spot popular among the inhabitants; it is a little place called the "LDA Buffet." Sooner or later all the writers go there to find themes for their novels...

One afternoon Herman Melville bumps into Jane Austen at the bocce ball court, and they get to talking.

"You know," says Austen, "I have not written a thing in weeks."

"Arrrrgh," Melville replies, "me neither."

So hand in hand they stroll down Gibbs Lane to the LDA Buffet. Now, down at the LDA Buffet no one gets fat. The buffet only serves light (leit?) motifs, themes, topics, and tropes (seasonal). Melville hands a plate to Austen, grabs another for himself, and they begin walking down the buffet line. Austen is finicky; she spoons a dainty helping of words out of the bucket marked "dancing." A slightly larger spoonful of words, she takes from the "gossip" bucket and then a good ladle's worth of "courtship."

Melville makes a bee line for the "whaling" trough, and after piling on an Ahab-sized handful of whaling words, he takes a smaller spoonful of "seafaring" and then just a smidgen of "cetological jargon."

The two companions find a table where they sit and begin putting all the words from their plates into sentences, paragraphs, and chapters.

At one point, Austen interrupts this business: "Oh Herman, you must try a bit of this courtship."

He takes a couple of words but is not really fond of the topic. Then Austen, to her credit, asks permission before reaching across the table and sticking her fork in Melville's pile of seafaring words, "just a taste," she says. This work goes on for a

© Springer Nature Switzerland AG 2020
M. L. Jockers, R. Thalken, *Text Analysis with R*, Quantitative Methods in the Humanities and Social Sciences,
https://doi.org/10.1007/978-3-030-39643-5

little while; they order a few drinks and after a few hours, voila! Moby Dick and Persuasion are written . . .

[Now, dear reader, our story thus far provides an approximation of the first assumption made in LDA. We assume that documents are constructed out of some finite set of available topics. It is in the next part that things become a little complicated, but fear not, for you shall sample themes both grand and beautiful.]

. . .Filled with a sense of deep satisfaction, the two begin walking back to the lodging house. Along the way, they bump into a blurry-eyed Hemingway, who is just then stumbling out of the Rising Sun Saloon.

Having taken on a bit too much cargo, Hemingway stops on the sidewalk in front of the two literati. Holding out a shaky pointer finger, and then feigning an English accent, Hemingway says: "Stand and Deliver!"

To this, Austen replies, "Oh come now, Mr. Hemingway, must we do this every season?"

More gentlemanly then, Hemingway replies, "My dear Jane, isn't it pretty to think so. Now if you could please be so kind as to tell me what's in the offing down at the LDA Buffet."

Austen turns to Melville and the two writers frown at each other. Hemingway was recently banned from the LDA Buffet. Then Austen turns toward Hemingway and holds up six fingers, the sixth in front of her now pursed lips.

"Six topics!" Hemingway says with surprise, "but what are today's themes?"

"Now wouldn't you like to know that you old sot." Says Melville.

The thousand injuries of Melville, Hemingway had borne as best he could, but when Melville ventured upon insult he vowed revenge. Grabbing their recently completed manuscripts, Hemingway turned and ran toward the South. Just before disappearing down an alleyway, he calls back to the dumbfounded writers: "All my life I've looked at words as though I were seeing them for the first time. . . tonight I will do so again! . . ."

[Hemingway has thus overcome the first challenge of topic modeling. He has a corpus and a set number of topics to extract from it. In reality determining the number of topics to extract from a corpus is a bit trickier. If only we could ask the authors, as Hemingway has done here, things would be so much easier.]

. . . Armed with the manuscripts and the knowledge that there were six topics on the buffet, Hemingway goes to work.

After making backup copies of the manuscripts, he then pours all the words from the originals into a giant Italian-leather attache. He shakes the bag vigorously and then begins dividing its contents into six smaller ceramic bowls, one for each topic. When each of the six bowls is full, Hemingway gets a first glimpse of the topics that the authors might have found at the LDA Buffet. Regrettably, these topics are not very good at all; in fact, they are terrible, a jumble of random unrelated words . . .

[And now for the magic that is Gibbs Sampling.]

. . . Hemingway knows that the two manuscripts were written based on some mixture of topics available at the LDA Buffet. So to improve on this random assignment of words to topic bowls, he goes through the copied manuscripts that he kept as back ups. One at a time, he picks a manuscript and pulls out a word. He examines the word in the context of the other words that are distributed throughout each of the six bowls and in the context of the manuscript from which it was taken. The first word he selects is "heaven," and at this word he pauses, and asks himself two questions:

"How much of 'Topic A,' as it is presently represented in bowl A, is present in the current document?" "Which topic, of all of the topics, has the most 'heaven' in it?" . . .

[Here again dear reader, you must take with me a small leap of faith and engage in a bit of further make believe. There are some occult statistics here accessible only to the initiated. Nevertheless, the assumptions of Hemingway and of the topic model are not so far-fetched or hard to understand. A writer goes to his or her imaginary buffet of themes and pulls them out in different proportions. The writer then blends these themes together into a work of art. That we might now be able to discover the original themes by reading the book is not at all amazing. In fact we do it all the time—every time we say that such and such a book is about "whaling" or "courtship." The manner in which the computer (or dear Hemingway) does this is perhaps less elegant and involves a good degree of mathematical magic. Like all magic tricks, however, the explanation for the surprise at the end is actually quite simple: in this case our magician simply repeats the process 10 billion times! NOTE: The real magician behind this LDA story is David Mimno. I sent David a draft, and along with other constructive feedback, he supplied this beautiful line about computational magic.]

. . . As Hemingway examines each word in its turn, he decides based on the calculated probabilities whether that word would be more appropriately moved into one of the other topic bowls. So, if he were examining the word "whale" at a particular moment, he would assume that all of the words in the six bowls except for "whale" were correctly distributed. He'd now consider the words in each of those bowls and in the original manuscripts, and he would choose to move a certain number of occurrences of "whale" to one bowl or another.

Fortunately, Hemingway has by now bumped into James Joyce who arrives bearing a cup of coffee on which a spoon and napkin lay crossed. Joyce, no stranger to bags-of-words, asks with compassion: "Is this going to be a long night."

"Yes," Hemingway says, "yes it will, yes."

Hemingway must now run through this whole process over and over again many times. Ultimately, his topic bowls reach a steady state where words are no longer needing to be being reassigned to other bowls; the words have found their proper context.

After pausing for a well-deserved smoke, Hemingway dumps out the contents of the first bowl and finds that it contains the following words:

"whale sea men ship whales penfon air side life bounty night oil natives shark seas beard sailors hands harpoon mast top feet arms teeth length voyage eye heart leviathan islanders flask soul ships fishery sailor sharks company. . ."

He peers into another bowl that looks more like this:

"marriage happiness daughter union fortune heart wife consent affection wishes life attachment lover family promise choice proposal hopes duty alliance affections feelings engagement conduct sacrifice passion parents bride misery reason fate letter mind resolution rank suit event object time wealth ceremony opposition age refusal result determination proposals. . ."

After consulting the contents of each bowl, Hemingway immediately knows what topics were on the menu at the LDA Buffet. And, not only this, Hemingway knows exactly what Melville and Austen selected from the Buffet and in what quantities. He discovers that Moby Dick is composed of 40 percent whaling, 18 percent seafaring and 2 percent gossip (from that little taste he got from Jane) and so on ...

[Thus ends the fable.]

For the rest of the (LDA) story, see David Mimno's *Topic Modeling Bibliography* at https://mimno.infosci.cornell.edu/topics.html.

Appendix C: Practice Exercise Solutions

C.1 Solutions for Chap. 1

1. In the first expression, the multiplication operation is computed first: 10 * 2 = 20. The division is computed second: 20/5 = 4. The subtraction is completed last: 4 − 1 = 3. In the second expression, the multiplication operation is computed first: 10 * 2 = 20. Next the part of the expression in parentheses is computed: 5 − 1 = 4. The division is then computed 20/4 = 5.

2. The xy variable is a vector containing two numerical values: 5 and 6. xyz is a vector containing three character values: 5, 6, and whale. Notice that when you combine variables that are of different types, i.e. numerical and textual, the numerical values are converted to characters. Because the values in xyz are not numerical, R gives us an error.

3. In the practice exercise 1.2 x was set to 5 and y was 6. Since 5 is not equal to 6, R returns FALSE. Note that the equivalence operator can also evaluate if two character strings are identical.

4. R uses something called vector recycling. So in this example, each value of the vector x is multiplied by 2.

5. df[3,2]

C.2 Solutions for Chap. 2

1. The top ten most frequent words are found in the first through tenth position in the sorted vector:

© Springer Nature Switzerland AG 2020
M. L. Jockers, R. Thalken, *Text Analysis with R*, Quantitative Methods in the Humanities and Social Sciences,
https://doi.org/10.1007/978-3-030-39643-5

```
top_ten <-sorted_moby_freqs_t[1:10]
top_ten
```

2. Visualizing the results is as simple as using

```
plot(top_ten)
```

But adding a few more arguments to the `plot()` function gives you a more informative graph.

```
plot(top_ten, type = "b",
    xlab = "Top Ten Words", ylab = "Word Count", xaxt = "n")
axis(1, 1:10, labels = names(top_ten))
```

C.3 Solutions for Chap. 3

1. First load Moby Dick.

```
text_v <- scan("data/text/melville.txt", what = "character", sep = "\n")
```

Now remove the boilerplate and create a sorted frequency table.

```
start_v <- which(text_v == "CHAPTER 1. Loomings.")
novel_lines_v <-  text_v[start_v:length(text_v)]
novel_v <- paste(novel_lines_v, collapse = " ")
novel_lower_v <- tolower(novel_v)
moby_words_l <- strsplit(novel_lower_v, "\\W")
moby_word_v <- unlist(moby_words_l)
not_blanks_v  <-  which(moby_word_v != "")
moby_word_v <-  moby_word_v[not_blanks_v]
moby_freqs_t <- table(moby_word_v)
sorted_moby_freqs_t <- sort(moby_freqs_t, decreasing=TRUE)
```

Multiply the relative frequencies by 100 and plot the results for the first ten values.

```
sorted_moby_rel_freqs_t <- 100 * (
  sorted_moby_freqs_t/sum(sorted_moby_freqs_t)
  )
plot(sorted_moby_rel_freqs_t[1:10],
    main = "Moby Dick",
    type = "b",
    xlab = "Top Ten Words",
    ylab = "Percentage",
```

```
        xaxt = "n")
axis(1,1:10, labels = names(sorted_moby_rel_freqs_t[1:10]))
```

Now do something similar by loading *Sense and Sensibility*.

```
text_v <- scan("data/text/austen.txt", what = "character", sep = "\n")
start_v <- which(text_v == "CHAPTER 1")
novel_lines_v <-  text_v[start_v:length(text_v)]
novel_v <- paste(novel_lines_v, collapse=" ")
novel_lower_v <- tolower(novel_v)
sense_words_l <- strsplit(novel_lower_v, "\\W")
sense_word_v <- unlist(sense_words_l)
not_blanks_v  <-  which(sense_word_v != "")
sense_word_v <-  sense_word_v[not_blanks_v]
sense_freqs_t <- table(sense_word_v)
sorted_sense_freqs_t <- sort(sense_freqs_t , decreasing=TRUE)
sorted_sense_rel_freqs_t <- 100 * (
  sorted_sense_freqs_t/sum(sorted_sense_freqs_t)
  )
plot(sorted_sense_rel_freqs_t[1:10],
    main = "Sense and Sensibility",
    type = "b",
    xlab = "Top Ten Words",
    ylab = "Percentage",
    xaxt = "n")
axis(1,1:10, labels = names(sorted_sense_rel_freqs_t[1:10]))
```

2. Answer shown in the code below.

```
unique(c(names(sorted_moby_rel_freqs_t[1:10]),
         names(sorted_sense_rel_freqs_t[1:10])))
```

3. Answer shown in the code below.

```
names(sorted_sense_rel_freqs_t[
  which(names(sorted_sense_rel_freqs_t[1:10])
        %in% names(sorted_moby_rel_freqs_t[1:10]))])
```

4. Answer shown in the code below

```
presentSense <- which(names(sorted_sense_rel_freqs_t[1:10])
  %in% names(sorted_moby_rel_freqs_t[1:10]))
names(sorted_sense_rel_freqs_t[1:10])[-presentSense]
presentMoby <- which(names(sorted_moby_rel_freqs_t[1:10])
  %in% names(sorted_sense_rel_freqs_t[1:10]))
names(sorted_moby_rel_freqs_t[1:10])[-presentMoby]
```

C.4 Solutions for Chap. 4

1. To find the occurrences of the whale variants, we can use the same code as before but replace which(moby_word_v == "whale") with grep() and the multiple whale variants. From this point, the code is the same.

```
w_varient_v <- rep(NA, length(n_time_v))
whale_hits <- grep(
  "whale|whales|whale's|monster|leviathan",
  moby_word_v
  )
w_varient_v[whale_hits] <- 1
plot(
  w_varient_v,
  main ="Dispersion Plot of 'whale' variants in Moby Dick",
  xlab = "Novel Time",
  ylab = "whale(s)",
  type = "h",
  ylim = c(0,1),
  yaxt = 'n'
  )
```

One thing you might notice when comparing the plots is that though the new plot is more concentrated with occurrences of "whale" and its variants, the overall pattern remains the same. Even when accommodating for synonyms of whale, the plot shows the most occurrences a little after the novel's halfway point.

2. Answer shown in the code below.

```
table(moby_word_v[grep("^wh..e$", moby_word_v)])
```

3. With function embedding:

```
sort(table(moby_word_v[grep("ly$", moby_word_v)]), decreasing = T)[1:3]
```

Or more verbose:

```
ly_positions <- grep("ly$", moby_word_v)
ly_hits <- moby_word_v[ly_positions]
ly_frequencies <- table(ly_hits)
sorted_lys <- sort(ly_frequencies, decreasing = T)
sorted_lys[1:3]
```

C.5 Solutions for Chap. 5

1. Answer shown in the code below.

```
for(i in 1:length(x)) {
  result <- mean(x[[i]])
  print(result)
}
```

2. Answer shown in the code below.

```
whales_l <- lapply(chapter_freqs_l, '[', 'whale')
whales_m <- do.call(rbind, whales_l)
whales_v <- whales_m[,1]

ahabs_l <- lapply(chapter_freqs_l, '[', 'ahab')
ahabs_m <- do.call(rbind, ahabs_l)
ahabs_v <- ahabs_m[,1]

queequeg_l <- lapply(chapter_freqs_l, '[', 'queequeg')
queequeg_m <- do.call(rbind, queequeg_l)
queequeg_v <- queequeg_m[,1]

whales_ahabs_queequeg_m <- cbind(whales_v, ahabs_v,queequeg_v)
barplot(whales_ahabs_queequeg_m, beside = T, col="grey")
```

3. Answer shown in the code below.

```
whale_raw_l <- lapply(chapter_raws_l, '[', 'whale')
whale_raw_m <- do.call(rbind, whale_raw_l)
whale_raw_v <- whale_raw_m[,1]
ahab_raw_l <- lapply(chapter_raws_l, '[', 'ahab')
ahab_raw_m <- do.call(rbind, ahab_raw_l)
ahab_raw_v <- ahab_raw_m[,1]
whales_ahabs_raw_m <- cbind(whale_raw_v, ahab_raw_v)
barplot(whales_ahabs_raw_m, beside = T, col="grey")
```

C.6 Solutions for Chap. 6

1. Answer shown in the code below.

```
my_l  <- lapply(chapter_freqs_l, "[", "my")
my_m <- do.call(rbind, my_l)
```

```
my_v <- my_m[,1]
i_l  <-  lapply(chapter_freqs_l, "[", "i")
i_m <- do.call(rbind, i_l)
i_v <- i_m[,1]
whales_ahabs_my_i_m <- cbind(whales_v, ahabs_v, my_v, i_v)
whales_ahabs_my_i_m[which(is.na(whales_ahabs_my_i_m))] <- 0
cor(whales_ahabs_my_i_m)
```

2. Answer shown in the code below.

```
my_i_m <- cbind(my_v, i_v)
my_i_m[which(is.na(my_i_m))] <- 0
my_i_cor_data_df <- as.data.frame(my_i_m)
cor(my_i_cor_data_df$i, my_i_cor_data_df$my)
i_my_cors_v <- NULL
for(i in 1:10000){
  i_my_cors_v <- c(
    i_my_cors_v,
    cor(sample(my_i_cor_data_df$i),
        my_i_cor_data_df$my)
    )
}
min(i_my_cors_v)
max(i_my_cors_v)
range(i_my_cors_v)
mean(i_my_cors_v)
sd(i_my_cors_v)
```

C.7 Solutions for Chap. 7

1. Answer shown in the code below.

```
ttr_v <- as.vector(ttr_m)
chapter_lengths_m <- do.call(
  rbind, lapply(chapter_raws_l, sum)
  )
chap_len_v <- as.vector(chapter_lengths_m)
cor(ttr_v, chap_len_v)
```

A correlation coefficient of -0.7971711 indicates strong negative correlation. As the length of the chapter increases, the TTR scores decrease.

2. Answer shown in the code below.

```
mean_word_use_v <- as.vector(mean_word_use_m)
cor(mean_word_use_v, chap_len_v)
```

A correlation coefficient of 0.8924156 indicates a strong positive correlation. As the length of the chapter increases, the overall mean word frequency increases as well. More words in the chapter means more repeated words.

3. Answer shown in the code below.

```
cor(ttr_v, chap_len_v)
my_cors_v <- NULL
for(i in 1:10000){
  my_cors_v <- c(my_cors_v, cor(sample(ttr_v), chap_len_v))
}
min(my_cors_v)
max(my_cors_v)
range(my_cors_v)
mean(my_cors_v)
sd(my_cors_v)
```

The permutation test reveals that the observed correlation is highly unlikely to be seen by mere chance alone. In 10,000 iterations the highest positive correlation in our test was 0.3132262 and the lowest negative correlation was -0.311472. The mean() hovered near zero indicating that the observed correlation was far outside the norm expected by chance.

C.8 Solutions for Chap. 8

1. After using order() to figure out the ranks, you can use data.frame() to create a table with columns for each of the values. If you want, you can then order the values in the data frame by their ranks. The Cetology chapter is 76th.

```
ranks <- order(hapax_percentage, decreasing=TRUE)
df <- data.frame(hapax_percentage, ranks)
df[order(df$ranks),]
```

3. A correlation coefficient of 0.8673559 indicates that Jane Austen is less consistent than Melville when it comes to the introduction of new words into her novel even while she increases the length of her chapters. It turns out, in fact, that in terms of vocabulary size and richness, Austen is very consistent. Her working vocabulary in *Sense and Sensibility* contains 6325 unique word types and from one of her novels to the next she rarely de-

viates far from a base vocabulary of about 6300 word types. For comparison, recall that Melville's vocabulary in *Moby Dick* contains 16,872 unique word types spread over 214,889 tokens. Austen uses 6325 types over 120,766 tokens. Even though Austen's *Sense and Sensibility* is much shorter than *Moby Dick*, Austen has a smaller vocabulary, and she repeats words much more often. Austen uses each word an average of 19 times whereas Melville uses each word in his vocabulary only about 13 times on average.

```
text_v <- scan("data/text/austen.txt", what="character", sep="\n")
start_v <- which(text_v == "CHAPTER 1")
end_v <- which(text_v == "THE END")
novel_lines_v <-  text_v[start_v:end_v]
novel_lines_v <- unlist(novel_lines_v)
chap_positions_v <- grep("^CHAPTER \\d", novel_lines_v)
last_position_v <-  length(novel_lines_v)
chap_positions_v  <-  c(chap_positions_v , last_position_v)
sense_raws_l <- list()
for(i in 1:length(chap_positions_v)){
  if(i != length(chap_positions_v)){
    chapter_title <- novel_lines_v[chap_positions_v[i]]
    start <- chap_positions_v[i]+1
    end <- chap_positions_v[i+1]-1
    chapter_lines_v <- novel_lines_v[start:end]
    chapter_words_v <- tolower(paste(chapter_lines_v, collapse=" "))
    chapter_words_l <- strsplit(chapter_words_v, "\\W")
    chapter_word_v <- unlist(chapter_words_l)
    chapter_word_v <- chapter_word_v[which(chapter_word_v!="")]
    chapter_freqs_t <- table(chapter_word_v)
    sense_raws_l[[chapter_title]] <-  chapter_freqs_t
  }
}
sense_chapter_hapax_v <- sapply(sense_raws_l, function(x) sum(x == 1))
sense_chapter_lengths_m <- do.call(rbind, lapply(sense_raws_l,sum))
sense_hapax_lenghts_m <- cbind(
  sense_chapter_hapax_v,
  sense_chapter_lengths_m
  )
cor(sense_chapter_hapax_v, sense_chapter_lengths_m)
```

4. In both novels, the observed correlations are way beyond (many standard deviations) the means found in random sampling.

```
# Test the Moby Dick Result
moby_cors_v <- NULL
for(i in 1:10000){
  moby_cors_v <- c(
    moby_cors_v,
```

```
      cor(
        sample(chapter_hapax_v),
        chapter_lengths_m
      )
    )
}

# Test the Sense and Sensibility Result
sense_cors_v <- NULL
for(i in 1:10000){
  sense_cors_v <- c(
    sense_cors_v,
    cor(
      sample(sense_chapter_hapax_v),
      sense_chapter_lengths_m
    )
  )
}

# Combine and compare the discriptive stats

moby_stats_v <- c(
  observed = cor(chapter_hapax_v, chapter_lengths_m),
  random_mean = mean(moby_cors_v),
  random_std = sd(moby_cors_v)
  )

sense_stans_v <- c(
  observed = cor(
    sense_chapter_hapax_v,
    sense_chapter_lengths_m
    ),
  random_mean = mean(sense_cors_v),
  random_std = sd(sense_cors_v)
)

data.frame(moby_stats_v, sense_stans_v)
```

C.9 Solutions for Chap. 9

1. Answer shown in the code below.

```
austen_word_v <- make_token_v("data/text/austen.txt")
moby_word_v <- make_token_v("data/text/melville.txt")
```

```
context <- 5
dog_positions_sense <- which(austen_word_v == "dog")
dog_positions_moby <- which(moby_word_v =="dog")

# Answer for Sense and Sensibility
for(i in seq_along(dog_positions_sense)){
  start <- dog_positions_sense[i]-context
  end <- dog_positions_sense[i]+context
  cat(austen_word_v[start:end], "\n")
}

# Answer for Moby Dick
for(i in seq_along(dog_positions_moby)){
  start <- dog_positions_moby[i]-context
  end <- dog_positions_moby[i]+context
  cat(moby_word_v[start:end], "\n")
}
```

2. What follows below is not a perfect solution, but it has the advantage of being simple. In the sixth line, we use which() with paste() to find and replace instances of the keyword with the same keyword surrounded by brackets. In the next chapter, you will learn about some cases that would make this loop break and how to fix them.

```
for(i in seq_along(dog_positions_moby)){
  start <- dog_positions_moby[i]-context
  end <- dog_positions_moby[i]+context
  output <- moby_word_v[start:end]
  keyword <- moby_word_v[start+context]
  output[which(output == keyword)] <- paste("[", keyword, "]", sep = "")
  cat("----------------------", i, "----------------------", "\n")
  cat(output, "\n")
}
```

C.10 Solutions for Chap. 10

1. The key changes to the doitKWIC() function we wrote in the chapter are in the 7th line where we instantiate a data frame object with a number of rows equal to the number of hits found for the user's keyword and in the last few lines where we populate the rows of the data frame with data that is bound together into columns using cbind(). By instantiating the data frame to the exact size we need, R is able to work more efficiently by setting aside the amount of memory it needs for the final size of the object.

```
doItKwicBetter <- function(directory_path){
  file_id <- as.numeric(readline(show_files(directory_path)))
  keyword <- readline("Enter a Keyword: ")
  context <- as.numeric(readline("How many words of context? "))
  word_v <- make_token_v(
    file.path(directory_path, dir(directory_path)[file_id])
    )
  hits_v <- which(word_v == keyword)
  results_df <- data.frame(
    matrix(nrow=length(hits_v),
    ncol=4)
    ) # create an empty data frame
  colnames(results_df) <- c("position", "left", "keyword", "right")
  for(i in seq_along(hits_v)){
    start <- hits_v[i] - context
    if(start < 1){
      start <- 1
    }
    end <- hits_v[i] + context
    if(end >= length(word_v)){
      end <- length(word_v)
    }
    position <- hits_v[i]
    left <- paste(word_v[start:(hits_v[i] - 1)], collapse = " ")
    right <- paste(word_v[(hits_v[i] + 1):end], collapse = " ")
    df_row <- cbind(position, left, keyword, right)
    results_df[i,] <- df_row
  }
  return(results_df)
}
```

2. The solution below is better because it gives the user an option to save
   the KWIC output to a csv file.

```
doItKwicStillBetter <- function(directory_path){
  file_id <- as.numeric(readline(show_files(directory_path)))
  keyword <- readline("Enter a Keyword: ")
  context <- as.numeric(readline("How many words of context? "))
  word_v <- make_token_v(
    file.path(directory_path, dir(directory_path)[file_id])
    )
  hits_v <- which(word_v == keyword)
  results_df <- data.frame(
    matrix(nrow=length(hits_v), ncol=4)
    ) # create an empty data frame
  colnames(results_df) <- c("position", "left", "keyword", "right")
  for(i in seq_along(hits_v)){
```

```
  start <- hits_v[i] - context
  if(start < 1){
    start <- 1
  }
  end <- hits_v[i] + context
  if(end >= length(word_v)){
    end <- length(word_v)
  }
  position <- hits_v[i]
  left <- paste(word_v[start:(hits_v[i] - 1)], collapse = " ")
  right <- paste(word_v[(hits_v[i] + 1):end], collapse = " ")
  df_row <- cbind(position, left, keyword, right)
  results_df[i,] <- df_row
}
toprint <- readline(
  "Would you like to save this
  result to afile: enter y/n \n"
  )
if(toprint == "y"){
  file_name <- paste(
    keyword, "in",
    context, "in",
    dir(directory_path)[file_id],
    "csv",
    sep = "."
    )
  write.csv(results_df, file.path("results", file_name))
}
return(results_df)
}
```

3. The solution here allows users to pass a regular expression through
   doItKwicBest() out to make_token_v().

```
doItKwicBest <- function(directory_path, regex){
  file_id <- as.numeric(readline(show_files(directory_path)))
  keyword <- readline("Enter a Keyword: ")
  context <- as.numeric(readline("How many words of context? "))
  word_v <- make_token_v(
    file.path(
      directory_path,
      dir(directory_path)[file_id]),
    pattern = regex
    )
  hits_v <- which(word_v == keyword)
  results_df <- data.frame(
    matrix(nrow=length(hits_v), ncol=4)
```

```
    ) # create an empty data frame
  colnames(results_df) <- c("position", "left", "keyword", "right")
  for(i in seq_along(hits_v)){
    start <- hits_v[i] - context
    if(start < 1){
      start <- 1
    }
    end <- hits_v[i] + context
    if(end >= length(word_v)){
      end <- length(word_v)
    }
    position <- hits_v[i]
    left <- paste(word_v[start:(hits_v[i] - 1)], collapse = " ")
    right <- paste(word_v[(hits_v[i] + 1):end], collapse = " ")
    df_row <- cbind(position, left, keyword, right)
    results_df[i,] <- df_row
  }
  toprint <- readline("Would you like to save this
                       result to a file: enter y/n \n")
  if(toprint == "y"){
    file_name <- paste(
      keyword,
      "in",
      context,
      "in",
      dir(directory_path)[file_id],
      "csv",
      sep = "."
      )
    write.csv(results_df, file.path("results", file_name))
  }
  return(results_df)
}
```

Despite the name, there is still a lot more we could do to improve this function. We might, for example, want to update the `make_token_v()` function to accept an argument directing the function to lowercase the text or not. We could then add that argument to `doItKwicBest()` as a further option. Here is how the two functions might be revised to be more flexible:

```
# Revised make_token_v() with option for lowercasing.
# Default behavior is strill to lowercase the input file.
make_token_v <- function(file_path, pattern = "\\W", lowercase = TRUE){
  text_v <- scan(file_path, what = "character", sep = "\n")
  text_v <- paste(text_v, collapse = " ")
  if(lowercase){
    text_v <- tolower(text_v)
```

```r
    }
    text_words_v <- strsplit(text_v, pattern)
    text_words_v <- unlist(text_words_v)
    text_words_v <-  text_words_v[which(text_words_v != "")]
    return(text_words_v)
}


# Slightly revised doItKwicBest() function that implements
# a "make_lower" argument that can be set to either TRUE or FALSE.
# This argument is passed to make_token_v() as the "lowercase"
# argument
doItKwicBest <- function(directory_path, regex, make_lower){
    file_id <- as.numeric(readline(show_files(directory_path)))
    keyword <- readline("Enter a Keyword: ")
    context <- as.numeric(readline("How many words of context? "))
    word_v <- make_token_v(
        file.path(directory_path, dir(directory_path)[file_id]),
        pattern = regex,
        lowercase = make_lower
        )
    hits_v <- which(word_v == keyword)
    results_df <- data.frame(
        matrix(nrow=length(hits_v), ncol=4)
        ) # create an empty data frame
    colnames(results_df) <- c("position", "left", "keyword", "right")
    for(i in seq_along(hits_v)){
        start <- hits_v[i] - context
        if(start < 1){
            start <- 1
        }
        end <- hits_v[i] + context
        if(end >= length(word_v)){
            end <- length(word_v)
        }
        position <- hits_v[i]
        left <- paste(word_v[start:(hits_v[i] - 1)], collapse = " ")
        right <- paste(word_v[(hits_v[i] + 1):end], collapse = " ")
        df_row <- cbind(position, left, keyword, right)
        results_df[i,] <- df_row
    }
    toprint <- readline("Would you like to save this
                        result to a file: enter y/n \n")
    if(toprint == "y"){
        file_name <- paste(
            keyword,
            "in",
```

```
      context,
      "in",
      dir(directory_path)[file_id],
      "csv",
      sep = "."
      )
    write.csv(results_df, file.path("results", file_name))
  }
  return(results_df)
}
```

With the two functions revised in this way, you should now be able to search
for the keyword "Ahab's" in *Moby Dick*.

C.11 Solutions for Chap. 11

1. We can use this code from the chapter to isolate the three chapters with
   a hapax percentage greater than .5.

```
filter(nice_df, hap_percent > .5)
```

They appear to be some of the shorter chapters when looking at the chapter
lengths column, but we can use dplyr to double check this hypothesis. If we
use summary(), we will note that the minimum chapter length is 49, and
the mean chapter length is 1587. The three chapters with hapax percentage
greater than .5 have lengths of 246, 427, and 49; all of which are much shorter
than the mean chapter length.

```
select(nice_df, chapter_lengths) %>%
  summary()
```

2. To find the chapters with hapax percentage less than .2, we can use the
   following code:

```
filter(nice_df, hap_percent < .2)
```

If we look at the chapter length column again for this new result, we will note
that the chapters all appear to be rather long. According to the summary
statistics we found in practice problem 1, the chapters with the least amount
of hapax are some of the longest chapters.

3. Chapter 19 of *Moby Dick* is not long. In fact, with a length of only 1258
   words, this is on the shorter end of *Moby Dick* chapter lengths.

4. Answer shown in the code below.

```
repeat_df <- mutate(
  nice_df,
```

```
  repeat_words = chapter_lengths - num_hapax
) %>%
filter(repeat_words > 3000) %>%
select(short_title, chapter_lengths, repeat_words) %>%
arrange(desc(repeat_words))
```

5. Answer shown in the code below.

```
done <- mutate(
  repeat_df,
  repeat_rate = chapter_lengths / repeat_words
) %>%
  arrange(desc(repeat_rate))
```

6. Answer shown in the code below.

```
final <- mutate(
  nice_df,
  chap_num = gsub("CHAPTER", "", short_title)
) %>%
filter(chapter_lengths > 3000) %>%
select(-chap_names) %>%
mutate(as_num = as.numeric(chap_num)) %>%
arrange(desc(as_num))
```

7. Because the value in the chap_num column was derived from character data, it must be converted to numeric data.

C.12 Solutions for Chap. 12

1. Answer shown in the code below.

```
chapter_title_l <- lapply(
  chapters_ns, get_node_text,
  xpath = ".//tei:head",
  ns = c(tei = "http://www.tei-c.org/ns/1.0")
)
```

2. Answer shown in the code below.

```
chapter_title_df <- do.call(rbind, chapter_title_l)
text_df <- do.call(rbind, text_l)
combined_df <- cbind(chapter_title_df, text_df)
```

3. Answer shown in the code below.

```
freq_table <- function(word_v){
  table(word_v)/length(word_v)
}
word_freq_tables_l <- lapply(word_tokens_l, freq_table)
barplot(
  unlist(lapply(word_freq_tables_l, '[', c('whale', 'ahab'))),
  names.arg = "Occurrence of Whale (blue) and Ahab (red)",
  col = c("blue", "red"),
  border = NA
  )
```

C.13 Solutions for Chap. 13

1. Answer shown in the code below.

```
receiver_names_l <- xml_find_all(xml_doc, ".//RECEIVER")
receiver_names_v <- xml_text(receiver_names_l)
sort(
  table(receiver_names_v)/length(receiver_names_v),
  decreasing = TRUE
  )
```

Unsurprisingly, Hamlet also accounts for the majority of heard speech acts. He receives 28% of the play's speech acts, with Horatio and Claudius behind him, at 10.5% and 7.6%, respectively.

2. Answer shown in the code below.

```
unique_speakers <- unique(speaker_names_v)
unique_receivers <- unique(receiver_names_v)
unique_receivers[-which(unique_receivers %in% unique_speakers)]
```

The characters who receive speech but never engage in speech are the Attendants, Players, and Soldiers.

3. Answer shown in the code below.

```
group_by(sorted_speeches_df, Receiver) %>%
  summarise(Total = sum(word_count)) %>%
  arrange(desc(Total))
```

Hamlet again hears the most words directed to him, hearing 6455 total words. Horatio comes in second, with 3565 words, and then Laertes comes in third, hearing 2849 words. Interestingly, if we compare this to exercise 13.1's result, even though Laertes only comes in 5th for total number of overheard speech acts, he comes in 3rd for most words directed to him. This means that even though he hears less speech acts than other characters, when characters are speaking to him they tend to be more verbose.

4. Answer shown in the code below.

```
tokenize <- function(text_v, pattern = "[^A-Za-z0-9']", lower = TRUE){
  if(lower){
    text_v <- tolower(text_v)
  }
  word_v <- unlist(strsplit(text_v, pattern))
  word_v[which(word_v != "")]
}

hamlet_speaks_df <- filter(
  speech_data_counts_df,
  Speaker == "HAMLET"
  ) %>%
  select(words = Speech)
ham_words_v <- paste(hamlet_speaks_df$words, collapse = " ")
sort(table(tokenize(ham_words_v)), decreasing = T)[1:20]
```

5. Answer shown in the code below.

```
QG_speaks_df <- filter(
  speech_data_counts_df,
  Speaker == "QUEEN GERTRUDE"
  ) %>%
  select(words = Speech)
QG_words_v <- paste(QG_speaks_df$words, collapse = " ")
sort(table(tokenize(QG_words_v)), decreasing = T)[1:20]
```

C.14 Solutions for Chap. 14

1. Answer shown in the code below.

```
summary(moby_sentiments_v)
summary(sense_sentiments_v)
```

2. Answer shown in the code below.

```
sentiment_df <- data.frame(
  "sentences" = moby_sentences_v,
  "sentiment" = as.numeric(moby_sentiments_v)
  )
sentiment_df[1, ] # show the first row
```

3. Answer shown in the code below.

```
library(dplyr)
# Finding the most positive sentences
positive_df <- sentiment_df %>%
  arrange(desc(sentiment))

# Finding the most negative sentences
negative_df <- sentiment_df %>%
  arrange(sentiment)
```

4. Answer shown in the code below.

```
positive_df[1,]
negative_df[1,]
```

C.15 Solutions for Chap. 15

1. Answer shown in the code below.

```
# still works at .0275 with 3 features left
keepers_test_v <- names(token_means[which(token_means >= .0275)])
length(keepers_test_v)
dist_m <- dist(wide_df[, keepers_test_v])
cluster <- hclust(dist_m)
cluster$labels <- rownames(wide_df)
plot(cluster)

# no longer works at .03
keepers_test_2 <- names(token_means[which(token_means >= .03)])
length(keepers_test_2)
dist_m <- dist(wide_df[, keepers_test_2])
cluster <- hclust(dist_m)
cluster$labels <- rownames(wide_df)
plot(cluster)
```

2. Answer shown in the code below.

```
# sample 50 random features
keepers_sample_v <- names(sample(token_means, size = 50))
dist_m <- dist(wide_df[, keepers_sample_v])
cluster <- hclust(dist_m)
cluster$labels <- rownames(wide_df)
plot(cluster)
```

```
# sample 100 random features
keepers_sample_v <- names(sample(token_means, size = 100))
dist_m <- dist(wide_df[, keepers_sample_v])
cluster <- hclust(dist_m)
cluster$labels <- rownames(wide_df)
plot(cluster)
```

C.16 Solutions for Chap. 16

1. With 681 features, the model is unable to detect a latent author signal because there are far too many open-class context words.

2. Solving this one is not easy and requires some out of the box thinking. We want to know whether an author uses or does not use a given feature in any one (or more) of his/her texts. If an author uses a feature at least once, we keep it. If an author never uses the feature in any text, we want to remove it from consideration. Another way of thinking about this is that we want to remove any feature in which the sum of that feature for any given author is equal to zero. The key part of that sentence was "the sum of that feature is equal to zero." To solve this problem we use the `aggregate()` function to group rows by author and then calculate the sum of the values in each column in that author group. Here is a dummy example. Below the example, we offer the solution for the problem in the chapter.

First we create a dummy data frame:

```
authors <- c("A","A","B","B","C", "C")
f1 <- c(0, 1, 2, 3, 0,0)
f2 <- c(0, 1, 2, 3, 0,1)
f3 <- c(3, 2, 1, 2, 1,1)
f4 <- c(3, 2, 1, 2, 1,1)
f5 <- c(0, 0, 1, 2, 1,1)
author_df <- data.frame(authors, f1,f2,f3,f4, f5)
author_df # Show the original data frame
```

Now we will use the `aggregate()` function to group rows and get the group sum for each author.

```
author_sums <- aggregate(author_df[, 2:ncol(author_df)],
  list(author_df[,1]), sum)
```

Examine the `author_sums` object to see that it includes one row for each author and the values in each cell are the sum of the values from that author for that feature (column). We can reduce that data frame to remove any columns with a 0. Then we grab the column names of the columns that survive the winnowing into `keepers_v`.

```
reduced_author_sums <- author_sums[, colSums(author_sums == 0) == 0]
keepers_v <- colnames(reduced_author_sums)[2:ncol(reduced_author_sums)]
smaller_df <- author_df[, c("authors", keepers_v)]
smaller_df # show the new data frame
```

Below is the solution using the `authorship_df` data frame from the chapter. Running `aggregate()` on this larger data frame is processor intensive and will take several minutes to complete. Notice that we use `4:ncol(authorship_df)` to omit the first three metadata columns.

```
author_sums <- aggregate(authorship_df[, 4:ncol(authorship_df)],
  list(authorship_df[,1]), sum)
reduced_author_sums <- author_sums[, colSums(author_sums == 0) == 0]
keepers_v <- colnames(reduced_author_sums)[2:ncol(reduced_author_sums)]
smaller_df <- authorship_df[, c("authors", keepers_v)]
dim(smaller_df) # show the new data frame
```

C.17 Solutions for Chap. 17

1. Answer shown in the code below.

```
for(i in 1:43){
  topic_top_words <- mallet.top.words(
    topic_model,
    topic_words_m[i,], 100)
  print(
    wordcloud(
      topic_top_words$words,
      topic_top_words$weights,
      c(4,.8), rot.per=0,
      random.order=F)
  )
}
```

2. Answer shown in the code below.

```
mallet_instances <- mallet.import(documents_df$id,
  documents_df$text,
  "data/stoplist-exp.csv",
  FALSE,
  token.regexp="[\\p{L}']+")
topic_model <- MalletLDA(num.topics = 43)
```

```
topic_model$loadDocuments(mallet_instances)
word_freqs <- mallet.word.freqs(topic_model)
topic_model$train(400)
topic_words_m <- mallet.topic.words(topic_model,
  smoothed=TRUE,
  normalized=TRUE)
vocabulary <- topic_model$getVocabulary()
colnames(topic_words_m) <- vocabulary

for(i in 1:43){
  topic_top_words <- mallet.top.words(topic_model,
    topic_words_m[i,], 100)
  print(
    wordcloud(
      topic_top_words$words,
      topic_top_words$weights,
      c(4,.8), rot.per=0,
      random.order=F)
    )
}
```

C.18 Solutions for Chap. 18

1. Simply change the "kind" argument to indicate the type of entity you wish
   to extract.

```
entity_tag_annotator <- Maxent_Entity_Annotator(kind = "date")
entity_tag_annotator <- Maxent_Entity_Annotator(kind = "organization")
entity_tag_annotator <- Maxent_Entity_Annotator(kind = "money")
entity_tag_annotator <- Maxent_Entity_Annotator(kind = "percentage")
```

Index

A
assignment operators, 11
authorship attribution, 178, 184, 189, 195

C
clustering, 195
code commenting, 11
console, 7
correlation, 70, 169

D
dendrogram, 192
dispersion plots, 38

E
equivalence operator, 95
Euclidean distance, 184, 190

F
feature winnowing, 189
for loop, 53, 101, 179
frequency tables, 198
function embedding, 180
functions
    annotate, 238
    arrange, 129, 150
    c, 26
    cat, 102, 201
    cbind, 65
    ceiling, 215
    class, 23, 83

cor, 71
cut, 196
data.frame, 183, 218
dist, 185
do.call, 64, 85, 187
filter, 127
get node text, 182
get sentiment, 162
grep, 41
group by, 155
gsub, 187
hclust, 192
head, 29
lapply, 61, 84, 139, 149
length, 20
load, 242
mallet.import, 221
mallet.top.words, 228
mallet.word.freqs, 223
mutate, 125
order, 87
paste, 21, 201
plot, 34
prop.table, 199
rbind, 59, 85
read xml, 136, 146, 179
readline, 111
rep, 39
rescale x 2, 167
sample, 76
sapply, 94
save, 242
scale, 86
scan, 15
select, 128

© Springer Nature Switzerland AG 2020
M. L. Jockers, R. Thalken, *Text Analysis with R*, Quantitative Methods in
the Humanities and Social Sciences,
https://doi.org/10.1007/978-3-030-39643-5

Printed in the United States
by Baker & Taylor Publisher Services